FREEDOM UNDER THATCHER

Freedom Under Thatcher

Civil Liberties
in Modern Britain

K. D. EWING AND C. A. GEARTY

CLARENDON PRESS · OXFORD

Oxford University Press, Walton Street, Oxford OX2 6DP

Oxford   New York   Toronto
Delhi Bombay Calcutta Madras Karachi
Kuala Lumpur Singapore Hong Kong Tokyo
Nairobi Dar es Salaam Cape Town
Melbourne Auckland Madrid

and associated companies in
Berlin Ibadan

Oxford is a trade mark of Oxford University Press

Published in the United States
by Oxford University Press Inc., New York

First published 1990

British Library Cataloguing in Publication Data
Data available

Library of Congress Cataloging in Publication Data
Ewing, K. D. (Keith D.)
Freedom under Thatcher: civil liberties in modern Britain /
K. D. Ewing and C. A. Gearty.
Includes bibliographical references.
1. Civil rights—Great Britain—History.
I. Gearty, C. A. II. Title.
KD4080.E95 1990 342.41'085—dc20 [344.10285] 89–71331
ISBN 0–19–825413–X
ISBN 0–19–825414–8 (pbk)

5 7 9 10 8 6

Printed in Great Britain
on acid-free paper by
Biddles Ltd, Guildford and King's Lynn

Preface

IN recent years, there has been a marked decline in the level of political freedom enjoyed in Britain. It is difficult if not impossible to point to a particular turning-point. The Labour Government of the 1970s tried to stop publication of the Crossman diaries, passed the first Prevention of Terrorism Act, deported an American journalist for allegedly obtaining security secrets, and pursued two other journalists under the Official Secrets Act 1911 (the ABC case). Repressive action, therefore, is not the preserve of any single political party. Since the first Conservative election victory in 1979, however, the process of erosion has become more pronounced. All our traditional liberties have been affected, partly by new statutory initiatives and partly by the Government and other public officials relentlessly pushing back the frontiers of the common law, the traditional guardian of the people. It is these developments which are dealt with in this book. In particular, we are concerned first to demonstrate the extent to which core political freedoms have been compromised; and secondly to highlight the weaknesses of some of the proposals which have been made recently with a view to redressing the balance between the citizen and the state.

This is not to deny that the present Government is concerned with questions of liberty. These concerns have, however, an undeniable political content: the freedom to buy one's council house; to buy shares; to choose whatever hospital, doctor, lawyer, or school one wants. It is by these criteria that the Government claims to be adding to, rather than eroding, the liberty of its citizens. The traditional freedoms of the person, expression, assembly, and association come a poor second. Yet these are important precisely because, unlike the values promoted by the Conservatives, they have no political content. They are fundamental because they enable argument and debate about other matters to take place. The freedom to speak is not a freedom to say something in particular. The freedom to assemble is not the freedom to promote a particular point of view. The debates about socialism and capitalism, about the direction in which the country should go, about economic choices, and all the other myriad issues that make for a healthy democracy require the existence of our core civil liberties. They are the gloriously apolitical facilitators of political debate. A nation that tampers with them risks its vitality and its originality. A government that does not believe in them threatens its country's well-being.

5 September 1989   K. D. E.
                                                         C. A. G.

Contents

1

Introduction

IT was not so long ago that British Democracy was synonymous with liberty and freedom. The 'Westminster model' of government was envied by Europeans, rebuilding after the Second World War, and studied by conscientious foreign politicians, engaged in the planning of new nations. The United States proudly acknowledged the dependence of its founders upon the principles of the 'glorious revolution', and continued to express profound regard for the tolerance and fair-mindedness of its erstwhile colonial master. Newly independent nations enlisted the aid of British constitutional lawyers and sought with them to translate the special qualities of 'the Mother of Parliaments' into their local legal vernacular. If a country enacted a bill of rights, then it was likely to be acknowledged as a written but inadequate consolation for the absence of that commitment to liberty which appeared to seep unconsciously and effortlessly through the British system of government.

The nation has always been aware of its pre-eminent position, and proud of a moral ascendancy in the political sphere which has been sustained for centuries. As early as 1752, David Hume noted that 'the plan of liberty is settled, its happy effects are proved by experience, [and] a long tract of time has given it stability' (Hume, 1906: 203). Britain still maintained 'her station as guardian of the general liberties of Europe and patron of mankind' (Hume, 1906: 76). To Macaulay, the 'highest eulogy which [could] be pronounced on the revolution of 1688 [was] this, that it was our last revolution'. In all 'honest and reflecting minds', there was 'a conviction, daily strengthened by experience, that the name of effecting every improvement which the constitution requires may be found within the constitution itself' (Macaulay, 1861: ii. 669). Dicey described how, when

'Voltaire came to England—and Voltaire represented the feeling of his age—his predominant sentiment clearly was that he had passed out of the realm of despotism to a land where the laws might be harsh, but where men were ruled by law and not by caprice' (Dicey, 1959: 189–90).

From Complacency to Concern

Confidence in this traditional system of government was enhanced by its absorption of democratic reform in the nineteenth century and by its survival through two world wars in the first half of the twentieth. Textbooks catering for the upsurge in legal education in the 1950s and 1960s sought to capture in print the mysterious unwritten secrets of a constitution which had emerged into the democratic world without appearing to have changed at all. Incongruities and idiosyncracies were seen as strengths not as weaknesses, as indicators of a capacity for quiet change rather than as evidence of a tendency towards obfuscation. Even less complacent works shared common assumptions about the essential good qualities of the British approach: pragmatic legislation, a benevolent executive, and a general culture of tolerance and forbearance. So although Attlee's cabinet of the post-war years was instrumental in promoting and drafting the European Convention on Human Rights and Fundamental Freedoms, few thought it necessary or desirable that this guarantee of freedom should become part of English law. In this era of consensus, there was general agreement within the kingdom that the British constitution was 'the envy of the world'.

Times have changed. Such an assertion today would be greeted with incredulity and disbelief. The omnipotence of the British Prime Minister, unparalleled in any other liberal democracy, is undreamt of by an American President or West German Chancellor—and undesired by any of their peoples. Britain has an unenviable reputation as one of the most consistent transgressors against human rights in the Council of Europe. The manic international campaign to prevent publication of Peter Wright's *Spycatcher* advertised to the world an obsession with secrecy that seemed better suited to the other side of the Iron Curtain. Earlier, this obsession had been carried to absurd lengths with the determined pursuit of Sarah Tisdall and Clive Ponting. Whilst other nations wrestle with the complex problems of a modern democracy, the questions of press ownership, the funding of political parties, wire-tapping, privacy, freedom of information, the control of the security services, and so on, Britain has been content either to stand aside altogether or to legislate for continuing trust and deference. A special report on censorship in the UK by the *New York Times* magazine in March 1989 was headed simply, 'Thatcher puts a lid on'.

Puzzlement outside the country has been matched by even greater anxiety within it. The old certainty is gone. Labour has committed itself to a wide range of civil-liberties legislation and constitutional reform when it returns to government, to counter what its Deputy Leader, Mr Hattersley, has described as the vulnerability of traditional freedoms to the dual threat of 'legal restriction and a cynical partnership between Government and private enterprise'. Many of its leading members have spoken in favour of some measure of electoral reform. Others have called for the enactment of a bill of rights. The tercentenary of the first Bill, passed in 1688, has provided a stimulus for some earnest reflection. Macmillan published a book, edited by Richard Holme and Michael Elliott, simply entitled *1688–1988: Time for a New Constitution*. One of its editors describes modern Britain as 'a constitutional shambles'. A group of academics and intellectuals has gathered together under the title Charter 88 to campaign for a written constitution to rectify the 'implausibility' of the country's current protection of liberty and freedom. The journal *Samizdat* started the same year and has followed a similar line. Under the banner of 'Liberty', the National Council for Civil Liberties launched, in January 1989, a counter-offensive to ten years of sustained attacks on individual freedom, detailed in Peter Thornton's book, *Decade of Decline: Civil Liberties in the Thatcher Years*.

The internationally respected journal *Index on Censorship* devoted the whole of its September 1988 issue to the question of liberty in Britain, because, as its opening article entitled 'Why Britain?' put it, 'if freedom is diminished in the United Kingdom, where historically it has deep roots, it is potentially diminished everywhere'. Even the *Sunday Telegraph* has castigated Mrs Thatcher for the 'almost messianic bigotry and enthusiasm' with which she has 'trampled on genuine ideals with deep roots in our national history' and 'enjoyed doing so'.[1] In less emotive terms, the *Daily Telegraph* has devoted a page to what it called the 'cracks in the image of justice' which are being identified—'and not only by predictable critics'.[2] *The Economist* has called for a bill of rights as a bulwark against what Lord Hailsham once described as an 'elective dictatorship'. Conservative back-benchers like Richard Shepherd and Jonathan Aitken have voiced their concern at many of the Government's anti-libertarian actions; and Enoch Powell has written of 'this atmosphere of near-hysteria in which, with general applause, Parliament gets to trample upon the rights and freedoms which it has nurtured and protected through its long history'.[3]

The Constitutional Context

One might well ask what has happened to transform the public mood from complacency to crisis in so short a time. The answer, in institutional terms, is almost nothing at all—and this is precisely the problem. The constitutional framework set in place after the 'Glorious Revolution' was, rightly, one of the wonders of its age. The monarch was head of the executive branch, in fact as well as in theory. Law emerged from a partnership between the Crown's ministry and Parliament. Neither slavishly followed the views of the other. The end-product was interpreted and enforced by judges who were independent of both the legislature and the executive and whose jobs were guaranteed regardless of how inconvenient they proved to be. Blackstone thought it 'highly necessary for preserving the balance of the constitution that the executive power should be a branch, though not the whole, of the legislature. The total union of them . . . would be productive of tyranny' (Blackstone, 1830: 153–4). It was this element of genuine separation of powers that appealed to Blackstone. It also strongly influenced the European and American theorists of the following century. This is the formal arrangement that pertains to

[1] 27 Nov. 1988.   [2] *Daily Telegraph*, 7 Dec. 1988.
[3] *Guardian*, 23 Feb. 1989.

this day. Under this cover of tradition and past glory, however, the executive has bustled through informally to seize almost total power.

The royal drift to impotence began almost immediately after the Whig victory over James II. The Hanoverians of the early eighteenth century diluted their grip on power both by their frequent absences from executive meetings and by their occasional lack of command of the nation's language when they did attend. By the third decade of that century, the idea of a prime minister had emerged and in its first physical manifestation it took the imposing form of Sir Robert Walpole. For another 130 years, and in particular in the period 1830–70, a succession of prime ministers and cabinets wrestled to impose their will on parliaments that were riven by faction and driven by independence of view. It may have been an aristocratic élite, but it was also unruly, unpredictable, and extremely difficult to manage. The change came with parliamentary reform in the nineteenth century and the emergence of large disciplined political parties in the 1860s and 1870s. In 1988 Lord Scarman perceptively observed that the momentum created by the democratization of Parliament was a major factor behind the marked increase in executive power at this time. Certainly Disraeli and Gladstone thrived on the electoral reform of the 1860s and quickly learned how to discipline their followers and manage them so as to translate the wishes of the executive into votes in the House. They were more akin to the machine politicians we know today than to the noble coalition builders and power-brokers who preceded them.

The result of this historical trend is a Parliament that for most of the time now exists to do the executive's bidding. Unlike America or France, the Government is defined by reference to its ability to command majority support in the lower House. This quickly reverses itself into cabinet control. The payroll vote (those members of the Government who sit in the two Houses), back-bench ambition, and the vigilance of the Whips' Office ensure that executive will invariably prevail. The House of Lords may be an irritant, but its powers are restricted by the Parliament Acts. In any event, a Conservative Cabinet can always rely on its 'backwoodsmen' to get it out of trouble if its more usual supporters amongst the Peers show an inclination to reject an executive decision. Thus, in May 1988, one of the highest turn-outs of Lords this century saw the Government home on the introduction of a flat-rate poll tax, a measure which had caused great concern amongst regular attendants. In July 1988 the Lords voted by 120 to 94 to reject the imposition of charges for eye tests. The Government's response was to call on its country support and put the matter before the Lords again. This time, they won by 257 to 207 votes. It was once again one of the highest turn-outs of the century.

The Government controls Parliament's time and it is therefore able to limit debate where its proposals are proving controversial or where a rational examination of them is turning out to be embarrassing. One device for curtailing debate and the detailed examination of a bill is the so-called 'guillotine' motion. The Government's official secrets legislation in 1989 was guillotined after only two days in committee in the lower House. Discussion on the Prevention of Terrorism Bill 1989 was also arbitrarily curtailed. The control of Parliament is perhaps even better illustrated by the fact that few pieces of legislation have been lost in the Commons in the ten years since Mrs Thatcher became prime minister—the Shops Bill comes to mind, but there is talk of its reintroduction in a future session. A whole series of laws bears the personal imprint of the Prime Minister—the abolition of the Greater London Council, the poll tax, identity cards for football supporters, to name but a few. All that unpopularity in the country or in the Commons manages to achieve is a revolt by a handful of predictable Tory rebels, a few careful speeches about the need to present policy better, and a vague anxiety about the results of an election not due to be held for years. The real power struggle is behind the scenes, in the informal advisory bodies with access to Secretaries of State, in the Cabinet committees, in the meetings of Ministers with their powerful back-benchers, and in the informal cabals that focus energies on future policy. A bill before the House signals the end of the real battle and the start of a squabble over detail. It is the tiresome but essential task of window-dressing.

The lack of any real constraints on the executive branch has led to a crisis of overgovernability, in which executive proposals quickly become law via a quiescent Parliament without sufficient consultation, scrutiny, or debate and without any possibility of subsequent judicial challenge. Yet it is worth pausing at this point to remind ourselves that throughout her years in office, the Prime Minister has not created any new constitutional structures from which she and her Cabinet have been able to benefit. The two major attempts at reform in the ten years before Mrs Thatcher, the reform of the House of Lords in 1969 and Scottish and Welsh devolution in 1978, were both conspicuous failures. Few institutional changes have occurred since 1979. The structure of government has stood still, but about it all has changed. Because of this failure to develop, the great debate about liberty and the control of power in the technological age, which we see in other Western nations, is passing the country by, almost unnoticed. The result is that, in international terms, where once it was the paradigm, Britain is now little more than a jaded footnote. Pride in the nation's system of government, once shared by all, has degenerated into complacency about its superiority, believed only by the few who exercise the near despotic powers that its outmoded forms have given them. Mrs Thatcher has merely utilized to the full the scope for untrammelled power latent in the British Constitution but obscured by the hesitancy and scruples of previous, consensus-based, political leaders. Her great good fortune has been an electoral system that has given her power on a minority vote. Her great success has lain in her willingness to use the vagueness and flexibility of the Constitution to her own ends. In so doing, she has both accelerated a process of institutional decline that was well in place before she arrived, and, by the extent of her unchallenged success, signalled the need for new forms and structures. Mrs Thatcher's greatest service to the nation may yet be the institutional reforms that take place on her departure.

The Influence of Dicey

It is, perhaps, unsurprising that individual liberty should be one of the chief casualties of a system of government that rests so much power in the executive branch. A major contribution to the growth of state power has also been the ineffective protection traditionally provided for political freedom by the British Constitution. Historically, the principal safeguard was the doctrine of the rule of law, first given widespread currency in A. V. Dicey's extraordinarily influential *Introduction to the Study of the Law of the Constitution*, the first edition of which appeared in 1885. For Dicey, the rule of law involved three propositions. First, it meant that 'no man [was] punishable or [could] be made to suffer in body or goods except for a distinct breach of law established in the ordinary legal manner before the ordinary courts of the land'. Secondly, it also meant 'not only that no man [was] above the law, but (what is a different thing) that here every man, whatever be his rank or condition, [was] subject to the ordinary law of the realm and amenable to the jurisdiction of the ordinary tribunals'. Thirdly, it involved saying that 'the general principles of the constitution (as for example the right to personal liberty, or the right of public meeting) are with us as the result of judicial decisions determining the rights of private persons in particular cases brought before the courts'.

What this entailed for civil liberties may be gleaned by looking at the way in which Dicey dealt with traditional freedoms in the body of his work. 'The right to personal freedom' was secured in England by 'the strict maintenance of the principle that no man [could] be arrested or imprisoned except in due course of law . . . under some warrant or authority'. Freedom of expression was treated in the same way: 'Any man may . . . say or write whatever he likes, subject to the risk of, it may be, severe punishment if he publishes any statement (either by word of mouth, in writing or in print) which he is not legally entitled to make'. Finally, there was freedom of assembly:

[I]t can hardly be said that our constitution knows of such a thing as any specific right of public meeting. . . . The right of assembling is nothing more than a result of the view taken by the courts as to individual liberty of person and individual liberty of speech. There is no special law allowing A, B, and C to meet together in the open air or elsewhere for a lawful purpose, but the right of A to go where he pleases so that he does not commit a trespass, and to say what he likes to B so that his talk is not libellous or seditious, the right of B to do the like, and the existence of the same rights of C, D, E, and F and so on *ad infinitum*, lead to the consequence that A, B, C, D and a thousand or ten thousand other persons, may (as a general rule) meet together in any place where otherwise they each have a right to be for a lawful purpose and in a lawful manner.

There was 'in the English constitution an absence of those declarations or definitions of rights so dear to foreign constitutionalists', but this was a strength rather than a weakness; whereas 'general rights guaranteed by the constitution may be, and in foreign countries, constantly are, suspended', the English emphasis on specific remedies protected by legislation and the courts meant that 'the suspension of the constitution, as far as such a thing can be conceived possible, would mean with us nothing less than a revolution'.

These ideas of political liberty have lain behind traditional British attitudes to rights and freedoms ever since Dicey first conceived of them. But as a theoretical basis for the protection of these rights and freedoms, such ideas are woefully inadequate. In the first place the guarantee afforded liberty in Dicey's scheme is a negative rather than a positive one. Freedom is not something that can be asserted in opposition to law; it is the residue of conduct permitted in the sense that no statute or common-law rule prohibits it. Undoubtedly, there was such a reservoir of unregulated behaviour in Dicey's day. His unspoken premiss was that such a space for freedom would always continue to exist; he saw Parliament and the courts as guardians of liberty. Accordingly, nothing in his framework was designed to stand up for liberty where the legislature saw fit to intervene with new restrictive laws, or where the courts contrived to discover or develop them; Dicey simply assumed that this would not occur. Yet, as we shall see, this has been by far and away the most prevalent trend in terms of legislation, at least since the start of the 1970s. And, as we shall also see, the courts have not been adverse to developing the common law to like restrictive effect. The Dicey approach has no answer to this. The residue of liberty just gets smaller and smaller, until eventually, in some areas, it is extinguished altogether, with freedom becoming no more than the power to do that which an official has decided for the time being not to prohibit. The British approach of refusing to assert positive rights gives freedom no weapons with which to retaliate.

The point is nicely illustrated by an important case arising out of the miners' strike of 1984–85.[4] Virtually all the members of the South Wales Area of the NUM had obeyed the strike call when it had gone out in 1984. By November, however, a small number of them had returned to work. The practice developed of ferrying this minority of strike-breakers to their collieries in NCB vehicles, protected all the way by large numbers of police officers. Pickets were unable to communicate with the strike-breakers as they were whisked by—peaceful persuasion was not possible. Demonstrators also began to gather outside the pit gates. Sometimes there were several hundreds of them. They shouted and roared as those whom they saw as traitors sped by. The languaged used was often abusive and insulting. An official described this conduct as 'symbolic and "ritualistic" and merely a gesture'. The question arose as to whether this behaviour was unlawful. Scott J. scoured the common law for the right restrictive formula—but without success. There was no assault because, cocooned within their vehicles and surrounded by the police, the working miners had no genuine fear of immediate physical violence, as required by that tort. For the same reason, there was no obstruction of the highway—the miners were getting from home to colliery far more quickly than normal, thanks to the chauffeur and the VIP escort. Nor was there the tort of interference with contract—work was being done (theoretically at least) just as the NCB wanted.

Dicey's theory, therefore, seemed to favour the demonstrators. At this point, however, the judge played an elegant legal game. He turned to private nuisance, a tort which he admitted was 'strictly concerned with, and [could] be regarded as confined to activity which unduly interferes with the use or enjoyment of land'. This should have made it irrelevant to the case before him. The miners owned neither the buses nor the land over which they travelled. However, this was how the judge saw it:

[T]here is no reason why the law should not protect on a similar basis the enjoyment of other rights. All citizens have the right to use the public highway. Suppose an individual were persistently to follow another on a public highway, making rude gestures or remarks in order to annoy or

---

[4] *Thomas* v. *NUM (South Wales Area)* [1985] 2 WLR 1081.

vex. If continuance of such conduct were threatened no one can doubt that a civil court would, at the suit of the victim, restrain by an injunction the continuance of the conduct. The tort might be described as a species of private nuisance, namely unreasonable interference with the victim's rights to use the highway. But the label for the tort does not, in my view, matter.

The demonstrators were therefore in the wrong and the union could properly be held responsible for their actions. In the absence of earlier cases to rely upon, the judge simply invented a new tort, and granted an injunction compelling the union to call off the pickets. Dicey allowed that legislation and the common law could restrict liberty. But now we see that even the absence of law is no guarantee against the possibility of retrospective regulation. Freedom retreats in the face of laws that are constantly emerging, evolving, and accumulating—but very rarely disappearing. They originate not only in Parliament but also in the courts. The residual nature of liberty means that it can never fight back.

This case highlights a second weakness of Dicey's approach, namely his assumption that individual liberty can be adequately protected by the decisions of English judges. The 'law of the constitution' was 'not the source but the consequence of the rights of individuals, as defined and enforced by the courts'. It was the judges' commitment to freedom that was the main guarantee against despotism. It is true that the potential is clearly there: judges retain the independence they won after the 'Glorious Revolution'; members of the senior judiciary may only be removed by the Queen on an address presented by both Houses of Parliament. There is, however, some potential for abuse in the system, with senior appointments being made by the Prime Minister. Other writers have emphasized the narrow social strata from which judges are drawn and have questioned the degree to which they are able to relate to ordinary people and to stand up against the powerful and the rich. These are familiar criticisms. But our concern in this book is more with the civil-liberties record of the judges as reflected in the cases they have decided. It is not a salutary one. The courts have invented new laws, as in the new liabilities to restrain picketing during the miners' strike. They have also rediscovered long-forgotten old ones, such as the Home

Secretary's prerogative to do whatever is 'reasonably necessary to preserve the peace of the realm', which in the case in question meant supplying plastic bullets and CS gas to the police without consultation with Parliament and against the wishes of local police committees (see Chapter 4). The existing common law on breach of the peace has been continuously expanded so that it now adds greatly to the non-statutory powers of the police to restrict peaceful assembly (see Chapter 4).

The courts have identified the interests of the state with the interests of the government of the day (see the Ponting case and the law on secrecy detailed in Chapter 5). They have accepted that Government can avoid scrutiny of its conduct by calling to its aid a concept, 'national security', the definition of which the judges are content to leave to the executive (see the GCHQ case in Chapter 5). Their willingness to grant ex-parte and interlocutory injunctions has meant that liberties are sometimes extinguished without proper adjudication, and on other occasions that their vindication has been crucially delayed (see the Zircon affair and the *Spycatcher* litigation in Chapter 5). There are, of course, exceptions: the various judgments by Sir Nicolas Browne-Wilkinson and Lord Bridge's dissent in *Spycatcher*; the ultimate failure of the Government in that case; and Glidewell J.'s first-instance decision in the GCHQ case. But these are deviations and dissents rather than the mainstream that Dicey would have expected. Our leading civil-liberties cases are still those old authorities with which he was familiar, *Entick* v. *Carrington*[5] and *Beatty* v. *Gillbanks*.[6] The breakthroughs in administrative law that have occurred since the war have concerned issues like the marketing of milk, the dismissal of a chief constable, and the allocation of foreign compensation.[7] Civil-liberties litigation has been dismally deferential to authority. As we see when we examine the *Spycatcher* cases, in the area of civil liberties the courts seem to have come to regard themselves as the partners of the executive, tackling difficult problems together, rather than as a separate, autonomous, and sometimes necessarily antagonistic

[5] (1765) 2 Wils. 275.
[6] (1882) 9 QBD 308.
[7] See *Padfield* v. *Minister of Agriculture* [1968] AC 997; *Ridge* v. *Baldwin* [1964] AC 40; *Anisminic Ltd.* v. *Foreign Compensation Commission* [1969] 2 AC 147.

branch of government. This is a long way from Dicey's reliance on them as the guardians of our rights.

The European Convention on Human Rights

There has been one dramatic innovation since the days of Dicey, though he would not have approved of its European focus and its impact on British law is confusingly oblique. The European Convention on Human Rights was signed at Rome in 1950 and was ratified by the United Kingdom in 1951. It came into force for those states which had ratified it in 1953. The inspiration for the Convention came from the wide principles declared in the United Nations Universal Declaration of Human Rights in 1948. It was a direct result of the move towards greater political co-operation in Western Europe which had led to the creation of the Council of Europe in 1949. The overriding influence was, of course, the Second World War, with its terrible suffering and sacrifice of human life. The Convention set down certain human rights and created a political and judicial procedure to secure their protection. The European Commission of Human Rights was created to receive complaints of abuses from states and (where the country concerned had agreed to such a procedure) from individuals. The Commission's job is to make a preliminary decision on the admissibility of the complaint. An individual, for example, is required to have exhausted all local remedies. If the Commission thinks the case admissible and worth proceeding with, it sees if it can achieve a friendly settlement. If this is not possible, the case may then be referred to the European Court of Human Rights, whose decision on the matter will be binding on the nation concerned. The vast majority of cases begin as applications by individuals against their own states.

A glance at the provisions of the Convention makes interesting reading. The assertion of rights is its starting-point. 'Everyone has the right to respect for his private and family life, his home and his correspondence' (Article 8); 'everyone has the right to freedom of thought, conscience and religion' (Article 9); 'everyone has the right to freedom of expression' (Article 10); 'everyone has the right to freedom of peaceful assembly and to freedom of association with others' (Article 11). These rights are then made subject to exceptions, and these can be very broad. Rather typical are those to be found in Article 10:

The exercise of these freedoms, since it carries with it duties and responsibilities, may be subject to such formalities, conditions, restrictions or penalties as are prescribed by law and are necessary in a democratic society, in the interests of national security, territorial integrity or public safety, for the prevention of disorder or crime, for the protection of health or morals, for the protection of the reputation or rights of others, for preventing the disclosure of information received in confidence, or for maintaining the authority and impartiality of the judiciary.

Two things are clear from this very brief summary of the content of the Convention. First, its approach is completely different to that which pertains in the United Kingdom. The British emphasis, as we have seen, is on liberty as the residue, the bit left over after the law has had its say. The European method is exactly the reverse: the right exists unless it has been abridged by a law which, moreover, has to be specifically justified. It is just the sort of Continental charter that was despised by Dicey. This structural contradiction may explain, though it does not excuse, why Britain has been brought to book so frequently by the European judges. The Court has had occasion to condemn our laws on contempt of court, on prisoners' rights, on terrorism, on telephone-tapping, on birching (in the Isle of Man), on homosexuality (in Northern Ireland), on detention, and on freedom of association. We look at some of these cases in more detail in the chapters that follow. In recent years, the Court's decisions have invariably been the impetus behind that small ration of liberalization that has been forced upon Mrs Thatcher.

Secondly, the wording of the Convention is vague and decisions in individual cases may very largely depend on the preferences of the individual judges involved. The *Sunday Times* case which overruled the House of Lords on contempt was decided by 11 votes to 9. The rejection of Britain's seven-day detention period for terrorist suspects was by 12 votes to 7 (see Chapter 7). The inevitably open texture of such a document leaves a great degree of discretion in the hands of the judiciary. This is an important consideration which bears directly on the current debate as to whether the Convention should be incorporated into British law and made directly enforceable within the jurisdiction. At the moment, the Convention is not part of Britain's domestic law. Litigants may not argue on its basis before a local judge, but they may take their cases to the European Commission after they have exhausted all locally available remedies. Incorporation into domestic law to rectify this anomalous situation would have the attractive consequence of reversing the current bias against freedom inherent in the residual approach now applied. If it were enacted in isolation, however, and if, in particular, there were no new constitutional settlement to underpin it, it is hard to see how problems with parliamentary sovereignty could be avoided. The dogmatic resistance to entrenchment would raise its arid and pedantic head. We discuss this in more detail in our concluding chapter. But, more importantly perhaps, the question of incorporation, particularly of such an open-textured document, inevitably raises difficult questions about the commitment of the British judiciary to the fundamental freedoms that such a charter would be asking them to defend. As has already been suggested, their record does not inspire confidence. Even where legislation has been phrased in the European manner, like section 10 of the Contempt of Court Act, the courts have nevertheless contrived to let pro-executive exceptions swallow the supposed rule (see the *Guardian Newspaper* case, Chapter 5). This general question is one to which we also return, in Chapter 8.

Conclusion

The various issues raised here will receive closer attention as we work our way in greater detail through the law. The criticisms that we make derive strength from an analysis of other jurisdictions with similar common-law backgrounds and the same liberal democratic traditions as the United Kingdom. Australia, Canada, the Republic of Ireland, and the United States have nothing like the same concentration of unqualified power at the centre of government as this country has. As we shall see in subsequent chapters, the approach they have taken to fundamental freedoms has on a number of important occasions been radically different and altogether more liberal than has been the case here. These are the nations with which Britain should be compared and by reference to which her laws should be judged. The existence of totalitarian states elsewhere in the world should be a source of anxiety for us all, rather than an excuse for falling standards at home. Professor Dworkin (1988: 7–8) has summed up present atttitudes to liberty in his trenchant piece in *Index on Censorship*:

[T]his government's challenge to freedom has nothing to do with totalitarian despotism. It shows a more mundane but still corrupting insensitivity to liberty, a failure to grasp its force and place in modern democratic ideals. . . . Thatcher's government places liberty at a much lower level, it makes freedom just another preference, just something that some people want a great deal more than most people do, just something else to be balanced out with an eye to majority opinion and the next election . . . Thatcherism makes intellectual liberty just another commodity, to be enjoyed when there is no particular political or commercial or administrative price to be paid for it, but abandoned, with no evident grief, when the price begins to rise. That is not despotism. But it cheapens liberty and diminishes the nation.

Dworkin concludes that liberty 'is ill in Britain'. In this introduction we have diagnosed some of the causes of its illness and, in the substantive chapters that follow, we will draw attention to its various unpleasant symptoms.

2

The Extension of Police Powers

THE police have been in the front line of Thatcherism. Their diligent enforcement of the Government's industrial laws has helped to transform the role of the trade unions; their role as guarantors of public order has led them into bitter conflict with pickets and demonstrators. Their struggles on the streets of Britain during the riots of 1981 restored the public peace at a time when it looked as though the 'thin blue line' was all that stood between turmoil and a still nascent Thatcherite revolution. The police have also taken on the football hooligans, the hippies, and the criminal gangs. Apart from this industrial, political, and mob violence, however, there has been the ongoing pressure of the seemingly inexorably high level of 'ordinary' crime, the control of which has been high on the agenda for ten years. With a government that appears consciously to thrive on discord, and which has no policy on crime other than the obviousness of its being evil, the central role of the police has been inevitable. To advocates of the 'resolute approach', crime is simply a choice to do wrong; it is never the squalid last gasp of the outsider. The job of the police is to protect the purity of this image.

The Policing Context

For all these valuable services, the police have been well rewarded. Their numbers have jumped over the years. Between May 1979, when the Conservatives came into office, and January 1988 their strength in England and Wales had risen from 109,998 to 122,131, an increase of 11 per cent. In the London metropolitan area growth was in the order of 23.5 per cent, from 22,225 to 27,449. At the end of 1988 the Home Secretary promised an additional 1,230 officers for 1989/90. The Metropolitan Police are expected to cost £1,082.391 million in 1989/90—an increase of over 50 per cent in real terms since 1978/9. Officer remuneration has enjoyed an even more meteoric rise. At the start of 1988, the maximum basic pay for a constable was £13,938; for a superintendent £25,650; and for a chief constable £46,914. This does not include overtime pay, or the free accommodation, or rent allowance in lieu, to which officers are entitled. Constables with the Metropolitan Police can expect, on top of these extras, further sums of £945 (London weighting) and £1,011 (London allowance). On top of all this, the police received, during the autumn of 1988, an average pay rise of 8.5 per cent, well above the rate of inflation at the time.[1]

During the 1980s the police found themselves embroiled in a number of controversies. Whilst driving through London, Stephen Waldorf was shot several times and severely injured by officers who confused him with another person whom they said they were seeking to capture. In September 1985 Mrs Dorothy Croce was shot and paralysed after the police had entered her home in search of her son. Mrs Cynthia Jarrett died during a police search of her home in October 1985, as did a five-year-old boy, John Shorthouse, when a police gun went off accidentally during a search of his home. In 1987 the number of people shot dead in Britain by the police using firearms was five. The deaths in police custody of a number of detainees over the years have also been controversial. Allegations have been made that successful convictions in a number of key murder trials have been dependent upon confession evidence which has been improperly obtained during police interrogation. The cases of the Birmingham

---

[1] These various facts on police manpower, pay, and conditions have been obtained from written answers to parliamentary questions. See in particular: 119 HC Debs. (WA) 603 (16 July 1987); 125 HC Debs. (WA) 783 (21 Jan. 1988); 126 HC Debs. (WA) 250–2 (27 Jan. 1988); 132 HC Debs. (WA) 82 (26 Apr. 1988); 138 HC Debs. (WA) 1018 (21 Oct. 1988); 147 HC Debs. (WA) 111–12 (14 Feb. 1989). See also 140 HC Debs. (WA) 397–8 (14 Nov. 1988).

Six and the Guildford Four are only the best known in what is a disturbingly long list. Allegations about racial harassment simmer away in the background, unhelped by the tiny number of non-whites in police forces up and down the country. Following a serious and unprovoked attack on a number of youths in Holloway, the Police Complaints Authority castigated the 'shameful' silence of a large number of constables and criticized the 'moral failure' of sections of the service (Police Complaints Authority, 1988: 12). In August 1988 a number of police officers joined forces to pursue a person whom it was alleged had been driving recklessly. Quite by chance, and unknown to the police, the incident was filmed and broadcast later on national television news. The victim was charged with obstruction, and the passenger travelling with him was charged with assault. The driver was eventually sentenced to six months in prison for reckless driving. A police investigation has led to charges of assault against five officers.

Criticism has not always been related to specific cases. Various reports critical of CID standards have been issued. As reported in the press, an internal inquiry in 1989 into one police force recommended a radical rehaul in the way the force dealt with local crime. As reported, the authors found 'disturbing' the fact that half of the sample CID investigations they examined were 'lacking in some details or were actually unsatisfactory'. Most of the difficulties lay in 'deep-seated Force problems'.[2] Shortly afterwards, in the same year, a report by MPs criticized the appointments procedure for some senior officers as 'ramshackle . . . haphazard and amateurish in the extreme'. It recommended a radical change in approach (Home Affairs Committee, 1989). A long-term irritant to the police has been the ongoing allegation that some officers have been closely connected with freemasonry. This has recently been the subject of judicial review proceedings.[3] A police constable caused great concern with his assertions, made for the first time some years ago, that some Kent police officers were offering inducements to prisoners to make false admissions to offences, and to confess to crimes that they had not committed, so that the force could then add to the number of crimes they had 'detected', and thereby improve their crime clear-up statistics.

[2] *Independent*, 25 Apr. 1989.   [3] *Independent*, 12 May 1988.

After a three-year investigation involving the Police Complaints Authority, it was announced that a number of police officers were to be admonished or advised about their conduct and were to face disciplinary charges.

The Authority was less successful in its attempt to ensure that disciplinary proceedings were brought against a detective superintendent, whose early retirement from the Metropolitan Police in 1989 meant that he avoided questions about his links with drug smuggling and criminal gangs, queries that had arisen after a *World in Action* television programme which had made serious allegations about corruption in the London police. It is against this background that we examine the nature of police power more than ten years into the premiership of Mrs Thatcher and scrutinize the degree to which the individual is protected from the abuse of that power. The subject of police powers is of course an enormous one raising many diverse issues. In this chapter we are concerned with key aspects of the Police and Criminal Evidence Act 1984, an Act based to some extent on the report of a Royal Commission under the chairmanship of Sir Cyril Philips. When may the police arrest a suspected citizen? What rights do citizens have in custody? Here we are concerned in particular with the right to silence and the right of access to a solicitor. In concentrating on these issues, we are reminded of the comments made by a distinguished Scottish judge in 1954. He said that 'In the eyes of every ordinary citizen the venue [i.e. the police station] is a sinister one. When he stands alone in such a place confronted by several police officers, usually some of high rank, the dice are loaded against him, especially as he knows there is no one to corroborate him as to what exactly occurred during the interrogation, how it was conducted and how long it lasted'.[4]

Police Powers of Arrest

1. The scope of the power

In 1979 there were 1.4 million arrests in England and Wales. The powers underpinning this huge number of detentions were many

---

[4] *Chalmers* v. *HM Advocate* 1954 JC 66.

and varied—but there were some bewildering inconsistencies. A citizen could be arrested without a warrant under the Deer Act 1963, the Town Gardens Protection Act 1863, or the Public Stores Act 1875 for 'obliterating marks denoting that property in stores is HM property', but he or she could not be directly apprehended for an indecent assault on a woman. An important general rule was in an Act passed in 1967, which allowed arrest without a warrant for murder or for any other crime for which the jail sentence could be five years or more, but this was merely in addition to the motley of other provisions. Sir Cyril Philips's Commission observed that there was a 'lack of clarity and an uneasy and confused mixture of common law and statutory powers of arrest, the latter having grown piecemeal and without any consistent rationale'. The task of the police was made 'more difficult because of the complexity of the law', and it was 'scarcely surprising if the citizen [was] uncertain of his rights' (Philips, 1981: 41, 42).

The Royal Commission was anxious to produce order from this chaos in the fairest way possible. To this effect, it suggested that as a general rule the police should be able to arrest an individual without a warrant if the crime which was suspected was one for which the individual could be jailed rather than simply fined. This carried the law further than the 1967 Act because any term of imprisonment (rather than five years minimum) was now to be enough. To meet objections to this, the Commission added that an individual should only be held where, quite apart from being for an 'arrestable offence', the arrest was also 'necessary'. Philips emphasized this idea of 'necessity' as an extra qualification on police power. It had various elements: detention upon arrest should only continue if the person was unwilling to identify himself or herself; or if there was a likelihood that he or she would not turn up at court; or if there was a need to prevent the continuation or repetition of the offence; or if the arrest was essential to protect the arrested person or other persons or property or to secure evidence by questioning or other means. Thus the Commission saw these two vital controls on police power: the arrest had to be for an imprisonable offence and it had also, in addition to this, to be 'necessary'.

For their Police and Criminal Evidence Act 1984 the Government has fastidiously chosen from the menu of options offered by Philips only those dishes that it thought the most palatable. The real taste is disguised by the grandiose wording that accompanies them. The marginal note to section 24 refers to 'arrest without warrant for arrestable offences', an apparent tautology which will be explained later. It defines as 'arrestable offences' murder, treason, and other crimes imprisonable for five years or more. This seems to be a restatement of the old law and a rejection of Philips. All is not as it would appear, however. A number of modifications to this general rule lurk in the background. First, a variety of offences are deemed arrestable despite the fact that they do not fit into this general rule. Most of these are unexceptional. They cover a variety of sexual offences and crimes against property and customs and excise legislation. The Government could not resist adding offences under the Official Secrets Acts 1911 and 1920. This caught the notorious (and now repealed) section 2 for which the punishment was a maximum of two years. Why it should have been possible to arrest without warrant for this ridiculous crime was not clear. Secondly, conspiring or attempting to commit or inciting, aiding, abetting, counselling, or procuring the commission of any arrestable offence is in itself arrestable. Thirdly, a later section grandly describes itself as engaged in the '[r]epeal of statutory powers of arrest without warrant or order'. Clearly, removal of the old laws should be part and parcel of reform. In fact, the Act does not repeal all of them. There are preserved powers of arrest in relation to, among others, the Military Lands Act 1892, the Emergency Powers Act 1920, the Public Order Act 1936 (and now 1986), the Bail Act 1976, and the Prevention of Terrorism Act. The common-law power of arrest for breach of the peace remains untouched. Many of the powers of arrest enjoyed by the police in relation to civil liberties are, therefore, untrammelled by the restrictions introduced in the 1984 law.

These qualifications to section 24 dilute the meaning of 'arrestable offence'. Section 25 relegates it to the margins of police practice. The section could have been summarized in the sidenote as 'arrest for non-arrestable offences', but the draftsman did not dare to risk such Kafkaesque accuracy. Rather than ignore Philips's cherished necessity principle, the Government turned it on its head. The Act provides that where 'a constable has reasonable grounds for suspecting that any offence which is not an arrestable offence has been committed or attempted, or is being committed or attempted, he may arrest the relevant person if it appears to him that service of a summons is impracticable or inappropriate because any of the general arrest conditions is satisfied'. There are five of these general arrest conditions:

(a) he name of the person is not known to the police officer and he or she cannot 'readily ascertain' it.

(b) A name is provided, but the police officer has 'reasonable grounds for doubting' that it is genuine.

(c) A 'satisfactory address' is not provided or, if one is supplied, the constable has 'reasonable ground for doubting' it.

(d) There are 'reasonable grounds for believing' the arrest to be necessary to prevent physical injury to somebody, the loss of or damage to property, an offence against public decency, or an unlawful obstruction of the highway.

(e) There are 'reasonable grounds for believing' that the arrest is 'necessary to protect a child or other vulnerable person'.

All this is very much wider than anything envisaged by Philips. The outcome is a power which transforms the nature of the relationship between the police and the public. All crimes, no matter how trivial, no matter how minor, now expose the citizen to the risk of arrest without warrant and detention, with all the sordid and humiliating consequences that often attach to these upsetting experiences. How vulnerable is the exotically named individual, or anyone who happens to have no identification documents with him or her? Consider too the vulnerability of the homeless person with no fixed abode. By allowing the arbitrary arrest of such people, the Act explicitly recognizes that personal freedom in Britain depends in large measure on economic and material well-being.

In one extraordinary case in July 1988, the reason the officer gave for doubting the name and address of the person arrested was that 'suspects usually gave false names and addresses'. Unsurprisingly, the Divisional Court did not think this was enough.[5] In another case,[6] two police officers spotted a man cycling without his hands on the handlebars. They shouted from their car telling him to cycle properly. He ignored them. They then drew alongside him and told him again to put his hands on the handlebars. This time he did as he was told, but, when the police had driven off, he raised two fingers in their direction. They spotted him, came back, stopped his cycle, and demanded to know his name and address. When he refused to give this information, he was arrested 'for failing to give his name and address'. A struggle ensued, during which many blows were struck. In later proceedings, the validity of this arrest was upheld. The Divisional Court thought the matter 'a storm in a teacup which thereafter became unfortunately somewhat more serious'. It agreed with the police that he had been arrested for cycling without due care and attention and that this had been sufficiently communicated to him. It seems clear, however, that it would be possible in other similar circumstances for a police officer to detain such a person for what he or she did after the offence rather than for the crime itself. In such circumstances, it would be possible to employ section 25 to punish for insolence rather than illegality. The open-ended nature of the section is an invitation to the police to abuse their discretion in response to which there are no effective safeguards. It is difficult to see how the courts can scrupulously review the reasonableness of police discretion where the case comes up so long after the event when the wording in the Act is so very wide in the first place. The overriding criterion—that the service of a summons is impracticable or inappropriate—does not even have to be based on objective grounds; it is enough that it should appear to be so to the constable making the arrest. From being an additional safeguard for those already arrested, the necessity principle becomes, in the hands of the Home Office, the basis of a separate and quite independent set of criteria justifying arrests that would otherwise have been unlawful. Instead of protecting detainees, therefore, it simply adds to their number. It is an audacious transformation, managed by a confident government, and a reminder to Royal Commissions of the impotence of their prestige.

[5] *G.* v. *DPP* [1989] Crim. Law Rev. 150.
[6] *Nicholas* v. *Parsonage* [1987] RTR 199.

2. *The grounds for arrest*

It is one thing to identify the crimes for which an arrest is now possible; it is another to say when such arrests may lawfully take place. Here we have to distinguish between the police and ordinary mortals. Any one of us may arrest a person who is, or who is reasonably suspected to be, in the act of committing an 'arrestable' offence. Any one of us may also apprehend an individual whom we know to be, or whom we have reasonable grounds for suspecting to be, guilty of such an offence as long as it has been committed. However, the ordinary member of the public cannot go around arresting cyclists and homeless persons and so on under section 25. That is the preserve of the police. They have the same powers as the ordinary citizen—and more. If a constable reasonably suspects that an arrestable offence has been committed, he or she may detain anyone whom he or she reasonably suspects to be guilty of it. Furthermore, the constable may also arrest someone whom he or she suspects to be about to, or who is actually about to, commit an arrestable offence.

The key constraint here, of course, is this notion of 'reasonable suspicion'. In the early days, the higher courts provided some fairly clear ideas on what this involved. In one case in 1944, Scott LJ stated that the 'British principle of personal freedom, that every man should be presumed innocent until he is proved guilty, applies also to the police function of arrest—in a very modified degree, it is true, but at least to the extent of requiring them to be observant, receptive and open-minded and to notice any relevant circumstance which points either way, either to innocence or to guilt'. The court pointed out that reasonable suspicion did not require the police 'to have anything like a *prima facie* case for conviction'. They had, however, the 'duty of making such inquiry as the circumstances of the case ought to indicate to a sensible man is, without difficulty, presently practicable'. In the case itself, a man was arrested for having soap flakes (a rationed article) with him as he cycled home. The police did not get his name and address or make enquiries at his workplace to check out his story before they arrested him. Their hunch was held not to amount to a reasonable suspicion.[7] In a leading case in 1969, Lord

---

[7] *Dumbell* v. *Roberts* [1944] 1 All ER 326.

Devlin agreed that reasonable suspicion could be based on information that would not generally be admissible in court. On the facts before it, which concerned a death from a lorry shedding its load, the court held that the police were wrong to arrest for manslaughter the person whom they thought had been driving the truck: there was a wide gap between a suspicion that somebody was driving a truck, and a suspicion that they were driving it recklessly.[8]

These cases show that the courts took a fairly hard line when it came to police discretion in this area. There are a couple more cases of recent vintage,[9] but this is not an issue which the higher courts confront very often. It takes money, determination, and patience to launch a false imprisonment action; most detainees are happy simply to be out of the police station. A magistrates' or crown court will rarely second-guess a constable and it in turn will only very occasionally be overruled on this issue further up the judicial ladder. Hence there is a paucity of case-law. In any event, the courts now seem to take a softer line on police practice so far as this can be discerned from the undiscussed elements in cases that reach the law reports for other reasons. In one good example in June 1988,[10] a company was burgled some time after an employee was sacked. The police suspected that it was an inside job and promptly arrested the dismissed worker, for no reason other than that she might have borne a grudge against her erstwhile employer. After nearly four hours of questioning, she was released. The court accepted that these facts amounted to a reasonable suspicion. There was no need to pursue the matter any further prior to arrest. The fact that other courses of enquiry were open to the police officer did not affect the reasonableness of his suspicion and the lawfulness of the detention. In a 1984 case,[11] jewellery was stolen from a house in which the defendant was a temporary lodger. Shortly afterwards, some of the jewellery was sold to a shop in Portsmouth. More than four months later, the victim of the crime recognized her jewellery in the shop window

[8] *Hussien* v. *Chong Fook Kam* [1970] AC 942.
[9] *King* v. *Gardner* (1979) 71 Cr. App. R. 13; *R.* v. *Prince* [1981] Crim. Law Rev. 638.
[10] *Castorina* v. *Chief Constable of Surrey* (1988) 138 NLJ Law Reports 180.
[11] *Mohammed-Holgate* v. *Duke* [1984] AC 437.

and told the police. The jeweller's description of the person from whom he had bought the valuables was thought by the victim to resemble her former lodger. The police then went to the new home of the former lodger, entered it, and arrested her. They had no warrant. It is difficult to avoid the feeling that the evidence against the arrested person was distinctly shaky—but all the judges thought it enough to justify a reasonable suspicion.

But it is not only the concept of reasonable suspicion that has been diluted by police practice and judicial endorsement. It does not follow that because a police officer reasonably suspects a person of having committed an arrestable offence, that the person should for that reason alone be arrested. Detention of a person presumed to be innocent is a serious matter. In the past something more than this suspicion was required. The position used to be quite clear and is well summed up in what Scott LJ had to say in the wartime case concerning the soap flakes:

The duty of the police when they arrest without warrant is, no doubt, to be quick to see the possibility of crime, but equally they ought to be anxious to avoid mistaking the innocent for the guilty . . . They may have to act on the spur of the moment and have no time to reflect and be bound, therefore, to arrest to prevent escape; but where there is no danger of the person who has *ex hypothesi* aroused their suspicion that he probably is an 'offender' attempting to escape, they should make all presently practicable enquiries from persons present or immediately accessible who are likely to be able to answer their enquiries forthwith.

The whole emphasis here is on arrest to prevent escape. Later in the same judgment, Scott LJ referred to the appropriateness of delaying arrest where 'there [was] no probability . . . of the suspected person running away'. Lord Devlin expanded on this in the lorry accident case in 1969:

It is indeed desirable as a general rule that an arrest should not be made until the case is complete. But if arrest before that were forbidden, it could seriously hamper the police. To give power to arrest on reasonable suspicion does not mean that it is always or even ordinarily to be exercised. It means that there is an executive discretion. In the exercise of it many factors have to be considered besides the strength of the case. The possibility of escape, the prevention of further crime and the obstruction of police inquiries are examples of those factors with which all judges who have had to grant or refuse bail are familiar. (Emphasis added)

The Royal Commission also thought that the purpose of an arrest could be to prevent the destruction of evidence, or the warning of accomplices or the repetition of the crime, or any interference with witnesses. Unlike Scott LJ and Lord Devlin, it did not stop there. The Commission went on to say that detention could also be used 'to dispel or confirm . . . reasonable suspicion by questioning the suspect or seeking further material evidence with his assistance'. This had 'not always been the law or practice' but now seemed 'to be well established'. The development of the law along these lines is recent and confirmation of it by an august Commission is ominous. The earlier cases do not make any reference to the possibility of arresting someone for the sole purpose of questioning him or her with a view to obtaining a confession. As recently as 1978, the Court of Appeal was emphatic that 'police officers can only arrest for offences'. There was no power 'to arrest anyone so that they can make inquiries about him'.[12] Despite this, arrest for questioning has quickly become an attractive option for the police. Research done for Philips testifies to the importance that the police now attach to interrogation of suspects and the procuring of confessions from the guilty. From being a peripheral aspect of police practice, unrecognized in the courts and rarely adverted to as a ground for arrest, detention followed by interrogation has become a central pivot in the battle against crime. Quite imperceptibly, arrest has moved from a position at the end of the investigative process to a new niche right at the start. It is the beginning of the search for a confession rather than the conclusion of a well-managed police operation.

The House of Lords has upheld and indeed encouraged the development of this trend, in an important case in 1984, *Mohammed-Holgate* v. *Duke*.[13] This is the case concerning the burglary of jewellery which we have already encountered. Mrs Mohammed-Holgate was the temporary lodger whom the police

---

[12] *R.* v. *Houghton and Franciosy* (1978) 68 Cr. App. R. 197. The court made an exception for anti-terrorism legislation.

[13] [1984] AC 437.

arrested when, many months after the burglary, the original owner of the valuables thought that she recognized her from the description given by the shop owner of the person from whom she had bought the jewellery. After her arrest, Mrs Mohammed-Holgate was detained for six hours. She was then released on police bail. No charges were brought against her. In subsequent proceedings for false imprisonment, it was admitted that the sole reason for arresting her was the constable's opinion that 'police inquiries were more likely to be fruitful in clearing up the case if Mrs. Mohammed-Holgate were compelled to go to the police station to be questioned there'. The circuit judge translated this as implying that the 'greater stress and pressure' of an arrest made a confession more likely. She was awarded £1,000 damages. The House of Lords overturned the decision. The lower judge was castigated by Lord Diplock for having used 'emotive phraseology'. In the exercise of his power of arrest, it was perfectly proper for the constable to have taken into account that 'there was a greater likelihood . . . that Mrs Mohammed-Holgate would respond truthfully to questions about her connection with or knowledge of the burglary, if she were questioned under arrest at the police station, than if, without arresting her, questions were put to her . . . at her own home from which she could peremptorily order [him] to depart at any moment'. This drift towards investigation through interrogation is altogether clearer when one looks at the provisions on detention which are to be found in the Police and Criminal Evidence Act.

Detention in Police Custody

There was a benign vagueness to the law on detention before the 1984 Act. The police were required to bring the detained person before a magistrates' court 'as soon as practicable' after arrest. After twenty-four hours, the presumption was that the detainee had to be released: it was only if the offence 'appeared to be a serious one' that police bail could be postponed. These important phrases were not defined anywhere in the law. In reality, police practice drifted benevolently in the uncertainty. Three-quarters of all suspects were dealt with within six hours; 95 per cent emerged from custody within a day. A Metropolitan Police study conducted during a three-month period in 1979 found that 0.4 per cent of detainees were held for seventy-two hours or more. The judges, for their part, came increasingly to regard the law as embodying a legal limit of forty-eight hours, after which any detainee had to be brought before a court. A trilogy of cases in 1979 and 1980 reflected this development of a clearer rule.[14] By 1984, it had crystallized into a firm time control on the police power to detain without charge.

A weakness in this scheme was that the original limit of twenty-four hours—applicable to all except serious crimes—seemed to have been forgotten. The Royal Commission sought to rectify this by returning to the twenty-four-hour yardstick as the general rule. It recognized that a longer period of detention might also be required in a 'small minority' of cases concerned with 'grave offences'. There could be a need to check forensic evidence, for example, or to prevent a suspect absconding, or to travel to a far-away police station where the investigation was being conducted, and any of these could take more than a day. Significantly, the Commission did not suggest that such longer periods of detention could ever be justified by the desire to continue questioning or by the need further to interrogate. As a safeguard, they recommended that a magistrates' court should be required to sanction any detention after twenty-four hours and that the suspect should be legally represented at this stage, so that his or her point of view could be put across. The Government followed few of these suggestions when it came to the enactment of its Police and Criminal Evidence Act. Nor was it happy with the imprecision of the old days. To solve crimes, the police needed more time— not on the beat, but in their own cells. More time they were certainly given.

The police now have up to ninety-six hours, i.e. four days and nights, to detain people without charge. Nowhere is this said directly. The greatly increased power which flows from the Act is enshrouded in a mist of complicated statutory provisions. It is protected from public scrutiny by the technicality of its jargon. Words rarely mean what they seem to say. Grandiose guarantees

[14] R. v. Houghton and Franciosy (1978) 68 Cr. App. R. 197; R. v. Hudson (1980) 72 Cr. App. R. 163; Re Sherman and Apps (1980) 72 Cr. App. R. 266.

of freedom are liable to be contradicted in a couple of discreet subparagraphs, loitering at the end of a page. Safeguards offered to detainees turn out to be more apparent than real. Their world is filled with authority figures, some their interrogators, others—custody officers, review officers, superintendents—their statute-designated friends. It is a bureaucracy of incarceration beyond the dreams of the bleakest writer. An arrested person has to be 'taken to a police station by a constable as soon as practicable after the arrest'. Later, we read that 'nothing . . . shall prevent a constable delaying taking a person who has been arrested to a police station if the presence of that person elsewhere is necessary in order to carry out such investigations as it is reasonable to carry out immediately'. This is important because time begins to run only on arrival at a police station; there is no bar on preliminary questioning before detention proper commences. Thus, in the case of *Parchment*,[15] the police committed what would have been a number of breaches of the rules had the accused been in the police station, but, simply because the supposed infractions had taken place before his arrival, the crown court held that nothing wrongful had occurred.

Once at the station, the suspect meets the 'custody officer', a person at least of the rank of sergeant and somebody who is unconnected with the case. He or she is the 'fairy godmother' of the force, the suspect's friend, and the person the Act expects will stand up to his or her (often more senior) colleagues if there is anything amiss: a dramatic invitation to insubordinated heroics. The first job of the officer is to 'determine whether he has before him sufficient evidence to charge that person with the offence for which he was arrested'. If there is not the evidence, 'the person arrested shall be released'. Then comes the expected, 'unless the custody officer has reasonable grounds for believing that his detention without being charged is necessary to secure or preserve evidence relating to an offence for which he is under arrest or *to obtain such evidence by questioning him*' [emphasis added]. If there is no release, then after six hours' detention, in steps the 'review officer', at least of inspector rank, again unconnected with the investigation, who now determines whether there is sufficient

---

[15] [1989] Crim. Law Rev. 290.

evidence to charge. If not, the suspect is to be let go, unless, once again, detention is 'necessary to secure or preserve evidence relating to an offence or *to obtain such evidence by questioning*' [emphasis added]. The same event takes place after fifteen hours and thereafter at nine-hourly intervals. Each time, the review officer asks 'is there the evidence?'; each time he or she is permitted to say that it may be obtained by further questioning. All these reviews may be postponed if the police decide that they are 'not practicable'. The suspect, or the solicitor dealing with the case on his or her behalf (subject to availability), may make representations to the review officer about the continuing detention—but the officer may refuse to hear these if he or she decides that the suspect is 'unfit . . . by reason of his condition or behaviour'.

This procedure takes us through to the end of the first day. Section 41 clearly states that 'a person shall not be kept in police detention for more than 24 hours without being charged'. But this turns out to be subject to 'the following provisions of [the] section and to sections 42 and 43'. In reality, a superintendent or above may authorize detention for up to thirty-six hours. Representations may be made, but, as before, the police can decide that the detained person's behaviour makes him or her unfit to communicate them. There are a number of supposed controls on this power. The offence must be a 'serious arrestable' one; the investigation must be being 'conducted diligently and expeditiously'; and there must be a need to secure or preserve evidence or '*to obtain such evidence by questioning him*' [emphasis added]. How real are these safeguards? First, we have 'serious arrestable offence'. This sounds pretty grave and terrible. In fact, a close examination of a section tucked away right at the end of the Act reveals that it is very vague. The formula includes the obvious, such as murder, rape, kidnapping, and so on. But it also covers all arrestable offences which have (or are likely to have or are intended to have) certain consequences like, among other things, 'serious harm to the security of the State or to public order', 'serious interference with the administration of justice', 'substantial financial gain to any person', and 'serious financial loss to any person'. These words are not defined in the Act. A crime, therefore, is not in itself a 'serious arrestable' one. There is no conclusive schedule of offences to which the police and the suspect can refer. This goes much further than the recommendations of the Royal Commission. Everything depends on what is meant by 'financial gain', 'financial loss', 'security of the State', and so on. The 'gain' and 'loss' provisions bring all thefts potentially within the definition. The courts usually allow the Government to define national security in whatever way it pleases. 'Serious harm to public order' is also a vague phrase undefined in the Act.

The police do not need to know that such an offence is involved. All the superintendent must have are reasonable grounds for believing that an offence is a serious arrestable one; this safeguard, therefore, is obviated where the police think one of these vague and undefined consequences might occur. The second safeguard is even less commendable. This is the requirement that the investigation be conducted diligently and expeditiously— hardly worth putting in the statute, easily reduced to an empty formula, and unlikely significantly to assist the suspect. Finally, the twenty-four hours of detention do not have to have produced one jot of evidence to justify their continuation; it is enough that the police want to obtain such evidence by further questioning. The desire to persist in interrogation is a valid reason for keeping a suspect in custody for thirty-six hours and indeed beyond. For the police may apply to a magistrates' court which can issue a 'warrant of further detention' if it reasonably believes this course of action to be justified. The effect of such a warrant is to keep the suspect incarcerated for up to another thirty-six hours. The criteria that determine the court's decision are much the same as those employed earlier by the superintendent. There are the same imponderables about 'serious arrestable' offences. In particular, it is enough for the police to maintain that 'detention without charge is necessary . . . to obtain evidence by questioning'. Once again, there is no requirement that any evidence than that which grounded the original 'reasonable suspicion' should actually exist—and we have already seen that this formula is sometimes rather loosely interpreted at the arrest stage.

If the police have still not got what they want, there is a final option open to them. Before the seventy-two hours are up, they can go back to the court and apply for an extension of the warrant of further detention by up to another thirty-six hours. The criteria are the same as before, so the desire to pursue still further the questioning of the suspect may be enough to justify the court's sanction for this additional detention. The suspect must appear and may be legally represented at the various hearings before the magistrates, though the utility of this safeguard is reduced by the breadth of the statutory language justifying continued incarceration. A heavy burden is placed on the magistrates to protect individual liberty from the abuse of police power. Much may thus depend on how seriously they rise to the challenge. In London, in 1986, 101 warrants of further detention were sought; 100 were granted. In 1987, the Metropolitan Police asked for 66, and got 57. Much also hinges on how willing the police are to push their powers to the limit. The information available so far is slight. In each of 1986 and 1987, a little less than a couple of dozen suspects would seem to have been detained long into the fourth day in the London area (Metropolitan Police Commissioner, 1987, 1988). A Home Office Research Study published in 1989 found that in the 111 cases in the survey which the police judged to involve serious arrestable offences, the suspect was detained over twenty-four and under thirty-six hours in 44 of them. Warrants of further detention were sought in 14 cases, with 3 such warrants being refused by magistrates (Brown, 1989). But whatever the current practice, the potential breadth of the provisions is clear. Their overall effect is to permit detention for up to ninety-six hours, a far cry from the limit of twenty-four hours suggested by section 41, and to allow it notwithstanding that its primary purpose is nothing more than the questioning and interrogation of the suspect. We have come a long way since the idealism of Lord Devlin—and that was only twenty years ago.

Questioning of Suspects

1. The right to silence

One important omission from the 1984 Act is the right to silence. In the last century, the form of the right was that the police were not to ask any questions of a detained person. It was up to them to prove their case. The 'best maxim' for a constable, according to Lord Brampton's preface to *Vincent's Police Code* in 1882, was:

'keep your eyes and your ears open, and your mouth shut.' By silent watchfulness you will hear all you ought to hear. Never act unfairly to a prisoner by coaxing him by word or conduct to divulge anything. If you do, you will assuredly be severely handled at the trial and it is not unlikely your evidence will be disbelieved.

Out of this rather extreme position developed a more moderate line, involving the notion of a caution, first formalized in the Judges' Rules in 1912, and finding expression today in the Code of Practice for the Detention, Treatment and Questioning of Persons by Police Officers (Home Office, 1985c). Arrested persons must be cautioned in the following terms: 'You do not have to say anything unless you wish to do so, but what you say may be given in evidence.'

Refusing to speak is an exercise of the right to silence. It is a 'right' to the extent that, at the trial, the prosecution may not comment at all on the accused's failure to answer questions and the judge may refer to it, but not adversely: the point is that in no circumstances should silence be used against an accused person. What is the purpose of this rule? It is part of a broader privilege against self-incrimination. The Royal Commission explained it in the following way:

In the accusatorial system of trial the prosecution sets out its case first. It is not enough to say merely 'I accuse.' The prosecution must prove that the defendant is guilty of a specific offence. If it appears that the prosecution has failed to prove an essential element of the offence, or if its evidence has been discredited in cross-examination, there is no case to answer and the defence does not respond. There is no need for it to do so. To require it to rebut unspecific and unsubstantiated allegations, to respond to a mere accusation, would reverse the onus of proof at trial and would require the defendant to prove the negative, that he is not guilty. Accordingly, 'it is the duty of the prosecution to prove the prisoner's guilt,' which is, in Lord Sankey's words, the 'golden thread' running through English criminal justice.

The second element in the right of silence is that no one should be compelled to betray himself. It is not only that those extreme means of attempting to extort confessions, for example the rack and thumbscrew, which have sometimes disfigured the system of criminal justice in this country, are abhorrent to any civilised society, but that they and other less awful, though not necessarily less potent, means of applying pressure to an accused person to speak do not necessarily produce speech or the truth. This is reflected in the rule that statements by the accused to be admissible must have been made voluntarily. (Philips, 1981: 80, 81)

The American Supreme Court has long been a proponent of the rule:

Our system of criminal justice demands that the government seeking to punish an individual produce the evidence by its own independent labours, rather than by the cruel, simple expedient of compelling it from his own mouth.[16]

It is quite clear that this thread of non-incrimination is at variance with the recent emphasis on obtaining confession evidence. Silent detainees reduce the effectiveness of the Police and Criminal Evidence Act. They deprive officers of the interrogation that is often the sole or main purpose behind an individual's detention. Surprisingly, there were very few who argued, during the passage of the Police and Criminal Evidence Act, for the removal of the right to silence. On the contrary, its continued existence was soon recognized by lawyers to be a vital counterbalance to the new powers the police had secured. Certain aspects of its exercise had, however, attracted criticism in the past. In 1972 the Criminal Law Revision Committee had been particularly exercised by the fear that silent suspects could 'ambush' the prosecution with evidence at their trial which they did not mention during questioning and which the police now had no time independently to verify. They had proposed a new rule to the effect that, i. during an interrogation, a suspect omitted to mention some fact which would exculpate him or her, but kept this back until the trial, the court or jury could infer that the evidence was untrue (Criminal Law Revision Committee, 1972). This proposal would have involved a different, immensely complicated, and, for suspects, terrifying new caution which could easily fatally have undermined the whole rule. It was very controversial and was never acted upon by government.

The Royal Commission rejected the proposal for a number of reasons, and it was not to the fore of government thinking when

[16] *Miranda* v. *Arizona* 384 US 436 (1966).

the Police and Criminal Evidence Bill was being drafted. In recent years, however, a dramatic change in emphasis has begun slowly to come about. The whole momentum of the 1984 Act, with its emphasis on detention, interrogation, and confessions, has made the right to silence more vulnerable than ever to allegations that it is out of date, too favourable to criminals, and anachronistic. The logic of the Act makes it appear an eccentric indulgence rather than a guarantee of fair procedures. In late 1988 the right was rendered well-nigh obsolete in Northern Ireland, by changes that were introduced without any consultation—we shall examine this further in Chapter 7. In the same year, the Home Secretary set up an internal committee to examine how the right to silence might best be modified in England and Wales. At the time of writing, its report is still awaited, but it seems certain that legislation will shortly be introduced to end or sharply to modify the present law. If this does occur, then the Act will be seen to have been part of a 'softening-up' exercise, creating the conditions within which abolition of the right is capable of being presented as an inevitable rationalization, without actually tackling it directly. This is all the more so because other provisions in the Act, as they have been interpreted in the courts, amount to what is effectively an indirect attack on the right to silence. These concern in particular access to legal advice and the admissibility of confession evidence, and we shall now examine each of these in turn.

2. Legal representation of suspects

The law sets out a variety of safeguards to ensure that suspects are not unfairly or harshly treated when they are detained for questioning. Many of the relevant rules appear in a Code of Practice which was circulated to the police when the Act came into force. It covers issues like the treatment of the suspect in custody, the conditions of his or her detention, the form of interviews, the provision of rest periods, and so on. The most important safeguard is probably the entitlement to legal advice; this is also the one that may be most inconvenient for the police. An American Supreme Court judge once said that any 'lawyer worth his salt will tell the suspect in no uncertain terms to make no statement to the police under any circumstances'.[17] Lawyers can usually be relied upon to tell detainees of their rights in a way that suggests that some of them might actually be useful. Their conversations with suspects are likely to be more intelligible than the form-filling friendliness of any number of custody officers. But although the Act affects to recognize that lawyers are a 'good thing' it proceeds to undermine their utility in a number of important respects. First, there is the illusory general rule, with which, after looking at detention, we are now familiar. It is in section 58(1), which declares in ringing terms that a 'person arrested and held in custody in a police station or other premises shall be entitled, if he so requests, to consult a solicitor privately at any time'. The 'if he so requests' bit is a clever nuance which undermines the rest. The Royal Commission thought that the police should be under a duty to inform detainees. This obligation to inform now appears not in the Act but in the Code of Practice, which suggests not only that suspects should be told of their rights but also of 'the fact that they need not be exercised immediately'.

Section 58(1) is subject to a number of later subsections. The detainee making a request 'must be permitted to consult a solicitor as soon as is practicable except to the extent that delay is permitted by this section'. An officer of the rank of superintendent or above may delay access where the detainee is suspected of a serious arrestable offence and where the officer reasonably believes that one of the following will result from allowing such access:

(a) Interference with or harm to evidence connected with a serious arrestable offence.

(b) Interference with or physical injurty to other persons.

(c) The alerting of other persons suspected of having committed such an offence but not yet arrested for it.

(d) The hindering of the recovery of any property obtained as a result of such an offence.

Access can only be denied for a maximum period of thirty-six hours. These provisions are wider than what was proposed by the Royal Commission. The concept of a 'serious arrestable offence'

[17] *Watts* v. *Indiana* 338 US 49 (1949). The judge was Justice Jackson.

is, as we have seen, particularly vague. A broad interpretation of what it means would greatly expand the number of crimes for which access to legal advice could be delayed. A further debilitating gloss on section 58(1) is tucked away in the inner recesses of the police codes. It applies where access to a lawyer cannot be delayed, either because the offence is not a serious arrestable one or because none of the conditions for a temporary denial of access exist. The lawyer may have been notified, but the Act does not prohibit questioning before arrival. The Code allows it, where the suspect consents, or where a senior officer reasonably believes that delaying interrogation will 'involve an immediate risk of harm to persons or serious loss of, or damage to, property' or 'cause unreasonable delay to the processes of investigation'. This latter phrase is ominously open-ended. It must be frustrating to arrive at a police station after a hectic drive, only to find that 'the processes of investigation' necessitated a quick confession from the client.

So far we have referred exclusively to the rules. Our presumption has been that the police adhere to them. Certainly there are these useful exceptions and loopholes which entitle an officer to deny access. We may disapprove—but it is clearly within the law. What happens where the police flout the rules, for example by breaching the code or by denying a solicitor in a trivial case or by refusing access on grounds which are manifestly outside the statute and the code? There is no tort or crime, as there would be if the police were to beat up the suspect or wrongly apprehend him or her in the first place. The detainee can make a formal complaint after release, but this offers little solace to the aggrieved individual. The issue becomes especially important where, as a result of questioning, and without the benefit of the correct conditions or the advice from the solicitor, access to whom has been wrongly denied, the suspect makes a damaging confession which the police later try to rely upon at the trial in order to secure a conviction. Do the courts ignore the police malpractice and allow the jury to hear evidence of this confession, thereby, of course, greatly increasing the chances of a guilty verdict? Or do they say that, because the police behaved badly, the confession is, as a result, unreliable or unfair and it should not therefore be entered in evidence? The Act did not provide a clear answer to this crucial question and it depended very much on the courts.

The most important case, drawing together several decisions in the lower courts, is the Court of Appeal decision *R. v. Samuel*.[18] The police suspected that Samuel had been involved in a serious armed robbery at a building society in Birmingham. A cashier thought she recognized him as the man who had done it. On the basis of this suspicion he was arrested. A search of his house revealed evidence that was, to put it mildly, incriminating: two face masks, a building society pass book hidden under the carpet, lots of property from some other burglaries, and photographs of Samuel kissing bundles of banknotes. Samuel admitted to the burglaries but not to the robbery. The police were anxious to charge him with this as well. He had said that he did not want a solicitor when he first arrived at the police station, at 2 p.m. At 8.30 p.m. he asked for his lawyer. The superintendent refused access, recording that it was a serious arrestable offence and that there was a 'likelihood of other suspects to be arrested being inadvertently warned'. He was kept in overnight and questioned in more detail. At 11 a.m. the following day his mother was told of his detention. She managed to get the services of a highly respected Birmingham solicitor, a Mr Warner, but the police still refused to let him near his client. At 4.30 p.m. Samuel was charged with the burglaries, but questioning about the armed robbery went on. Mr Warner was still refused access. A new police questioner was drafted in. Samuel now faced three officers across the table, a detective inspector, a sergeant, and a detective, whereas before he had faced only two. At about 5.30 p.m., over twenty-seven hours into his detention and after four extended bouts of questioning, he confessed to the robbery. At 6.20 p.m. he was charged. At 7.25 p.m. he finally got to see his solicitor.

The Court of Appeal was scathing in its condemnation of this sequence of events. A suspect should always be able to see a solicitor after being charged, as Samuel was here at 4.30 p.m., with burglary. Access should only be denied before charge in very rare circumstances. Mistrust of a solicitor had to be based on tangible fact, and could not simply reflect a suspicion of the profession in general. Here, Samuel's mother knew all about where he was, and she could have tipped off any alleged accomplices long before the solicitor got a chance to do so inadvertently. In any event, 'a highly respected and very experienced professional lawyer [was] unlikely to be hoodwinked by a 24-year-old'. Denying access because the solicitor might advise his client to keep quiet was 'wholly unsustainable'. The court found the idea of Mr Warner unconsciously communicating coded messages to Samuel's fellow criminals quite ridiculous. The judges then went on to get through to the hub of the whole matter:

The more sinister side to the decision is, of course, this. The police had, over a period exceeding 24 hours, interviewed this young man four times without obtaining a confession from him in respect of the robbery. Time was running out for them. It was a Thursday evening. Thirty-six hours from the relevant time would expire in the early hours of the morning; then access to a solicitor would have to be permitted. On the following day the appellant would have to be taken before the magistrates' court: section 46. As he had already been interviewed four times and been in police custody for over 24 hours, the expectation would be that a solicitor might well consider that, at least for that evening, enough was enough and that he ought to advise his client not to answer further questions. . . . Regrettably we have come to the conclusion that whoever made the decision to refuse Mr Warner access at 4.45 pm was very probably motivated by a desire to have one last chance of interviewing the appellant in the absence of a solicitor.

The Court therefore excluded the confession wrongly obtained by the police and went on to quash Samuel's conviction for armed robbery.

After *R.* v. *Samuel* the police underwent a painful education, as a series of people charged with serious crimes on the basis of admissions went free because they had been wrongly denied access to a solicitor.[19] In January 1988 Leeds crown court excluded statements by the accused with the result that he was acquitted of the murder of a police sergeant and the attempted murder of a constable. In Manchester crown court a confession to two murders was disallowed because of improper denial of access;

[19] A number of these crown court decisions have been reported: *R.* v. *Davison* [1988] Crim. Law Rev. 442; *R.* v. *Vernon* [1988] Crim. Law Rev. 445; *R.* v. *Trussler* [1988] Crim. Law Rev. 446; *R.* v. *Cochrane* [1988] Crim. Law Rev. 449.

another man later pleaded guilty to the same charges. This shows up the reason for this tough line which, unfortunately, is no longer the stance that the Court of Appeal now unequivocally adopts. A notable judicial absentee in the *Samuel* case was the Lord Chief Justice, Lord Lane. In a case in May 1988,[20] a youth called Alladice confessed to armed robbery after the police had denied his request for a solicitor. He was sentenced to eight years in youth custody. Lord Lane accepted that the refusal to allow Alladice a lawyer was quite improper and a clear breach of section 58. It did not follow from this that the confession should therefore be excluded, however. This is where the case departed from the spirit of *Samuel*. The Chief Justice said that exclusion depended on all the circumstances: here the interview was conducted with propriety and the solicitor would have added nothing to the knowledge the detainee already had about his rights. The whole procedure, therefore, had been quite fair. On this basis, Lord Lane allowed in the confession and upheld Alladice's conviction. It is easy to see that there is potential here for an undermining of *Samuel*. Section 58 is not quite as absolutely critical as that case had suggested. Of course, Alladice can occupy his time in custody by lodging any number of formal complaints. One can imagine how severe the reprimand will be for the officer whose disregard of the rules has been decorated with a successful conviction.

Apart from qualifying the scope of *Samuel*, *Alladice* is important also for the interesting observations made by Lord Lane about legal advice and the right to silence. He said:

The result [of legal advice] is that in many cases a detainee who would otherwise have answered proper questioning by the police will be advised to remain silent. Weeks later at his trial such a person not infrequently produces an explanation of, or a defence to, the charge the truthfulness of which the police have had no chance to check. Despite the fact that the explanation or defence could, if true, have been disclosed at the outset and despite the advantage which the defendant has gained by these tactics, no comment may be made to the jury to that effect. The jury may in some cases put two and two together, but it seems to us that the effect of section 58 is such that the balance of fairness between prosecution and defence cannot be maintained unless proper comment is permitted on the

[20] *R.* v. *Alladice* (1988) 138 NLJ Law Reports 141. See also *R.* v. *Hughes* [1988] Crim. Law Rev. 519.

defendant's silence in such circumstances. It is high time that such comment should be permitted together with the necessary alteration to the words of the caution.

Abolition of the right to silence has been rejected by Parliament on a number of occasions, most recently when the Police and Criminal Evidence Act was enacted. It is a matter for elected representatives. Now Lord Lane has used the forum of a court of law in order to make his contribution to this political debate. More to the point, he has modified the right by taking a less than severe attitude to breaches of section 58. This point was made even clearer in a later case involving the Chief Justice, in which he stated that a 'breach of the Act or the Code did not mean that any statement made by a defendant after such breach would necessarily by ruled out. Every case had to be determined on its own particular facts'.[21] Certainly there have been cases after *Alladice*, including the one in which these remarks were made, where infraction of the rules has led to the resultant evidence being declared inadmissible.[22] The clear and simple message contained in the *Samuel* case has, however, been diluted. Since *Alladice*, the Divisional Court has accepted that access by a solicitor's clerk to a detained person may be refused if the police believe that the clerk is 'not capable of providing advice, whether because of his appearance, age, his mental capacity or because of the police knowledge of him'.[23] The police may form a view on capacity, but not, the Court insists, on quality. It is a line that will be difficult to draw in the adversarial atmosphere of the police station. The Haldane Society was reported in October 1988 to have claimed that the police had devised 'techniques and procedures' to bypass or avoid the safeguards in the Police and Criminal Evidence Act. After their brief scare in *Samuel*, it would appear that the police are now as protected as ever.

[21] *R. v. Parris* [1989] Crim. Law Rev. 214.
[22] See the following crown court cases: *R. v. Quayson* [1989] Crim. Law Rev. 218; *R. v. Fennelley* [1989] Crim. Law Rev. 142; *R. v. Williams* [1989] Crim. Law Rev. 66; *R. v. Fogah* [1989] Crim. Law Rev. 141. See also the Court of Appeal decisions in *R. v. Doolan* [1988] Crim. Law Rev. 747; *R. v. Absolam* [1988] Crim. Law Rev. 748; *R. v. Delaney* [1989] Crim. Law Rev. 139, and *R. v. Waters* [1989] Crim. Law Rev. 62.
[23] *Ex parte Robinson* (1989) 139 NLJ 186.

Conclusion: Police Accountability

The crux of recent difficulties in relation to the police lies in the ambiguity of our attitude to them. One view has it that they are the trusted preservers of law and order, men and women who do a difficult job very well and who deserve to be respected and admired throughout the communities which they protect. The other approach is less accommodating. It sees the police as powerful agents, people who are discriminatory in their exercise of might, and whose every action needs to be checked and controlled at every turn. Which of these views prevails today? The first is the traditional perception, the second the one that is gaining ground fast. Each new piece of police excess, each reported example of police harassment, each fresh scandal adds to the number of its converts. The Conservative Government under Mrs Thatcher tried in its Police and Criminal Evidence Act to steer a middle ground between these rival views. The result is, as we have seen, a difficult and sometimes contradictory compromise. On the one hand, Parliament did not trust the police enough to give them the power they wanted and then let them get on with it. The Act is a mass of technical paperwork and restriction. Each power is hedged about with qualifications and bureaucratic safeguards. On the other hand, the police are left largely to themselves when it comes to making sure that the Act is actually followed. Thus, 'reasonable suspicion', undefined and left to the discretion of the individual constable, is the key to many of their lavish powers. Detention is supervised by a custody officer who turns out on closer inspection to be a police officer with a different name. Senior officers have an exclusive say for thirty-six hours and thereafter an influential say before magistrates on how long a suspect should be kept in custody. Countless other powers depend upon note-taking and the keeping of records, all of which matters are inevitably in the hands of the police themselves.

External controls are secondary to this primary emphasis on self-policing. Police liaison consultative committees have been established in each of the London boroughs, though the majority party in five of the boroughs has refused to nominate represent-atives to their local groups. As we have seen the magistrates have an important role to play in overseeing the extension of detention beyond thirty-six hours. A potentially more important source of external control by the judiciary lies in the ability of the courts to exclude evidence obtained by sharp police practice. So far as confession evidence is concerned, the old law emphasized that, to be capable of being entered in evidence, a confession had to be obtained 'voluntarily'. This meant that it could not be used if it was the result of a 'fear of prejudice or hope of advantage, exercised or held out by a person in authority' or if it was occasioned by 'oppression'.[24] In the early 1970s the courts applied this test with extreme rigour. Gradually, during the decade, they began to relax it so as to admit more and more controversial confessions. This mirrored the increased emphasis on confession evidence within the police forces around the country. Public concern came to a head in the Maxwell Confait case, in which the reliability of confession evidence obtained from a mentally handicapped defendant became a particular source of anxiety (Fisher, 1977). In the Police and Criminal Evidence Act, the old idea of voluntariness, with its preoccupation with the mental state of the suspect, was dropped and replaced by a broader rule. A confession will now be excluded if it is the result of *'oppression'* or if it is the consequence of 'anything said or done which was likely, in the circumstances existing at the time, to render [it] *unreliable'* (emphasis added). Once the issue is validly raised, the prosecution has the burden of disproving it beyond reasonable doubt. The word 'oppression' is defined to include 'torture, inhuman or degrading treatment, and the use or threat of violence (whether or not amounting to torture)'. But crucially, although oppressive confessions may be ruled out, the Act goes on to provide that the fact 'that a confession is wholly or partly excluded . . . shall not affect the admissibility in evidence of any facts discovered as a result of the confession'. To take a wild hypothetical instance, the police could torture a suspect into revealing the location of stolen goods and then use the fact that his fingerprints are on them at his trial. In such circumstances, it is not such a blow to have lost the confession.

---

[24] *R.* v. *Prager* [1972] 1 WLR 260.

So far as evidence other than confessions is concerned, there is again no guarantee that unlawful police action will be punished by refusing to admit into court the evidence against an accused that their wrongdoing has secured. Indeed, the old common law was not in the least interested in how the police got their evidence; all that mattered was its probative value.[25] The European Court of Human Rights has left this general question to be dealt with by local law,[26] and the matter is, therefore, one for the discretion of British trial judges. Pressure from Lord Scarman and others in the House of Lords forced a change on the Government when it was enacting the Police and Criminal Evidence Act. The position now is that in any proceedings, 'the court may refuse to allow evidence . . . if it appears to the court that, having regard to all the circumstances, including the circumstances in which the evidence was obtained, the admission of the evidence would have such an adverse effect on the fairness of the proceedings that the court ought not to admit it' (section 78). It remains to be seen how this will operate in practice. In a recent case, the police posed as ordinary civilians in order to trap a shop owner, licensed to sell liquor by the case only, into selling them a few cans of lager and a bottle of wine. At his trial for this offence, he sought the exclusion of the evidence thereby obtained on the ground that he had been the victim of an entrapment. The Divisional Court said that this did not matter and was not caught by section 78, which the judges stressed was concerned with no more than the narrow question of the effect of the police practice on the fairness of the proceedings in court. The police could have adopted a different strategem but it would have been 'more time-consuming and difficult' than this 'simple procedure'.[27] The Scottish courts have been stricter than the English judges in this area, and the Americans exclude all evidence obtained in unlawful searches, subject to a 'good faith' exception developed in recent years.[28]

The weakness of these controls throws the spotlight on the Police Complaints Authority composed of lay persons. The

[25] *R.* v. *Sang* [1980] AC 402.

[26] *Schenk* v. *Switzerland*. Judgment of 12 July 1988. Series A, vol. 140.

[27] *DPP* v. *Marshall* [1988] 3 All ER 683.

[28] *Massachusetts* v. *Sheppard* 468 US 981 (1984); *United States* v. *Leon* 468 US 897 (1984).

complaints must be made to the police themselves in the first instance and all subsequent investigations are undertaken by police officers. Unsurprisingly, this hybrid procedure has caused problems. A number of prosecutions of constables arising out of the disorders at Wapping at January 1987 collapsed on account of delay. Others, such as those into an assault on youths in Holloway and into the 'crime-fixing' charges against Kent police, almost failed on account of a lack of sufficient police co-operation. The Authority handled 5,566 cases in 1987 and 5,516 in 1988 (Police Complaints Authority, 1988; 1989). In each year, less than 800 of these cases led to any form of criminal or disciplinary action, and the vast majority of even this small number involved nothing more severe than 'advice or admonishment'—651 of the 766 cases in 1987, for example. Yet even this relatively innocuous, and to some extent 'in-house', Authority has incurred the wrath of the police. An overwhelming vote of no confidence in it it was passed at the annual Police Federation conference in 1989, with one member being reported in the press as having described the Authority as 'hell-bent on depriving police officers of their civil rights'.[29] The previous year, the newspapers reported one memorable description of the Authority as a 'group of self-opinionated middle-class wallies playing Sherlock Holmes'.[30] Members of the Police Federation have admitted that 'anything short of total independence will fail to stifle the cry from outside the service that we are still judging our own'. How the Federation's members would respond to this is uncertain. One can only speculate about how a genuinely independent and effective complaints authority would be received. In this as in other areas, the fundamental error in our approach to policing is revealed: we do not trust the police so we build safeguards into the way they exercise their power. However, we have enough faith to allow them to police those very safeguards which mistrust has impelled us to impose. It is a curious paradox, that we should half mistrust the police in this way. The result is a muddle in which police efficiency and individual liberty are two certain losers.

[29] *Independent*, 18 May 1989.
[30] A member of the Police Federation as reported in the *Independent*, 20 May 1988.

3

The Interception
of Communications

THE interception of communications gives rise to something of a dilemma for a democratic society. As Lord Diplock pointed out in 1981, on the one hand it constitutes 'a major invasion of privacy', while on the other it is an important weapon available to the police and the security services, whose business it is to maintain law and order and protect national security. What this suggests then is that although it may be necessary to tolerate the practice, it should be conducted only in exceptional and highly controlled circumstances under which there is adequate scrutiny and review by institutions independent of the executive branch of government. The purpose of this chapter is to highlight the profound failure of British law and practice in this regard, concentrating mainly on telephone-tapping rather than on other forms of interception. We begin by tracing the position before 1985, when state agents were able to indulge in the practice of telephone-tapping without any direct legal authority. We then consider the judicial response to these arrangements before examining the Interception of Communications Act 1985, passed as a result of a decision of the European Court of Human Rights that British practice violated Article 8 of the Convention.

The Position before 1985

As might be expected, only a limited amount of information about the practice of telephone-tapping is made available to the public. The major sources of information about what happened before 1985 are two Home Office reports. The first is the Birkett Report of 1957 and the second is a White Paper published by the Home Office in 1980, updating the account given twenty-three years earlier. Access to information was otherwise protected by the Official Secrets Act 1911, section 2, and is perhaps now even more tightly controlled by the Official Secrets Act 1989. Until 1969 the Post Office was a department of government and at the time the telephone network was part of the Post Office. So there was no question but that section 2 of the 1911 Act applied to make it unlawful for any person to communicate information without authorization. Since 1969 many changes have taken place. The telephone network is now under the control and direction of British Telecom which has become a privatized monopoly. Nevertheless, by the Telecommunications Act 1984, section 2 was extended to BT employees (that is to say, private sector employees) and it is now an offence under the Official Secrets Act 1989 for Crown servants (which could be extended to cover BT employees engaged in this work) to disclose various types of information relating to telephone-tapping. These measures have not, of course, stopped information other than official information from being made public. Duncan Campbell and other journalists have been able to reveal intimate details of the workings of the system, as has Cathy Massiter, a former MI5 employee who 'went public' in a Channel 4 television programme. She was not prosecuted (though clearly she could have been) under section 2 of the Official Secrets Act 1911, possibly because the Government had just had its nose bloodied by a jury in the Clive Ponting trial, a case we deal with in Chapter 5.

1. The procedures for interception

According to the official version of events, interceptions were made before 1985 only on the authority of a warrant issued by the Home Secretary, the Secretary of State for Scotland, the Foreign Secretary, or the Secretary of State for Northern Ireland, with each warrant naming only one person and one number. So far as the grounds for issuing such warrants were concerned, these were first for the detection of serious crime, and, secondly, for safeguarding the security of the state. So far as serious crime was concerned, three conditions had to be satisfied: the crime had to be really serious; the normal methods of investigation had to have been tried and failed; and there had to be good reason to believe that the interception would result in a conviction (Birkett, 1957). The vague term 'really serious crime' was defined to mean an offence which carried the possibility of a three-year sentence for conviction on a first offence, or one in which large numbers of people were involved.[1] In 1982 this definition was extended (without parliamentary approval) to cover lesser offences where the financial rewards of success were very great.[2] As so defined, this ground for interception was wide enough to cover just about anything, from murder to breach of the peace. So far as the security of the state was concerned, two principles were stated to govern the granting of warrants. First, there had to be a major subversive or espionage activity that was likely to injure the national interest, and secondly the material likely to be obtained by the interception had to be of direct use in compiling the information necessary for the security services to carry out the tasks laid upon them by the state. The security services not being statutory agencies with statutory duties, their tasks were defined by the executive, without any parliamentary scrutiny. As so defined by the Home Secretary (Sir David Maxwell-Fyfe) these tasks were set out in 1952 as follows:

The Security Service is part of the Defence Forces of the country. Its task is the Defence of the Realm as a whole, from external and internal dangers arising from attempts at espionage and sabotage, or from actions of persons and organizations whether directed from within or without the country, which may be judged to be subversive of the State.

According to the official version of events, interceptions were made only on the authority of a warrant issued by the appropriate Secretary of State under his own hand. A number of safeguards were said to be in force, the first being that all applications had to be made in writing. Secondly, applications had to be made direct

---

[1] In the White Paper (Home Office, 1980a) it was revealed that warrants could be issued for lesser offences, not only where a large number of people were involved, but also where there was good reason to apprehend the use of violence.

[2] 22 HC Debs. 95 (WA) (21 Apr. 1982). This followed a recommendation by Lord Diplock in his second report as judicial monitor.

to the appropriate Secretary of State who, if not available, had to sign at the earliest possible opportunity (though they could be issued initially by a civil servant). Thirdly, it was claimed that no general warrants were issued. Birkett reported that on occasion a single warrant had been issued to cover a number of names, a practice which the committee criticized as being 'undesirable'. According to the White Paper, these criticisms were heeded, it being explained that 'As a general rule, each warrant names only one person and one address or telephone number' (Home Office, 1980a). Fourthly, a limit was imposed on the duration of each warrant. Until 1957 they were of unlimited duration. Thereafter, warrants were issued for only two months, though they could be renewed for one month at a time in the case of those issued to the police, and six months at a time in the case of those issued to the security services. Fifthly, regular reviews were made of outstanding warrants to see whether their continued operation was justified. Indeed, a quota was said to be imposed on the number of warrants which the Home Office would permit the police at any one time in order to ensure that the need for existing warrants was carefully scrutinized. There was, however, no quota on the number of warrants issued to the security services. Finally, in 1980 a senior judge was appointed to conduct a continuous independent check to ensure that interceptions were being conducted in accordance with the established procedures, with a duty to report to the Prime Minister.

2. Interception in practice

So warrants could be issued only on very limited grounds: either for *major* subversive or espionage activities, or for the *detection* of really serious crime. Yet although attempts were made to assure the British public that telephone-tapping was conducted in the most exceptional and in the most highly controlled circumstances, it was suspected by some that the practice was very different. Indeed, it is difficult to justify many of the cases where tapping is strongly suspected on the ground that it was necessary for the detection of really serious crime or to deal with major subversion, even allowing for the very wide definition of subversion announced by Lord Harris of Greenwich in 1975 when he said that

'Subversive activities are generally regarded as those which threaten the safety or well-being of the State and which are intended to undermine or overthrow Parliamentary democracy by political, industrial or violent means'.[3]

The following episodes are recent examples of allegations which have been made. If these can be confirmed and if the tappings were done with the authority of a Home Office warrant, it suggests that the guidelines were being interpreted with a remarkable degree of latitude.

(a) Questions surfaced about the tapping of the telephones of the Canadian High Commission at the time of the proposed repatriation of the Canadian Constitution.[4]

(b) Greenpeace, the environmental group, planned in September 1983 to row across the Thames, climb Big Ben, and unfurl a banner at the top. They arranged the protest at short notice over the phone and arrived at the river to find police everywhere.[5]

(c) The El Salvador Human Rights Campaign discovered at 1 o'clock one day that Henry Kissinger was due to pay a flying visit to London. At 3 o'clock they decided to organize a picket by phone. At 5 o'clock they turned up to find the police waiting for them.[6]

(d) Joan Ruddock, then chairperson of the Campaign for Nuclear Disarmament, heard her telephone conversation being played back to her at the end of a call. She called in a neighbour to witness what happened (Labour Research, 1984). CND in fact appears to be an established target for surveillance. The following story has been told on more than one occasion:

Tim and Bridie Wallis live near Molesworth and object to the Government's nuclear defence policy. They have a perfect right to object to it. As the Home Secretary has said several times, there is nothing illegal about that. On 31 January, someone dialled the Wallis's home number. After obtaining first the engaged tone and then the unobtainable tone—that would not happen now after privatisation—the caller was finally connected to an answerphone which said:

[3] 357 HL Debs. 947 (26 Feb. 1975).
[4] Financial Times, 12, 13 Feb. 1981.
[5] Guardian, 18 Apr. 1984.
[6] Guardian, 18 Apr. 1984.

'This is Tim and Bridie Wallis's number. We are out at the moment. Please leave your name, address and phone number and we will ring you back'.

Asked to leave his address on the answerphone? He rang the Wallis's number twice more during a period of five days and each time got the answerphone. The voice on the answerphone was described as male, with an Americanised accent. The caller did not know Tim Wallis well, but knew that he spoke with an American accent. He therefore assumed that it was Tim's voice on the machine. The Wallises report that the telephone regularly rings once or twice and then stops before they can answer it.[7]

(e) The independent inquiry established by NCCL on Civil Liberties and the Miners' Dispute referred in its interim report to a number of complaints which it received about tapping of telephones and the interception of mail. The inquiry reported that the evidence which they had received to date did not prove conclusively that such activities had taken place, but 'in some instances circumstantial evidence in support of the complaint has been very strong' (NCCL, 1984). On the question of the miners' strike, one study refers to an episode in South Wales where the owner of a bus company was phoned by strikers who wanted to be taken to Derbyshire. The owner was rung up minutes later by the Derbyshire police asking how many pickets he was bringing. The same study reports pickets laying traps for tappers by directing them to wrong venues (Coulter, Miller, and Walker, 1984: 46)

Although telephone-tapping during the miners' strike was relatively well publicized, it is allegedly by no means a new phenomenon in the policing of industrial disputes. Allegations of tapping of strikers and their leaders include claims that, during the General Strike in 1926, Ernest Bevin, then leader of the Transport and General Workers' Union, had his telephone tapped (Post Office Engineering Union, 1980: 15). It has been alleged by the director of a management investigation company that telephones in Transport House, then the headquarters of the Labour Party and still the headquarters of the TGWU, were tapped for long periods during 1972, a time of union opposition to the Industrial Relations Act 1971.[8] One journalist has written that

[7] 75 HC Debs. 229–30 (12 Mar. 1985).
[8] The Times, 4 Oct. 1974.

during the Grunwick dispute of the late 1970s a tap was attached to the telephone used by the strike committee in the Brent Trades' Council offices in Willesden Lane. Finally in this context, it has been alleged that 'ISTC offices at Rotherham were almost certainly tapped during the . . . steel strike [of 1980]. To test their belief, two officials organised a fictitious picket, by phone, for the next morning. When they arrived they found the police already there' (*Labour Research*, 1984).

If the tapping of telephones of trade unionists in industrial disputes is difficult to justify, even less justifiable is the evidence of the routine and systematic interception of telephones of a few key union leaders. Allegations of such activity were brought to light by Cathy Massiter, a retired MI5 official, and another unnamed former MI5 clerk. In a Channel 4 television programme it was alleged that whenever a major dispute comes up, it would immediately become an area for investigation. But it was also claimed that in the late 1970s certain telephones were tapped irrespective of any industrial dispute. Mr McGahey, a prominent communist and mineworkers' leader, was subjected to extensive surveillance, including the tapping of his home telephone. The phone of another leading miners' union official was also allegedly tapped in the late 1970s, as was the phone of a shop steward at the Ford plant at Dagenham. A particularly disturbing feature of the latter case was that instructions were allegedly given 'to listen out particularly for any reference to the Ford union's bottom line in the pay negotiations. It was considered of vital importance to obtain the union's private position'. The source of this allegation continued by saying that this was 'economic information from within a legally constituted trade union organisation which the Security Service and the government had no right to know'. As reported, the information was sought at the request of the Department of Employment.

These allegations led the Government to ask Lord Bridge of Harwich—the judicial monitor who replaced Lord Diplock in 1982—to examine whether MI5 had acted in breach of procedures. His appointment by the Prime Minister was announced on 1 March 1985 by the Home Secretary in the following terms:

In the light of recent allegations . . . the Prime Minister has asked Lord Bridge to examine the relevant papers to determine whether authorisations since May 1979 have named the individuals in question and, if so, whether those authorisations have been sought and given in accordance with the procedures and criteria in the Birkett report of 1957 and the White Paper of April 1980.[9]

According to Mr Gerald Kaufman Lord Bridge was able to complete his inquiry in five days, after which he was able to report that allegations of improperly authorized interceptions were without foundation. He reported to the Prime Minister that he was 'satisfied, after full examination of all the relevant documents, that no warrant for interception has been issued in contravention of the appropriate criteria'.[10] Unfortunately, however, the inquiry did little for public confidence in the independent judicial monitor. For the Labour Party, Mr Kaufman said that the report was 'an insult and an outrage',[11] while Mr David Steel for the Liberals is reported as having claimed that the report was 'totally inadequate', and that 'The secret state is out of control and democracy is threatened.'[12] More significantly, in a letter to *The Times*, Mr Roy Jenkins, a former Home Secretary, wrote:

On the narrowest criteria Lord Bridge appears cosily to exonerate us all [i.e. previous Home Secretaries]. I do not however believe that he exonerates himself. A judge of status and quality ought not in my view to have agreed to conduct such an enquiry within the limitations of time and scope imposed by the Prime Minister. He has made himself appear a poodle of the executive.[13]

Mr Jenkins continued by trusting that in future 'Lord Bridge will not be asked to pronounce on matters where the interests of authority and of liberty mingle uncomfortably. He no longer carries independent authority in this field.'

Legal Challenges to the Old Regime

It is surprising that such major intrusions by the state into the private lives of the people should take place without any clear

[9] 74 HC Debs. 450 (28 Feb. 1985).   [10] *The Times*, 7 Mar. 1985.
[11] *The Times*, 7 Mar. 1985.   [12] *The Times*, 7 Mar. 1985.
[13] *The Times*, 12 Mar. 1985. This was unreservedly withdrawn several years later following Lord Bridge's dissent in the *Spycatcher* case. See *The Times*, 3 Aug. 1987.

legal authority. It is perhaps unsurprising that the matter should have been challenged in the courts, given that it was an affront to the requirements of even the most basic conception of the rule of law. It was, however, only fairly recently that the first challenge occurred with Mr Malone attacking the practice on a number of grounds. His failure before the English courts led him directly to Strasburg where he successfully claimed that his rights guaranteed by the European Convention on Human Rights had been violated. Malone was not, however, the only challenger to these procedures in the English courts. Prominent members of CND tried a different strategy, but they too were unsuccessful. We now turn to consider these cases, before examining in the next section the legislation passed to implement the judgment of the European Court in *Malone*.

1. The Malone case

In the English courts, Mr Malone,[14] whose telephone had been tapped with the authority of a warrant, sought a declaration that the tapping was unlawful, as violating his rights of property, privacy, and confidentiality. So far as property rights were concerned the Vice-Chancellor held that words being transmitted by electrical impulses could not in themselves be the subject-matter of property rights. So far as privacy was concerned, Malone accepted that there was no general right to privacy in English law, but argued that there was a particular right of privacy, namely the right to hold a telephone conversation in one's home without molestation. The attempt to construct such a right was built upon a number of different grounds, perhaps the most important being the analogy with the Fourth Amendment to the US Constitution which protects people from unreasonable search and seizure, the analogy being drawn presumably because the Fourth Amendment is based upon English common law, particularly *Entick* v. *Carrington*,[15] where it was held that as a general rule search warrants may only be issued under the authority of a statute. In the US it has been held that the Fourth Amendment governs not only the seizure of tangible items, but

[14] *Malone* v. *Metropolitan Police Commisioner* [1979] 2 All ER 620.
[15] (1765) 2 Wils. 275.

extends also to the recording of oral statements.[16] In rejecting the view that *Entick* v. *Carrington* could thus form the basis of an action in privacy Sir Robert Megarry said:

The reason why a search of premises which is not authorised by law is illegal is that it involves the tort of trespass to those premises: and any trespass, whether to land or goods or the person, that is made without legal authority is prima facie illegal. Telephone tapping by the Post Office, on the other hand, involves no act of trespass. The subscriber speaks into his telephone, and the process of tapping appears to be carried out by Post Office officials making recordings, with Post Office apparatus on Post Office premises, of the electrical impulses on Post Office wires provided by Post Office electricity. There is no question of there being any trespass . . .

The confidentiality claim met the same fate as the other arguments. This is the action in the famous *Argyll* v. *Argyll*,[17] which concerned the possible disclosure of intimate marital secrets. In *Malone*, Sir Robert Megarry held that an action for breach of confidence does not lie where a person utters confidential information which is overheard by a third party. It is to be noted that this proposition appears to have been doubted by the Court of Appeal subsequently in *Francome* v. *Mirror Group Newspapers Ltd*,[18] where Sir Robert's remarks were distinguished as relating to a case involving the detection of crime. The court in *Malone* also held, however, that even if an action in confidence does apply to telephone conversations, in this case the circumstances would be governed by *Gartside* v. *Outram*,[19] where it was held that 'there is no confidence in the disclosure of an iniquity', observations subsequently explained by Lord Denning as merely an instance of just cause or excuse for breaking a confidence.[20] Lord Denning explained that 'There are some things which may be required to be disclosed in the public interest, in which event no confidence can be prayed in aid to keep them secret.' This was applied and extended by Sir Robert to safeguard the arrangements for telephone-tapping, even though when a tap is placed there may be no iniquity but only the suspicion of iniquity; and that entire conversations may be recorded and listened to 'when

[16] *Katz* v. *US* 389 US 347 (1967).
[17] [1967] Ch. 302.
[18] [1984] 2 All ER 408.
[19] (1856) 26 LJ Ch. 113.
[20] *Fraser* v. *Evans* [1969] 1 All ER 8.

much of the conversations may be highly confidential and untainted by any iniquity'. The willingness to bend the rules to authorize a major invasion of civil liberties contrasts sharply with the *Spycatcher* case. There, as we shall see, the judges wriggled furiously to avoid applying the principles outlined above in order to restrain the press from revealing the very serious iniquities disclosed by Mr Peter Wright, which included not only the bugging of embassies but also a conspiracy to assassinate the Egyptian President.

2. *The European Convention on Human Rights*

With the challenge to the extra-legal procedures having failed in the English courts, the matter was referred to Strasburg where it was argued that the British practice violated Article 8 of the European Convention on Human Rights which provides that everyone has the right to respect for his private and family life, his home, and his correspondence. This is qualified by paragraph (2) which provides that there shall be no interference by public authorities with the exercise of this right 'except such as is in accordance with law and is necessary in a democratic society in the interests of national security, public safety or the economic well-being of the country, for the prevention of disorder or crime, for the protection of health or morals, or for the protection of the rights and freedoms of others'. Malone had argued on the basis of the Convention before Sir Robert Megarry. He, however, rightly concluded that the Convention does not give rise to any enforceable rights under English law, but only a direct right in relation to the procedures established by the Convention. Thereupon Malone exercised his right of direct access under the Convention, with the first question for the European Court being whether the administrative arrangements in Britain (which restrict privacy) were 'in accordance with law'. At first sight, it seems arguable that the restrictions would meet this requirement following Megarry's decision that no unlawful acts were committed. The Court held, however, that the phrase 'in accordance with law' means that the law 'must be sufficiently clear in its terms to give citizens an adequate indication as to the circumstances in which and the conditions on which public authorities are empowered to resort to this secret and potentially dangerous interference with the right to respect for private life and correspondence'. The British Government stumbled at this hurdle, and in fact failed simply because domestic law did not regulate the circumstances in which the power could be exercised with sufficient clarity.[21]

The next question under the Convention was to determine what kind of legal regime would be acceptable under Article 8(2), assuming of course that it could meet the requirement of being 'in accordance with law'. And here lay the disappointment in the Court's decision. Having held that British practice was not in accordance with law, the judges found it unnecessary to address the question what would be regarded as acceptable limits on the right to privacy. So the British Government was required to introduce legislation to regulate the circumstances in which the power to tap may be used, but no guidance was given as to what should be the content of the legislation. It is quite possible that the legislation enacted to give effect to the decision (the Interception of Communications Act 1985) will be the subject of another application under the Convention. In the meantime the only guidance as to what would constitute an acceptable limit on Article 8(1) rights is the rather equivocal decision in the *Klass* case which concerned the operation of surveillance procedures in the German Federal Republic where legislation authorized telephone-tapping and other surveillance techniques if a number of conditions were satisfied.[22] The first of these conditions (which in some respects contrast sharply with the regulation in Britain before 1985) was that there had to be factual grounds to suspect a person of having committed a *crime* contrary to the security of the state.[23] Quite apart from this, the legislation required that the gathering of evidence by other means would be unlikely to succeed, or would be considerably more difficult; a warrant would apply to only one suspect, so that there were no general warrants; the warrants would remain in force for three months and thereafter had to be renewed; and the person concerned

---

[21] *Malone* v. *United Kingdom* (1985) 7 EHRR 14.

[22] *Klass* v. *Federal Republic of Germany* (1979) 2 EHRR 214.

[23] A separate regime, briefly alluded to in the case, dealt with interceptions in the course of investigating non-security criminal cases.

generally had to be notified as soon as possible after the surveillance ended that he or she had been the target of such surveillance. The application would be made by the Head of the Security Services to either the Minister of the Interior or the Minister of Defence. Unlike applications for interception in other criminal cases there was no procedure for judicial authorization in the case of security applications.

Although there was no judicial scrutiny in the case of security surveillance, there was a form of quasi-judicial scrutiny, as well as parliamentary scrutiny. A body known as the G10 Commission had the authority to decide, either *ex officio* or on application by a person believing himself or herself to be under surveillance, 'on both the legality of and the necessity for the [surveillance] measures'. In addition the competent Minister was obliged to report to a parliamentary Board at least once every six months and to the G10 Commission, in the latter case with an account of the measures he or she had ordered. Nevertheless it was argued that these procedures violated Article 8 of the Convention on two grounds, one because people were not always notified after the surveillance, the other because there was no judicial supervision of the procedures. Both arguments failed with the Court responding to the first by holding that the existing notification procedures were enough, there being no need for mandatory notification in all cases:

The activity or danger against which a particular series of surveillance measures is directed may continue for years, even decades, after the suspension of those measures. Subsequent notification to each individual affected by a suspended measure might well jeopardise the long-term purpose that originally prompted the surveillance. Furthermore . . . such notification might serve to reveal the working methods and fields of operation of the intelligence services and even possibly to identify their agents.

As to the second argument, the Court accepted that in principle it was desirable to entrust supervisory control to a judge, concluding that the rule of law implies that executive interference with individual rights should be subject to effective control which should normally be the judges on the ground that this offers the best guarantee of independence, impartiality, and proper procedures. Here, however, the Court held that the absence of judicial review and the provision of political control did not exceed the limits of what was permissible.

3. CND and judicial review

At about the same time that legislation was introduced to tackle the problems raised by the *Malone* decision, the Massiter revelations led to a second attempt to challenge the pre-1985 procedures in the domestic courts,[24] this time on different grounds from those which had failed before Sir Robert Megarry. Mr John Cox was a prominent member of the Campaign for Nuclear Disarmament (CND). He was also an active member of the Communist Party of Great Britain (CPGB). As a result of the public statements made by Cathy Massiter, it became known that Mr Cox had been the subject of a Home Secretary's warrant to intercept his telephone calls. According to Massiter:

from 1981 until December 1983 she had the task of investigating 'Communist and other forms of subversive influence and activity in the peace movement, including in particular the C.N.D.' She describes the collection of information and the keeping of files about persons classified as subversive. During the late 1960s to the mid-1970s she says CND was classified as subversive because it was a 'Communist dominated organisation'. In the late 1970s, since its leadership was no longer dominated by members of the Communist Party, it was no longer regarded as subversive, but merely as a 'Communist penetrated organisation'. Nevertheless, she says, investigation of CND and its leaders increased, and at the end she spent virtually all her time on it. She describes various sources and methods of acquiring information other than interception. When Mr Heseltine became Defence Secretary in January 1983 a briefing paper on CND had to be provided for him. Such briefing on security topics was a matter of routine when a new minister took office. In March 1983 Mr Heseltine set up a special unit, Defence Secretariat 19 (DS19), to combat CND propaganda on unilateral disarmament. Miss Massiter says DS19 requested information about any subversive political affiliations of CND's leaders. MI5 provided non-classified information, but none from secret or classified sources.

---

[24] R. v. *Secretary of State for the Home Department, ex parte Ruddock* [1987] 2 All ER 518.

In an affidavit, which is worth quoting at length—if only because information of this kind is so rare from the pen of a security officer—Massiter stated:

In or about February 1983, I received a message via my branch director that the deputy Director-General of MI5 was prepared to consider favourably an application from me for a telephone intercept on a member of the Communist Party within C.N.D. John Cox, a Vice-President of C.N.D., was selected since he was well known as a member of the Communist Party and had been involved in C.N.D. practically since its inception. Also, he lived in Wales and therefore would need to be in frequent telephone contact with C.N.D. headquarters. However, we had absolutely no evidence, as required by the guidelines, that he was concerned in any criminal activity or that he was engaged in a major subversive or espionage activity which was likely to injure the national interest. On the contrary, nothing from our coverage of the Communist Party and its Peace Committee gave us grounds to suspect that they were manipulating C.N.D.

My application for a warrant to monitor Mr. Cox's telephone communications was made in April 1983. It simply stated that Mr. Cox was a long term member of the Communist Party and prominent in C.N.D. and that it was desired to investigate his activities to ascertain whether the Communist Party was manipulating C.N.D. in a clandestine way. In August 1983 the Home Secretary signed the warrant. It was renewed after one month and was still in force when I left in December 1983. Judging by our previous experience, I do not think that the Home Secretary would have refused to renew it thereafter.

Pursuant to the warrant, an intercept was placed on Mr. Cox's telephone in or about August 1983 and I saw the products of the intercept in the form of transcripts of recorded telephone conversations. As Mr. Cox lived in Wales there was a fair amount of telephone communication between him and C.N.D. headquarters. He would routinely be in contact with the office and with, for example, Bruce Kent and Joan Ruddock. Accordingly, without intercepting their telephone communications we obtained a fair amount of information about their attitudes on quite a wide range of topics that were concerning C.N.D. at the time. As to Mr. Cox himself, we obtained very little information that we did not already have, although perhaps a bit more detailed. My own assessment before we had the check would have been that he worked within C.N.D. because he was a committed C.N.D. member rather than working in C.N.D. in order to further the interests of the Communist Party. Certainly nothing that I recall seeing as a result of the intercept ever contradicted that assessment.

On establishing that the warrant had been issued, Mr Cox and two other prominent members of CND (Joan Ruddock and Bruce Kent) sought judicial review of the Home Secretary's decision to issue the warrant. Cox argued that the interception had been unlawful because it did not meet the published criteria regulating such interceptions. Although the criteria did not have the status of legal rules, Cox argued nevertheless that he had a *legitimate expectation* that the Home Secretary would follow them when deciding whether the applicant's telephone would be intercepted. But before these matters could be considered the court had to address an argument for the Crown which, if it had succeeded, would have brought an immediate end to the matter. This was the contention that the court ought not to entertain the action 'because to do so would be detrimental to national security', the defence referring to the long-established practice of Secretaries of State not to disclose or discuss the existence of a warrant. In his affidavit Sir Brian Cubbon, Permanent Under-Secretary of State at the Home Office, explained the policy in the following terms:

To disclose whether or not a warrant has been issued in a particular case could establish means whereby those involved in serious crimes or espionage or subversion could learn the extent to which their activities had come to notice or—perhaps more damaging—could in some cases confirm whether their activities had come to notice at all. The revelation of such information could jeopardize sensitive investigations essential to the nation's security, could place at risk the lives of those who had come forward with their suspicions to the police and could undermine the efforts of the police to prevent or detect serious crime. It is equally important that the practice of not confirming or denying the existence of a warrant is maintained consistently. Successive Secretaries of State have stated that only by the unvarying observance of this practice is it possible to ensure that in no circumstances is anything said or not said which, by comparison with what was said on a different occasion, might imply that a warrant had or had not been issued. In the view of successive Secretaries of State it is essential in the interests of national security and of any other grounds for which a warrant may be issued that no such inference should ever be capable of being drawn.

This is by no means the first time that national security has been raised as a defence in legal proceedings against the Crown.

Indeed, the Crown has generally done rather well in such cases. In a well-known dictum, Lord Parker of Waddington said in a case in 1916: 'Those who are responsible for the national security must be the sole judges of what the national security requires. It would be obviously undesirable that such matters should be made the subject of evidence in a Court of law or otherwise discussed in public.'[25] This was adopted by the House of Lords in the GCHQ case,[26] where Lord Diplock said that 'National security is the responsibility of the executive government; what action is needed to protect its interests is . . . a matter upon which those upon whom the responsibility rests, and not the courts of justice, must have the last word.' As we shall see in Chapter 5, the defence in fact proved conclusive in the GCHQ case itself. *Ruddock*, however, differed from any of the cases which had gone before in the sense that the issue 'has usually been whether the admitted act or decision was justified on grounds of national security'. Where there was evidence to show that such a decision had been taken for reasons of national security, this would be accepted to 'preclude judicial investigation of [the] particular . . . grievance'. Here, however, 'no admission is made as to the existence of a warrant, so national security is not raised to justify an undisputed act. It is raised to preclude the court from considering the application at all.'

To his great credit, but contrary to the trend of recent decision-making, Taylor J. was unable to 'accept that the court should never inquire into a complaint against a minister if he says his policy is to maintain silence in the interests of national security'. He continued by asserting:

there could occur a case where the issue raised was so sensitive and the revelations necessarily following its decision so damaging to national security that the court might have to take special measures (for example sitting in camera or prohibiting the mention of names). Conceivably (although I would reserve the point) in an extreme case the court might have to decline to try the issues. But in all such cases, cogent evidence of potential damage to national security flowing from the trial of the issues would have to be adduced, whether in open court or in camera, to justify

[25] *The Zamora* [1916] 2 AC 77, at p. 107.
[26] *Council of Civil Service Unions* v. *Minister for the Civil Service* [1985] AC 374. See Ch. 5.

any modification of the court's normal procedure. Totally to oust the court's supervisory jurisdiction in a field where ex hypothesi the citizen can have no right to be consulted is a draconian and dangerous step indeed. Evidence to justify the court's declining to decide a case (if such a course is ever justified) would need to be very strong and specific.

In this case there was no such evidence with the result that the court did not decline to hear the case. This, however, did not conclude the matter in the applicants' favour for they then had to show that the warrant to intercept (which Taylor J. accepted was issued) was not granted in accordance with the established criteria. This they failed to do. Taylor J. held first that the Home Secretary did not knowingly flout the criteria, and secondly that he did not act unreasonably in granting the warrant. So far as the latter issue was concerned, to succeed the applicant had to show that the decision was 'so outrageous in its defiance of logic or of accepted moral standards that no sensible person who had applied his mind to the question to be decided could have arrived at it'. In holding that the decision to issue a warrant was not 'so outrageous in its defiance of logic', Taylor J. said:

In view of the evidence as to the history of CND, in its period of 'Communist domination' followed by its period of 'Communist penetration', vigilance was clearly required. The criteria placed a duty on the security service to keep up to date its information covering subversion . . . The applicant John Cox was involved at the highest level in both CND and the Communist Party of Great Britain, both in the period of 'Communist domination' and in the late 1970s when CND was growing. The applicant's case depends on the evidence and opinions of Miss Massiter . . . Against it is the evidence of Sir Brian Cubbon and his judgment that the criteria were always honoured.

The unanswered question, of course, is why is it a matter simply of judicial notice that the Communist Party of the 1980s is subversive?

The New Statutory Framework

With the failure of the Ruddock action, our attention now reverts to the legislation which the Government was compelled to introduce to meet the demands of the European Court of Human

Rights in the Malone judgment. In fact the legislation—the Interception of Communications Act 1985—was on the statute book while the *Ruddock* case was being decided. The legislation gave the Government generally and the Home Office in particular an opportunity to bare its liberal soul. Indeed, the Home Secretary, Mr Leon Brittan, took great pride in the fact that, unlike any of its predecessors, the Conservative Government had provided for the first time a clear and comprehensive statutory framework for the interception of communications. More importantly, he claimed, the Government had introduced a new offence of unauthorized interception.[27] More importantly still, it had provided for the first time an 'effective' means of redress for those wishing to complain that interception has been improperly authorized. This, however, seems rather sanguine. A more cynical assessment would be that the Interception of Communications Act 1985 is a crude example of political management. It appears to give legal authority for an apparently open-ended power to intercept and it fails to constrain that power by an adequate framework of judicial or parliamentary scrutiny. More troubling is that, as such, the Act provided the model for the Security Service Act which was enacted in 1989.

1. *The grounds for interception*

The Interception of Communications Act had a promising start. In 1957 the Birkett Committee recommended that unauthorized tapping should be a criminal offence. Some twenty-eight years later that proposal was finally implemented. Section 1 of the Act provides that it is an offence for a person intentionally to intercept a postal communication or a telecommunication. Conviction could lead to a fine or imprisonment of up to two years, or both. But here the progress ends. Section 2 authorizes warrants to be issued by the Home Secretary for the purposes of interception

---

[27] The parliamentary debates are located at 75 HC Debs. 151 (12 Mar. 1985) (2nd Reading); 76 HC Debs. 1091, 1241 (2, 3 Apr. 1985) (Committee); 77 HC Debs. 279 (17 Apr. 1985) (Report, 3rd Reading); 463 HL Debs. 1255 (16 May 1985) (2nd Reading); 464 HL Debs. 852, 865, 914 (6 June 1985) (Committee); 465 HL Debs. 956, 973 (1 July 1985) (Report).

and provides that a warrant shall not be issued unless the Home Secretary considers that it is necessary:

(a) in the interests of national security;
(b) for the purpose of preventing or detecting serious crime; or
(c) for the purpose of safeguarding the economic well-being of the United Kingdom.

The most troubling of these measures is the first, which is presumably for the benefit of the security services. The statute—which authorizes interception on grounds of national security without defining what is meant by national security—is clearly much wider than the old Home Office guidelines—which authorized warrants on the narrower grounds of '*major* subversive or espionage activity'. To the extent that the Home Secretary suggested that the Act did not involve any extension of the Government's powers, this could be only because in practice the guidelines were being exceeded for, as has been pointed out subsequently, the phrase 'national security' is not confined to major subversion or espionage (Lloyd, 1987). An attempt was made in Parliament to restrict the power to intercept for security reasons to cases where this was necessary for the defence of the realm or to prevent subversion, terrorism, or espionage—still wider than the guidelines but much closer to their spirit than the statute. The Opposition contended that the words 'in the interests of national security' were too vague and too wide and conferred too much discretion on the Home Office and the security services.

The amendment failed, being opposed not just by the Government but surprisingly also by the SDP spokesman, Mr Robert MacLennan, who said that 'senior Ministers who have the duty to authorise interception of communications must have a very wide—in many cases, almost unlimited—discretion'. For the Home Office this apparent extension of power was justified on four grounds. First, the term 'national security is no stranger to us' and was used often in statutes without being defined or restricted as to its meaning, with Parliament always accepting that 'decisions about questions of national security must be for Ministers'. Secondly, and most remarkably in view of Birkett and the 1980 White Paper, the phrase was appropriate 'because it properly reflects the way in which interception has been authorised by successive governments of the Left and Right', and it emphasizes the important point that the Act provides for no extension of existing practices. Thirdly, it was argued that the use of the phrase 'national security' was 'especially appropriate' because of the parallel with the European Convention on Human Rights which this measure was designed to implement. The fourth argument was that the amendment would have left the Government with inadequate powers. In the view of the Minister, 'There is obviously more to preserving the nation's security than safeguarding against subversion, terrorism and espionage.' In particular, 'Interception may be necessary to protect our national security at international level to provide secret intelligence in the foreign and defence areas. Undoubtedly, the acquisition of such intelligence may sometimes be essential in the interests of national security. Without it, the Government's ability to safeguard the country's vital interests would be undermined.' In fact, since the legislation was introduced warrants have been issued for unspecified reasons of national security but unrelated to subversion, terrorism, and espionage (Lloyd, 1987).

But although the first ground for the granting of warrants is, as drafted, the most troubling, the second (for preventing or detecting serious crime) is also a cause for concern. In contrast to the administrative procedures operating before 1986, the Act authorizes warrants to be granted for preventing as well as detecting crime, thereby compromising the important question of principle identified by Dicey that 'preventive measures are inconsistent with the pervading principle of English law, that men are to be interfered with or punished, not because they may or will break the law, but only when they have committed some definite assignable legal offence' (Dicey, 1959: 249). That is a principle which is now honoured in the breach, most notably in the power extended to police officers to issue instructions to prevent an apprehended breach of the peace, a power which apparently is subject to very little effective judicial scrutiny or control.[28] This does not, of course, necessarily justify further departures from principle, nor indeed does it justify a departure quite as significant as that contained in the 1985 Act. Of crucial

[28] *Piddington* v. *Bates* [1961] 1 WLR 162. See Ch. 4.

importance in determining the power to intercept in criminal cases is the definition of 'serious crime'. And here we find that the term is widely rather than narrowly defined to include an offence which carries a sentence of three years or more on first conviction; or involves the use of violence; or results in substantial financial gain; or involves conduct by a large number of people in pursuit of a common purpose. In other words a serious crime amounts to anything from murder to obstruction of the highway, the latter being committed where large numbers of people gather to march and demonstrate. The effect of the Act then is to give the police the legal power to intercept where there is the possibility that a public order offence might be committed. As it is possible that such an offence will be committed on any march or demonstration, the Act gives the power to tap any organization engaged in such activity.

2. Safeguards against abuse?

Despite criticisms voiced by the Post Office Engineering Union (1980) it is still the case that warrants are to be issued under the hand of the Home Secretary rather than a judge, there apparently being no concern that a major invasion of privacy can take place by executive act without the need for any judicial approval or authorization, as is required in other democracies.[29] Indeed in urgent cases (a term not defined), the warrant may be issued under the hand of an official in the Home Office. But before this is done the Home Secretary must expressly authorize the granting of the warrant which must be endorsed with a statement of that fact. Presumably this is intended as a safeguard: if the Home Secretary is not in his office, he must be contacted by telephone if necessary to give his consent. But this is hardly an effective safeguard: how much serious consideration can be given by a Minister absent from his office, engaged in pressing matters of state?

[29] See e.g. Criminal Code of Canada, s.178.12. It is interesting to note that Birkett (1957) recommended against judicial warrants on the ground that they would be easier to obtain. For an account of the position in Canada, see Burns (1976).

In view of the sheer volume of interception warrants, and in view of the sheer volume of the Home Secretary's other duties, it seems unlikely that his personal involvement can seriously be seen as an effective means of control. As a result effective safeguards must be found in the statutory restrictions on the grant of warrants. But these leave much to be desired—on three major grounds. The first relates to the extraordinarily wide scope of the warrants. Under the Act those executing a warrant are *required* (not empowered) to intercept *all* communications sent to or from one or more addresses specified in the warrant where the address in question is likely to be used for the transmission of communications to or from one particular person specified or described in the warrant. To illustrate the dangers of this measure, suppose that the Government took the view that membership of the Communist Party presented a threat to national security and that leading members of the party—including those holding positions in trade unions—were to be kept under surveillance. This would enable all telephone calls in and out of their homes to be intercepted. It would also enable *all* telephone calls in and out of their workplaces to be intercepted. As a result the legislation will authorize (and may indeed require) the interception of all the telephone calls to and from trade union head offices, as well as those of many other radical protest organizations.

The second area for concern relates to the duration of warrants. Although it is true that warrants must be for a fixed period and may not be open-ended, the period in question is a relatively long one and may exceed the purposes for which the warrant is initially granted. Take an absurd example. Suppose a warrant is granted to tap the telephones of an organization which is planning a march or demonstration. Under the statute, such a warrant may be granted on the spurious ground that the police suspect that public order offences may be committed by large numbers of people. Yet the warrant will be granted for two months—which may well include a period of time running after the demonstration in question has taken place. In other words, the period of fixed duration allows snooping of an unauthorized nature. But what is more troubling than the initial rigid fixed term is the fact that warrants may be renewed for longer periods still. It is true that warrants to the police in criminal investigations may be renewed only for one month. But it is also true that warrants to the security services may be renewed for six months at a time. Apart from the fact that the fixed periods are unreasonably long, they are unreasonably arbitrary and rigid. Much less unacceptable would be a shorter warrant period, which should be the maximum duration possible, rather than the standard period in every case. In other words, the Home Secretary would have a discretion to exercise from case to case, with the result that the duration of each warrant would vary, subject to a statutory maximum period.

The third area of concern relates to the adequacy of the remaining safeguards introduced by the Act. Two measures specifically are introduced as legal requirements. First, under section 6, when granting a warrant, the Home Secretary must make arrangements for the purpose of securing that:

(a) the extent to which the material is disclosed;
(b) the number of persons to whom the material is disclosed;
(c) the extent to which the material is copied; and
(d) the number of copies made of any material

is limited in each case to the minimum that is necessary. The second statutory safeguard is that copies of any intercepted material must be destroyed as soon as they are no longer required. But that is all: the Act fails to incorporate other safeguards said to be embodied in the pre-statutory warrant procedures. Far less does it make any attempt to improve these procedures to meet their critics. In particular, the statute does not incorporate the review procedures whereby the Home Secretary reviewed police warrants every month and security warrants every six months. But more significant omissions relate to the removal of the qualification for granting warrants which were claimed to operate under the pre-statutory arrangements. For security warrants, there had to be evidence of major subversive or espionage activity. For police warrants, normal methods of investigation must have been tried and failed and there must have been good reason to believe that interception would result in a conviction. None of these very significant substantive safeguards has been formally retained.[30]

---

[30] According to the Commissioner, however, the quota system still operates for

3. The Tribunal and the Commissioner

Apart from the administrative safeguards referred to above, the Act introduces a remedy by way of a right of complaint to a quasi-judicial Tribunal. It may be noted, however, that the Tribunal (all lawyers) is appointed by the Prime Minister (nominally the Queen) for fixed periods of five years. Although the members of the Tribunal may be reappointed by the Prime Minister for a further five-year period, under the Act they thus have no security of tenure, long recognized as the hallmark of judicial independence. Quite apart from this, the Tribunal has no real powers. Thus it has no power to determine whether unauthorized interceptions are taking place. Such claims may only be investigated by the police and prosecuted in the normal way. But if the police or the security services are perpetrating the illegal acts there may be little incentive for them to deal with such complaints seriously. The Tribunal is thus limited to determining whether a warrant to intercept has been properly issued under the Act, that is to say, that there are adequate grounds for the issuing of a warrant and that the statutory procedures have been complied with. But even this is not as extensive as it appears at first sight for, in conducting an investigation on a complaint, the Tribunal must apply 'the principles applicable by a court on an application for judicial review'. This means that the Tribunal has to ask whether the Minister acted reasonably in exercising his discretion to grant a warrant. That discretion would not be exercised reasonably if no reasonable Minister could conclude that the issuing of the warrant was necessary in the interests of national security or for the prevention or detection of crime.

The application of the principles of judicial review vary according to the circumstances. As the *Ruddock* case has shown, the standard of review employed in national security cases is set so high that it is possible that the Tribunal could be compelled to refrain from interfering with discretionary decisions taken for this reason. Much the same is true of the discretionary powers of the police. Although the courts do not refuse in principle to review

police and customs warrants, but not for the security services, though in this case the scope for interception is restricted by the limited availability of transcribers. See Lloyd (1987).

the exercise of police discretionary powers, they do nevertheless exercise a great deal of caution and restraint to such a degree that it is difficult to see how in practice the principles of judicial review are capable of being used to challenge decisions to issue warrants where these are considered to be necessary for the prevention or detection of crime. The point is nicely illustrated by one case[31] where the Central Electricity Generating Board unsuccessfully sought a court order to require the Chief Constable of Devon and Cornwall to compel his officers to remove or assist the Board in removing people obstructing a survey site. The Court of Appeal made it clear that the Chief Constable had authority to intervene, but it declined to compel him to do so. Lord Denning cited his own judgment in an earlier case where he said:

it is for the Commissioner of Police, or the chief constable, as the case may be, to decide in any particular case whether enquiries should be pursued, or whether an arrest should be made, or a prosecution brought. It must be for him to decide on the disposition of his force and the concentration of his resources on any particular crime or area. No court can or should give him direction on such a matter. He can also make policy decisions and give effect to them, as, for instance, was often done when prosecutions were not brought for attempted suicide. But there are some policy decisions with which, I think, the courts in a case can, if necessary, interfere.[32]

He continued by saying that 'the decision of the chief constable not to intervene in this case was a policy decision with which . . . the courts should not interfere'.

So the Act provides for the appointment by the Prime Minister of a Tribunal with very limited powers to regulate the way in which Ministers use the very extensive powers given to them under the Act. It is not clear whether it is the limited powers of the Tribunal or the wide powers of the Government which led to none of the first sixty-eight complaints to the Tribunal being upheld. One of the first complaints was made by three members of CND who were told on 7 July 1986 by the Tribunal 'that after careful investigation it was satisfied no contravention of the

[31] R. v. *Chief Constable of the Devon and Cornwall Constabulary, ex parte Central Electricity Generating Board* [1982] QB 458.
[32] At p. 472.

[statutory] criteria had occurred'.[33] In addition to the Tribunal, however, the 1985 Act makes provision for the appointment of a Commissioner to supervise the use of the new statutory powers. This in effect gives statutory force to the judicial monitoring procedure which was introduced in 1980. Under the Act, the Commissioner is also appointed by the Prime Minister, and it is required that the person appointed should hold or have held a high judicial office. Like the members of the Tribunal, there is no provision for security of tenure for the Commissioner, it being provided only that he 'shall hold office in accordance with the terms of his appointment'. Specifically, the Commissioner has three functions:

(a) to keep under review the carrying out by the Home Secretary of the functions conferred upon him or her by the Act;

(b) to keep under review the adequacy of any arrangements made for the purposes of restricting the use and distribution of the intercepted material;

(c) to give the Tribunal all such assistance as the Tribunal may require for the purpose of enabling it to carry out its statutory functions.

In fulfilling these three functions, two duties are imposed upon the Commissioner. First, where it appears that there has been a breach of the statutory provisions, he or she must make a report to this effect to the Prime Minister. Secondly, the Commissioner must make an annual report to the Prime Minister about his or her activities in the year in question. The annual report is to be published. This is a major advance on the pre-existing system of judicial monitoring where the Government agreed only to the publication of the first but not the succeeding reports of the monitor. Nevertheless, the significance of this development ought not to be exaggerated. There is no duty on the Prime Minister to publish any interim reports highlighting specific abuses. Also, although the annual report is to be published, the Prime Minister may exclude from publication any matter in an annual report if it appears to the Prime Minister that publication would be

---

[33] *R.* v. *Secretary of State for the Home Department, ex parte Ruddock* [1987] 2 All ER 518, at p. 528.

prejudicial to national security, the prevention or detection of crime, or the economic well-being of the country. In a very real sense the concept of a Commissioner is open to criticism. The Commissioner is appointed by the Prime Minister on terms determined by the Prime Minister, and reports to the Prime Minister who has the power to censor his or her report for the purposes of publication.

These arrangements for review of the procedures were strongly condemned by the Opposition which argued that the monitoring function should be undertaken by a Select Committee of the House of Commons which would 'oversee the work of any person responsible for, or making use of, the interception of communications'. So far as the Commissioner is concerned there was a fear that the Prime Minister's power of censorship could lead to an 'extremely thin' annual report being laid before Parliament, with little opportunity for informed debate. As a result there were other, more fundamental problems. Speaking for the Opposition, Mr Clive Soley said:

let us assume that a full report, with virtually nothing excluded, is laid before the House. It is then available for us to read, and we may be able to arrange a debate. Let us assume that we persuade the Government of the day to allow one day of prime Government time for that debate. That is one day's debate on an extremely serious matter, compared to what could be done by a Select Committee over many weeks of sitting, bringing evidence before it, questioning people involved, looking at the matter in depth. Which system protects the democratic rights best? The answer is clear. It is the Select Committee system, which can report to the House, after which a full debate can take place. In other words, we would have the best rather than the worst of both worlds.

Mr Soley was correct at least in his prediction that the published parts of the Commissioner's reports would be very thin. The published part of the first report amounted to only twelve pages (Lloyd, 1987) (with an appendix of one page giving details of the number of warrants issued by the Home Office and the Scottish Office, but with no information about the numbers issued by the Foreign Office or the Northern Ireland Office), and the second being a mere five pages (with an appendix of one page), yet priced at £1.90 (Lloyd, 1988).

The reports of the Commissioner provide some information about the number of warrants in force albeit that they are incomplete. In 1987 the Home Secretary was responsible for 223 telecommunications warrants and 71 letters warrants. The Scottish Secretary was responsible for 29 and 1 respectively. In the first two reports of the Commissioner, he drew attention to a few technical problems, such as wrong numbers being intercepted, and he did make recommendations as to how the procedures should be modified, describing these as being of 'no great importance'. For the most part, however, the procedures were given a clean bill of health, with the Commissioner examining warrants drawn at random, but also examining all new warrants issued on grounds of subversion. In conducting this exercise the Commissioner has explained that he has adopted the wide test of subversion formulated by Lord Harris in 1975 and that his duty 'is to look at each case individually and say whether the Home Secretary could reasonably take the view that the warrant was necessary in the interests of national security' (Lloyd, 1987). 'Applying that test, and bearing in mind that there are persons on the fringes of subversion that may make it difficult to draw the line', the Commissioner has been satisfied that the Home Secretaries' warrants have always been justified.

In his second report, the Commissioner wrote that the confidential part of his report discussed individual warrants which called for comment and also some examples of recent operations. But he also pointed out that if this information could be included in the published part of the report, it would do much to reassure members of the public who feel uneasy about interception. The Commissioner also accepted assurances by the five Secretaries of State involved that they never issue warrants without a careful review of the papers and a proper consideration of the matters which they are required to consider and take into account under the Act. Nevertheless, it is still open to question whether these arrangements are an adequate substitute for parliamentary scrutiny. Certainly the Home Office was unable to come up with a convincing case against such scrutiny by a House which is 'elected to protect the democratic rights of [the] people'. Mr David Waddington, the responsible Minister, lamented that 'parliamentary accountability is an easy cause always to espouse'.

But this resistance is weakened in the present context by allegations of misuse of power by the security services. Whatever the merits of the arguments against Mr Soley's proposal for a Select Committee in place of the Commissioner, they are much less convincing when applied to the more modest proposal put forward at the time by the SDP that there could be a Select Committee confining itself to the Commissioner's report 'so that in turn it would report and give some reality to parliamentary accountability'.

4. *The exclusion of the courts*

It has been argued so far that the methods of control and accountability introduced by the 1985 Act leave much to be desired. The statute has provided for the creation of a Tribunal with very little power. It has also given legal effect to the judicial monitoring procedure, but there is no accountability of the Commissioner to Parliament despite the concern about this type of procedure which was raised in public after the Massiter affair. Apart from these weaknesses, the Government has seen fit to deny an additional safeguard which might have been presumed to operate. This is judicial scrutiny and the power of the courts to regulate telephone-tapping and to deal with illegal or improper conduct. Yet judicial scrutiny has been expressly excluded: first by denying the courts the power to question decisions of the Tribunal, and secondly and more importantly by denying the courts the power to refuse to admit evidence obtained as a result of illegal or improper interceptions.

(a) The exclusive jurisdiction of the Tribunal   It is a general principle of English law that the decisions of inferior tribunals (such as social security appeal tribunals, industrial tribunals, or immigration appeal tribunals) should be the subject of appeal to the higher courts. Exceptionally the statutes creating these bodies may omit to provide for an appeal in which case the decisions of the tribunals in question may be the subject of review by the High Court, and if the decisions reveal an error of law they may be quashed by what is known as an order of *certiorari*. More exceptionally still, Parliament may endeavour to prevent judicial

review and may wish the decisions of the tribunal to be final and beyond the supervisory jurisdiction of the ordinary courts. As a result, Parliament may insert what is known as an exclusion or privative clause to achieve this result. An example of such a clause is the following which was found in the Foreign Compensation Act 1950, a statute setting up a body known as the Foreign Compensation Commission: 'The determination by the commission of any application made to them under this Act shall not be called in question in any court of law.' There is some justification for such clauses, despite questions about their constitutional propriety. If Parliament wishes to create a specialist body to adjudicate in a given field, it makes little sense to have the decisions of that body reviewed by courts which have no such expertise. On the other hand, however, such clauses are not without danger. They would not enable the courts to interfere where there clearly has been a breach of procedural fairness; and they would permit the inferior tribunals to exceed the limited powers which Parliament has conferred upon them. It is important to note that for a variety of reasons clauses of this kind have been heavily criticized. They have been attacked by Parliament, with the Tribunals and Inquiries Act 1971 providing that:

As respects England and Wales or Northern Ireland, any provision in an Act passed before 1st August 1958 that any order or determination shall not be called into question in any court, or any provision in such an Act which by similar words excludes any of the powers of the High Court, shall not have effect so as to prevent the removal of the proceedings into the High Court by order of certiorari or to prejudice the powers of the High Court to make orders of mandamus.

They have also been attacked by the courts, with the result that it is difficult to see what practical effect such clauses might be thought to have. The leading case is *Anisminic Ltd* v. *Foreign Compensation Commission*,[34] where the House of Lords held that the effect of an exclusion clause is only to prevent errors of law by a tribunal which are within its jurisdiction: the clause would not prevent the review of decisions outside jurisdiction. It thus becomes crucial to determine what errors fall outside jurisdiction.

[34] [1969] 2 AC 147.

Here the answer is just about any error the superior courts wish. In *Anisminic*, Lord Reid gave the following examples:

It may have given its decision in bad faith. It may have made a decision which it had no power to make. It may have failed in the course of the inquiry to comply with the requirements of natural justice. It may in perfect good faith have misconstrued the provisions giving it power to act so that it failed to deal with the question remitted to it and decided some question which was not remitted to it. It may have refused to take into account something which it was required to take into account. Or it may have based its decision on some matter which, under the provisions setting it up, it had no right to take into account. I do not intend this list to be exhaustive. But if it decides a question remitted to it for decision without committing any of these errors it is as much entitled to decide that question wrongly as it is to decide it rightly.

It is difficult to see what errors are left to make! In fact, since *Anisminic* the courts have gone one step further and now presume that any error of law by an administrative tribunal is subject to review by the higher courts, even where there is an exclusion clause purporting to prevent such review. The presumption is rebuttable. Yet despite this trend away from leaving sole jurisdiction with administrative tribunals, the Interception of Communications Act 1985 not only contains an exclusion clause to prevent review of the decisions of the Tribunal, but it contains one of unprecedented scope. Section 7 provides simply that 'The decisions of the Tribunal (including any decisions as to their jurisdiction) shall not be subject to appeal or liable to be questioned in any court.' The Government has thus done what no government before has done—it has given an inferior tribunal the power to determine the extent of its own jurisdiction. As Lord Wilberforce said in *Anisminic*: 'Although, in theory perhaps, it may be possible for Parliament to set up a tribunal which has full and autonomous powers to fix its own area of operation, that has, so far, not been done in this country.' It has now. As a result there can be no review of the decisions of the Tribunal, regardless of the merits and substance of the decision and regardless of the procedure by which it is reached. It is true of course that the device could potentially backfire: having equipped this Tribunal with so much power, it might begin to use it and impose demands on the executive which exceed those which the courts would demand. The Government would be powerless, having denied itself the right of access to the ordinary courts in such an eventuality. It will, however, be no surprise to learn that the Government is protected against that risk. The law of contempt does not apply to reinforce the decisions of administrative tribunals.[35] As a result there is no remedy available to an aggrieved party if a tribunal's decision is not complied with— unless the statute should expressly create such a remedy. This was not done in the 1985 Act—with the result that it would be open to the Government not to comply with an order if it takes the view that the Tribunal's decision clearly exceeds its powers under the statute. It is to be noted further that the Act, no doubt inadvertently, facilitates such behaviour by providing that the Tribunal shall give reasons for its decisions only to the Prime Minister.

(b) The admissibility of illegally obtained evidence   As we discussed in Chapter 2, one way of controlling the activities of the police and of ensuring that they do not act unlawfully is to prevent the admissibility of evidence which is obtained by illegal means. Such an approach was adopted by the US Supreme Court in the famous case, *Mapp* v. *Ohio*,[36] where it was held that to admit evidence obtained by means of an illegal search would make the constitutional guarantees against such arbitrary conduct worthless. A less absolute position now operates in the United States, as *Mapp* v. *Ohio* has been revised and qualified. A less absolute position is also adopted in Australia and in Scotland (Ewing and Finnie, 1988: 99–102) where the courts have a discretion to admit illegally obtained evidence. In exercising this discretion the courts will balance the public interest in the prosecution of crime against the interest of the accused in securing a fair trial. The more serious the violation by the police and the less serious the charge the more likely it is that the evidence will be inadmissible, though there are occasions in Scotland where crucial evidence has been struck out in serious cases which include murder.[37]

In England and Wales the position is now governed by the Police and Criminal Evidence Act 1984, section 78, the terms of

[35] *Attorney-General* v. *BBC* [1981] AC 303.   [36] 367 US 643 (1961).
[37] *Chalmers* v. *HM Advocate* 1954 JC 66.

which we encountered in the previous chapter. Although it is unclear precisely what the section actually means, at least on one view it does permit the courts to refuse to admit police evidence which has been obtained illegally. Yet in sharp contrast to this development, the 1985 Act provides expressly that evidence which tends to suggest that illegal tapping has taken place is not to be admitted in court.[38] Thus section 9 provides that in any proceedings before a court no evidence shall be adduced and no question in cross-examination shall be asked which tends to suggest that an interception has taken place without a warrant— that is, illegally. This exclusion does not apply to a prosecution for a breach of section 1. There is then no effective sanction against illegal tapping. The fruits of such conduct cannot be excluded. The only remedy lies in prosecution at the instance of the police. But, as already suggested, if it is the police who are doing the tapping what is the prospect of effective steps to stop it? More significantly, if questions may not even be asked in open court about illegal tapping, how is the victim to find out about it in order to bring it to the attention of the police? It would of course be possible for a British Telecom engineer to disclose such information to the targets of the tapping. But, as civil servants have discovered in the past, prosecution under the Official Secrets Act may be brought even where the civil servant (or the engineer in this case) is exposing improper or even illegal conduct by the executive.[39] But, in any event, there is no compelling reason to justify section 9. In Canada illegally obtained wire-tapping evidence can be excluded just as any other illegally obtained evidence may be excluded.[40] There is no reason why the same should not be the position here.

---

[38] This appears to have been the position adopted by the Court of Appeal (Criminal Division) before the Act came into effect. In *R.* v. *Murineddu*, *LEXIS*, 13 July 1984, the Court stated that '. . . during the course of a trial, is not a place where defending counsel should seek to get information about suspected telephone tapping. For these reasons we adjudge that both trial judges were right to refuse to allow any fishing questions to be asked about telephone tapping.'

[39] This is now even more clearly the position under the Official Secrets Act 1989.

[40] Criminal Code of Canada, s.178.16(2).

Conclusion

The practice of telephone-tapping in Britain is a symptom of the deep-rooted problems facing civil liberties in this country. Until the decision of the European Court in the *Malone* case this major invasion of privacy was conducted without any legal authority. Indeed the decision in *Malone* is an indication of the extent to which the British courts are willing to tolerate major invasions of civil liberties without any express authority vested in state agents. The rather weak response of Sir Robert Megarry stands in sharp contrast to the decision in *Kennedy* v. *Ireland*,[41] where the High Court of Ireland was faced with a much more difficult question, also in the context of telephone-tapping. In *Malone*, the Court was asked to recognize a limited common-law right to privacy whereas in *Kennedy* the Court was asked to take the much bolder step and apply in this sensitive area an implied constitutional right to privacy which was not to be found in the Constitution. This it was willing to do,[42] for although 'not specifically guaranteed by the Constitution, the right of privacy is one of the fundamental personal rights of the citizen which flows from the . . . democratic nature of the State'. The Court continued by asserting that the nature of the right to privacy must be such as to ensure the dignity and freedom of an individual in the type of society envisaged by the constitution, namely, 'a sovereign, independent and democratic society'. In a strong judgment the Court also claimed that the 'dignity and freedom of an individual in a democratic society cannot be ensured if his communications of a private nature, be they written or telephonic, are deliberately, consciously and unjustifiably intruded upon and interfered with'.

It is true that in Britain the matter is now regulated by statute and to that extent it has been flushed into the open. Yet the statute authorizes interception on wider grounds than those previously acknowledged and fails to provide some of the safeguards against abuse which were claimed to operate under the old administrative regime. But clearly the most significant feature of the Act is the

[41] [1988] ILRM 472.
[42] In so holding the Court paradoxically found support in the decision of the Supreme Court of Ireland in *Norris* v. *Attorney-General* [1984] IR 36.

reluctance on the part of the executive to subject the process to any satisfactory scrutiny or control. The torch of accountability shining from this statute is one which has failed to ignite. This is demonstrated most clearly in the lengths to which the courts have been excluded from the process, even though they have been only rarely a threat to the Thatcher Government. Thus, so far as the Tribunal is concerned, Parliament accepted a privative clause of a kind which is unprecedented in modern English law, purporting to do what no Parliament has done before—it has given an administrative tribunal the power to determine its own jurisdiction. This is despite the fact that the Tribunal is appointed by the Government; that it has no real powers; and that it is under a duty not to give published reasons for any decision it makes. Yet the exclusion of the courts is not confined to the question of judicial review of the Tribunal, with section 9 precluding any indirect judicial monitoring of unauthorized interceptions. The effect of section 9 is that the Crown cannot rely directly on wire-tapping evidence in legal proceedings, but may use only the fruits of the interception. More significantly, perhaps, it also means that no attempt may be made in the course of a prosecution to determine that in their investigations the authorities have committed one or more criminal offences. Even the most naïve of British people must be left to suspect that the reason for this is that unauthorized tapping may continue despite section 1. If it does, there is no institution which can intervene to regulate the practice except the police.

4

Freedom of Assembly and Public Order

WE now turn our attention to the law on peaceful processions and public assemblies. A noticeable change in the nature of protest has occurred in recent years. In the 1970s the police were often concerned with the need to keep apart two rival groups, each of which had gathered together for a demonstration in the same place and at the same time. Typically, the National Front would announce an intention to meet in or march through a racially sensitive area, and the Socialist Workers Party would then declare their determination to demonstrate against fascism at the same time. It was, for example, a National Front meeting in Southall Town Hall on St George's Day 1979 that sparked off the clashes between police and members of the local community during which Mr Blair Peach was fatally injured (NCCL, 1980). Such confrontation has been less frequent in the last ten years, probably because of the decline in popular support for extreme right-wing groups. Instead, where disorder has occurred, it has more often been between the police and a faction or factions within the demonstration itself. The clearest example of this is in the area of industrial protest, where alleged disorder on the picket line has been a routine justification for robust police action. It also occurs in the context of political protest. Meetings called to complain about Salman Rushdie's *Satanic Verses* and marches organized to oppose student loans, for example, have both occasioned violent encounters with the police. This type of disorder raises difficult questions about when and how the police should respond which are different in kind from those of the previous decade. Allegations of over-reaction by the authorities are, as we shall see, a common feature of modern protest. This makes the accountability of the police as important here as it was in our earlier discussion of their general powers.

In this chapter, we shall look first at the laws that were available to the authorities in the years before Mrs Thatcher's Government came into office in 1979. Then we shall examine how these laws were utilized to deal with large-scale public protest during the 1980s. The two most important episodes in public order policing during this period were the CND campaign against cruise missiles in the first half of the decade, and the miners' strike during 1984/5; we will examine each of these in turn. The miners' strike will give us an opportunity to discuss the militarization of the police, one of the most noticeable as well as one of the most controversial trends of recent years. Having looked at these particular protests, we will then turn our attention to the Public Order Act 1986, and examine why the Government thought the Act to be necessary. A recurrent theme in this area is how broad the law has always been, and how much the discretion of the authorities has been what has really mattered. In this context, we shall assess how the Act has added to police power and what effect it has had when it has been used in tandem with the pre-existing law. We shall conclude with an examination of the controversy over the use of Stonehenge as a site of pilgrimage during the summer solstice. This ongoing conflict serves as a useful example of the interrelationship of the various legislative and common-law powers. It also neatly illustrates the vulnerability of dissenting groups to the battery of laws which, as we shall see, is always available to the authorities.

The Legal Position in 1979

In our Introduction we examined the eccentric way in which this country has traditionally approached questions of liberty. The great British bluff on freedom is nowhere more clearly exposed than in relation to freedom of assembly. There is not and never has been a 'right' to demonstrate. A citizen on a march, or on a picket, or at a public meeting, has never been able to respond to the repressive exercise of authority by calling in aid a legally enforceable right to do that which is impugned. All such a person can say, quoting Dicey, is that he or she is free to do that which no law prohibits. Historically, it is true, the freedom did have some content. In *Beatty* v. *Gillbanks*,[1] the Salvation Army was stopped from marching because of fears that it would incite a disorderly rabble, loosely organized as a so-called 'skeleton army', to acts of violence against it. This preventive action was castigated by the judges on the Queen's Bench. The Salvationists associated together 'for a purpose which cannot be said to be otherwise than lawful and laudable, or at all events cannot be called unlawful'. What disturbances there had been or might be were or would be caused entirely by 'a body of persons opposed to the religious views of . . . the Salvation Army'. To prevent the procession amounted to saying 'that a man may be punished for acting lawfully if he knows that his so doing may induce another man to act unlawfully—a proposition without any authority whatever to support it'. Yet despite this decision—always regarded as a classic illustration of the common-law presumption in favour of freedom of assembly—the law has developed to the point where we can say with reasonable assurance that the residue of which Dicey was so proud has narrowed to the point of extinction. There may be a freedom to protest—but it exists only to the extent that it is permitted by the police.

1. The Public Order Act 1936

This was reasonably clear even by 1979. Both legislation and common law played a part. As regards the first of these, the most important statute was the Public Order Act 1936. Section 3 was concerned with public processions (stationary assemblies were not covered by the Act). In the first instance, the section permitted a chief officer of police who reasonably apprehended that a procession 'may occasion serious public disorder' to impose such conditions 'as appear[ed] to him necessary for the preservation of public order'. If it was felt that these conditions would be insufficient to prevent 'serious public disorder', then the chief

[1] (1882) 9 QBD 308.

officer could apply for a banning order—from the Home Secretary in London, or from the local council in any other part of the country. Such an order would be for up to three months and would have to be a ban on all or any class of processions in a given area. The idea behind this imposition of blanket bans was to prevent the temptation to discriminate against particular marches. In June 1937, a six-week ban on all political processions in a part of the East End of London was imposed. Over the years, however, such dramatic action proved to be the exception rather than the rule. Until 1980 the power to ban was employed sparingly. If a peaceful march threatened to attract an antagonistic rival mob, then the standard police procedure was to allow the march to go ahead, with as much protection as was necessary. This was regardless of the unpopularity or obnoxiousness of the views that were being expressed—and protected. This was the basis upon which many National Front marches proceeded during the 1970s. The spirit of *Beatty* v. *Gillbanks* was alive and reasonably well.

Apart from these preventive powers, section 5 of the 1936 Act also contained an important statutory offence which for fifty years was one of the central tools in the control of political assembly and public nonconformity. This section had its origins in police efforts in the 1930s to deal both with left-wing demonstrators and with Sir Oswald Mosley's Fascists. Over the years, it became the standard public order offence. As amended in 1965, it covered any person who in any public place or at any public meeting used threatening, abusive, or insulting words or behaviour or distributed or displayed any writing, sign, or other visible representation which was threatening, abusive, or insulting. None of these actions was criminal in itself. The conduct had also to be intended to provoke a breach of the peace or to have been of such a nature as to have been likely to have occasioned such a breach. As we shall see presently, 'breach of the peace' is a notoriously imprecise notion. Flexible attitudes to its definition, facilitated by the summary nature of the proceedings, led to some curious prosecutions under this provision. A leading textbook noted:

the convictions of (1) the person who took off his clothes in one of the fountains in Trafalgar Square; (2) the persons who shouted 'Remember Biafra' during the two minutes' silence at the 1969 Remembrance Day ceremony in Whitehall; and (3) the person who painted the word 'Jews' in two foot high letters on the garden wall of a house occupied by a Jewish family, the father of whom had been a prisoner at Dachau. (Bailey, Harris and Jones, 1985: 153–4)

Miaowing at a police dog brought the wrath of the section upon one tactlessly witty accused, though his conviction was quashed on appeal.[2]

The section took as its task the prevention of disorder. To the extent that freedom of expression figured at all, it was no more than as an implicit principle sitting silently in the gaps between the words. Not unnaturally, therefore, it was often squeezed. Peaceful demonstrators were vulnerable if their espousal of an unpopular cause moved to violence a hostile crowd or those who saw the message as threatening or insulting. Anti-apartheid demonstrators were prosecuted for invading court number 2 at Wimbledon during a match involving the South African, Cliff Drysdale; the House of Lords ultimately decided that the meaning of 'insulting' was properly a matter for the magistrates (who had acquitted in this case) and allowed the defendant's appeal against the Divisional Court's decision that the conduct had been insulting.[3] In 1968 a man handed out to US servicemen leaflets which opposed the war in Vietnam and invited them to consider deserting. For this, he was convicted of distributing insulting material whereby a breach of the peace was likely to be occasioned.[4] When Pat Arrowsmith gave out similar anti-war material to British troops, this time related to Northern Ireland, the justices before whom she appeared acquitted her because they did not think the publication to be 'insulting'. (When Ms Arrowsmith returned to her pacifist work, she was again arrested, but this time prosecuted and convicted under the more severe Incitement to Disaffection Act 1934. Her eighteen-month jail sentence was reduced on appeal—but not before she had been in prison for six months.)[5] In one leading case from 1963, a Fascist leader was convicted under the section for making a speech at a public meeting which deliberately provoked to fury the Jews, the members of CND, and the communists who had come to

---

[2] *The Times*, 4 Apr. 1985.   [3] *Brutus* v. *Cozens* [1973] AC 854.

[4] *Williams* v. *DPP* [1968] Crim. Law Rev. 563.

[5] *R.* v. *Arrowsmith* [1975] QB 678.

Trafalgar Square with the express intention of stopping the meeting. The appeal court took the view that a speaker must take the audience as he or she finds it—this contradicted *Beatty* v. *Gillbanks* and revived all the fears about 'mob rule' which had been to the forefront of the judges' minds in that case.[6]

2. Breach of the peace and police powers of arrest

These two sections in the Public Order Act were not all that were available to the authorities before 1979. A third power was also of critical importance. Throughout the century, there has lurked in the undergrowth of the common law a judge-made weapon of great flexibility and force which has never been defined with any great precision or examined closely by either House of Parliament. Lord Diplock accurately described the relevant legal rule in the following passage:

> every citizen in whose presence a breach of the peace is being, or reasonably appears to be about to be, committed has the right to take reasonable steps to make the person who is breaking or threatening to break the peace refrain from doing so . . .[7]

Whereas the ordinary person has a choice whether or not to act, the police officer, in view of his or her status, has a positive obligation to take action. Failure to obey any instructions he or she might issue in this context may amount to the statutory offence of obstruction of a police officer in the execution of his duty, for which the sentence can be either imprisonment or a substantial fine. This power is still available to the police today and three questions arise in relation to it: first, what is the meaning of breach of the peace?; secondly, when may the police act?; and thirdly, what may they do?

Given that it is the crucial phrase, it is perhaps surprising that the definition of breach of the peace has always been vague. As we have seen, section 5 of the Public Order Act 1936, which contained the formula, was used by the police to prosecute all sorts of odd and eccentric types of conduct. A fairly narrow meaning has been ascribed to it by the Court of Appeal:

[6] *Jordan* v. *Burgoyne* [1963] 2 QB 744.
[7] *Albert* v. *Lavin* [1982] AC 546.

we cannot accept that there can be a breach of the peace unless there has been an act done or threatened to be done which either actually harms a person, or in his presence his property, or is likely to cause such harm, or which puts someone in fear of such harm being done.[8]

At one level, this definition is rather broad; it refers to threatened acts and the likelihood (rather than the actuality) of damage to person or property. It does, however, link the law to the idea of harm and this is valuable in so far as it reduces the risk that boisterous behaviour, or other non-violent activity, can by itself amount to a breach of the peace. Whether it has always been strictly adhered to by magistrates and the police is, of course, another matter. Earlier cases had tended to defer to the judgment of the police officer on the spot without setting out an objective definition to which he or she was required to adhere.[9] In a Court of Appeal decision, reported in the same volume as the case from which the passage above is taken, Lord Denning thought that there was a breach of the peace 'whenever a person who is lawfully carrying out his work is unlawfully and physically prevented by another from doing it'. This would include many forms of peaceful protest, including sit-ins, certain public meetings, and even some pickets. His fellow judges disagreed with Lord Denning and his opinions probably do not reflect the law, though the emergence of such views from a source so eminent as Lord Denning demonstrates clearly the common law's culture of uncertainty, within which repressive rules can emerge without embarrassment.[10]

It is obvious that, if harm is occurring, the police should act to stop it. So much is clear from Lord Diplock's speech. The authorities do not have to wait for it to happen, however. If a police officer reasonably anticipates a breach of the peace, he or she is required to do whatever is thought necessary to prevent its occurrence. This may involve interference with otherwise lawful conduct. The threat of criminal sanction hangs over those who refute the constable's perception of events. This is potentially a wide-ranging power. In theory, the police are controlled by the

[8] *R.* v. *Howell* [1982] QB 416.
[9] See e.g. *Piddington* v. *Bates* [1961] 1 WLR 162.
[10] *R.* v. *Chief Constable of the Devon and Cornwall Constabulary, ex parte Central Electricity Generating Board* [1982] QB 458.

requirement that their suspicions about the future be reasonable, i.e. based on objective facts. The courts are supposed to be vigilant on behalf of the citizen, and mindful of the liberty to go about one's lawful business. Their job is to check the factual basis behind the police suspicion and the real likelihood of the breach of the peace ostensibly anticipated. In this way, the individual is supposed to be protected against any over-zealous use of this powerful and vague discretion. There is no doubt that the courts are rhetorically committed to such a role. The practice of the police, and the case-law surrounding it, tell a different story. In reality, it is this power, rather than any other provision, that has been vital to the police in their control over the years of pickets, protesters, and political demonstrators.

Three cases, two from that other period of great division, the 1930s, set the tone for the law as it stood in 1979. The first is *Thomas* v. *Sawkins*,[11] where a public meeting was called in Glamorgan to protest against the Incitement to Disaffection Bill then before Parliament and to call for the dismissal of the Chief Constable of the county. The organizers hired the local library for the occasion and decided, on account of tension at previous gatherings, that they did not want any police officers present. Despite this stipulation, two policemen—sitting in the front row—were among the 600 present. They refused to leave on request and attempts to eject them failed on account of the sudden arrival of reinforcements from the local station. In subsequent criminal proceedings, the High Court held that the police had a power to enter and remain on private property, against the wishes of the occupier, if they reasonably apprehended either that the commission of an offence was 'imminent or likely' or that any breach of the peace was likely to occur. The justices in the court below had been right to conclude that the police had 'reasonable grounds for believing that, if they were not present at the meeting, there would be seditious speeches and other incitements to violence and breaches of the peace would occur'. Beyond this bland assertion, there was no further scrutiny of the way in which the police had acted. No evidence emerged to justify the apprehension of the authorities, but this did not trouble the

[11] [1935] 2 KB 249.

court. It went 'without saying' that the rule was devoted 'not to the interests of the police, but to the protection and welfare of the public'.

Our second decision concerned Mrs Kate Duncan who, as a member of the National Unemployed Workers' Movement, wanted to give a speech outside an unemployment training centre.[12] A number of people gathered to hear her. Worried staff at the centre called in the police, who instructed Mrs Duncan to make her speech not in front of the centre but rather in an unobtrusive site on another street 175 yards away. She refused and was promptly arrested. In due course, she was charged with and convicted of obstruction of a police constable in the execution of his duty. Her appeal to the Divisional Court was rejected. The judges thought that the police anticipation of a breach of the peace was reasonable because there had been a 'disturbance' after a similar meeting addressed by Mrs Duncan—fourteen months before. The Lord Chief Justice, Lord Hewart, was able to turn Dicey's complacency to useful account:

There have been moments during the argument in this case when it appeared to be suggested that the court had to do with a grave case involving what is called the right of public meeting. I say 'called' because English Law does not recognise any special right of public meeting either for political or other purposes. The right of assembly, as Professor Dicey puts it, is nothing more than a view taken by the court of the individual liberty of the subject. If I thought that the present case raised the question which has been held in suspense by more than one writer on constitutional law—namely, whether an assembly can properly be held to be unlawful merely because the holding of it is expected to give rise to a breach of the peace on the part of persons opposed to those who are holding the meeting—I should wish to hear much more argument before I expressed an opinion. This case, however, does not even touch that important question.

Our third decision dates from 1960 and concerns an industrial dispute at a printers' works in London.[13] The police decided to allow only two pickets at each of the two entrances to the works. Mr Piddington disagreed with this decision. He felt that this number was not enough to communicate with workers entering

[12] *Duncan* v. *Jones* [1936] 1 KB 218.
[13] *Piddington* v. *Bates* [1961] 1 WLR 162.

and leaving the premises (usually at the same time) or with transport workers as and when they delivered goods to the place. So, with the brave words, 'I'm going there and you can't stop me; I know my rights', he attempted to join one of the pairs of pickets. He was arrested and, although there was no blockage of the highway, disorder, or violence, he was later charged with obstruction of a police officer in the execution of his duty. The police argued that they had reasonably apprehended that a breach of the peace might occur if there had been more than two pickets at each entrance. The Divisional Court, presided over by the Lord Chief Justice, Lord Parker, emphasized that there had to be a 'real possibility' of a breach of the peace, but went on to find that just such a situation of menace existed here: eighteen people 'milling about' when there were only eight people in the works created a 'real danger of something more than mere picketing'. The authorities, therefore, were entitled to act as they did. The exact number to be allowed was entirely a matter for the constable who 'must be left to take such steps as on the evidence before him he thinks are proper'. The police are thus empowered arbitrarily to limit numbers and to form cordons to allow lorries and workers through to work. The requirement that there be a real possibility of a breach of the peace before they act is rarely subject to close judicial scrutiny. This power, ostensibly the exercise of discretion by an individual constable, has in practice hardened into a set of rules for the management of industrial disputes. The emergence of these rules out of a common law which denies their existence has the added consequence, attractive to those who make them, that they are not subject to parliamentary or to adequate judicial control. They are the invisible force of the criminal law.

Policing the Peace Movement

Although the three powers we have just outlined were the principal measures available to the police to prevent or to control public assemblies, it would be a mistake to think that they were the only ones. The police could also rely on the statutory offence of obstruction of the highway,[14] and the common-law offence of

---

[14] *Arrowsmith* v. *Jenkins* [1963] 2 QB 561.

public nuisance.[15] The civil law, mainly through the torts of trespass and private nuisance, also had a role to play.[16] The practical consequence of the range of laws we have described was that, by 1979, the freedom to engage in peaceful protest in this country was traditionally dependent not on the law but rather on the benevolent exercise of discretion by those in power. In the first half of the 1980s, two events more than any others tested the malleability and breadth of the law that was available to the authorities. These were first the CND campaign against cruise missiles and secondly the miners' strike.

1. CND: the first phase

Opposition to nuclear weapons has proved to be an enduring source of popular protest in Britain in the 1980s. The origins of this popular movement lie in the first wave of pressure for disarmament, which began with the emergence of the Campaign for Nuclear Disarmament (CND) in 1958 and ended in 1964, with its decline in the face of the new Labour Government's failure to rid itself of nuclear weapons. Resistance focused initially on nuclear testing and the existence of American bases on British soil, but it quickly broadened to encompass unilateral nuclear disarmament in general and a rejection of the Polaris missiles favoured by the then Conservative Government in particular. The period was marked by mass demonstrations, of which the Aldermaston marches were the most successful as well as the best remembered, and by more direct forms of action such as well-planned and highly publicized sorties against selected US rocket bases situated in Britain. This latter tactic was favoured by the Committee of One Hundred, a radical CND faction led by the 89-year-old philosopher, Bertrand Russell.

After some initial successes, the authorities cracked down on the protesters. A sit-down in Trafalgar Square on 17 September 1961 resulted in the arrest of more than 1,300 people; nearly a third of the organizing committee (including Russell) had already been detained, two weeks before the event. A further 850 protesters were arrested when the police moved against simul-

[15] R. v. Clarke [1964] 2 QB 315.
[16] Hubbard v. Pitt [1976] QB 142.

taneous actions at a US air base at Wethersfield and six other locations. Six members of the Committee of One Hundred, who had planned to enter the air base and immobilize it by sitting in front of its planes, were charged with conspiracy to commit offences under section 1 of the Official Secrets Act 1911. Jail sentences of eighteen months each were meted out to five of them, with the sixth (the only woman) receiving twelve months. The House of Lords afterwards unanimously upheld these convictions.[17] Their Lordships agreed that the plan to immobilize the base was a purpose 'prejudicial to the safety or interests of the State' as required by the words of the section. The case was noteworthy for the fact that a section hitherto thought to be aimed only at espionage had been employed against peaceful protesters. Their Lordships also upheld the trial judge's refusal to allow the defendants to put any evidence before the jury about why they believed that nuclear weapons, rather than their own actions, were 'prejudicial to the safety . . . of the State'. The majority of the law lords seemed to regard the interests of the state as coterminous with the interests of the government of the day; executive-minded comments to that effect have lingered on in the textbooks ever since, an unwanted legal legacy from this period of popular protest.

2. CND: the second phase

The second great phase of CND activity occurred, of course, in the first half of the 1980s. The turmoil of those years seems now, in this new era of superpower co-operation, to be very far away. Shortly after the Soviet Union's invasion of Afghanistan at the end of 1979, the Western alliance decided to deploy new intermediate range nuclear missiles in Europe. These weapons, called cruise and Pershing, were to be land-based and many of the cruise missiles were to be sited in the United Kingdom. The idea was to demonstrate the solidarity of the NATO alliance with a view to ensuring that negotiations with the Eastern bloc would be from a position of strength. The policy was enthusiastically adopted by the new American President, Ronald Reagan, and by

[17] *Chandler* v. *DPP* [1964] AC 763.

Mrs Thatcher, who had assumed office some months before his election. Her Government also decided to expand Britain's own nuclear capacity by purchasing missiles for Trident submarines from the Americans.

These policies soon proved extremely controversial. NATO strategists talked of the need for a 'flexible response' and of the possibility of a 'limited' nuclear war; translated into the ordinary language of British voters, this seemed to many to amount to a willingness to contemplate nuclear war restricted to European soil. The words of one American ex-Admiral were frequently quoted: 'We fought World War One in Europe. We fought World War Two in Europe. And, if you dummies let us, we'll fight World War Three in Europe' (Hinton, 1989: 183–4). Tension was exacerbated by the cold-war rhetoric which both President Reagan and Mrs Thatcher consciously adopted, with the former referring to the 'Evil Empire' in Eastern Europe and the latter revelling in the 'Iron Maiden' label which the Russians themselves had affixed to her. The Government's ill-considered attempt to prepare the populace for civil defence in the face of nuclear attack, in the pamphlet *Protect and Survive*, provoked derision and added to the level of anxiety. Fears about a 'nuclear winter' destroying half the globe after a nuclear strike made Whitehall's advice about staying indoors seem curiously dated, and NATO's talk of limited war a dangerous self-delusion.

The Alliance's 1979 decision gave 1983 as the planned deployment year for cruise and Pershing. This gave the protest movements plenty of time to galvanize support. CND emerged once more as the focal point of popular dissent. Under the astute leadership of its general secretary, Bruce Kent, it made room for the various local and single-issue groups that were mushrooming around the country. At its height, the organization claimed 90,000 national members and 250,000 additional supporters organized at local level. As in the first phase of its activity, it sought to rely on a mix of massive public protest with occasional more direct forms of action. In October 1980, 70,000 people were estimated to have packed into Trafalgar Square for CND's first public demonstration of its strength. A rally in Hyde Park on 6 June 1982 drew a crowd which the police estimated at 115,000 (the Department of the Environment banned the playing of music at the demonstration). Its march through London on 22 October 1983 was 'probably the largest in British history, with the possible exception of the women's suffrage rally of 1909' (Hinton, 1989: 183). During the autumn of that year, more than five million people took to the streets of Europe in support of the cause of European disarmament.

One year missing from this litany of successful street protest is 1981. CND had planned a number of marches in London for that summer but they were affected by a ban on all public processions (other than those traditionally held) in the Metropolitan Police District which was imposed for a twenty-eight-day period by the Metropolitan Police Commissioner, with the consent of the Home Secretary, under section 3 of the Public Order Act 1936. CND's challenge to the legality of this banning order emphasized its breadth (786 square miles) and its near-absolute nature, but neither the High Court nor the Court of Appeal were willing to overturn the Commissioner's opinion about the risk of an outbreak of serious public disorder.[18] This was despite the fact that one member of the Court of Appeal, Sir Denys Buckley, thought the reasons for the order to be 'meagre'. All the judges emphasized that the danger of disorder came not from the CND marchers but rather from the fact that '[h]ooligans and others might attack the police who were doing their duty in escorting a peaceful procession' (Lord Denning). As Ackner LJ put it, the marchers might become a 'target for their viciousness'. The judgment of the Commissioner on this and the other issues was not to be gainsaid.

Apart from marches, CND fuelled their anti-cruise campaigns with demonstrations around the bases that were scheduled to take the new missiles. At Easter 1983, a crowd the police estimated at 40,000 linked hands to form a human chain that ran from the air base at Greenham Common to Aldermaston and the Royal Ordnance Factory at Burghfield in Berkshire. During the same weekend, 1,500 demonstrators gathered at the Royal Navy Polaris submarine base at Faslane on the Clyde. Two months later, there were 752 arrests when 3,000 demonstrators participated in a four-day attempted blockade of the Upper Heyford base in

[18] *Kent* v. *Metropolitan Police Commissioner*, *The Times*, 15 May 1981.

protest at the F1-11 nuclear bombers located there. Direct action did not always take place under the aegis of CND. Peace camps were formed around some of the RAF air bases which it was thought would house the new cruise missiles. The most famous of these was the first, at Greenham Common. Organized exclusively by women, it quickly became a symbol not only of peace but also of the values of the women's movement. On 12 December 1982, 30,000 women linked hands to 'Embrace the Base'. They adorned the perimeter fence with pictures, flowers, and messages of peace. Further peaceful actions followed at other bases, and these were more directy sponsored by CND. Unlike in the early 1960s, section 1 of the Official Secrets Act was not employed against the protesters at any point during this period though clearly it could have been.

3. The peace movement and the criminal law

None of these protests proved of any avail. Buoyed by an election victory in which the Opposition's commitment to unilateral nuclear disarmament had appeared a vote loser, the Government proceeded to deploy cruise on schedule in 1983. Plans for Trident continued apace. Weakened by internal conflict, CND was unable to mount an effective large-scale protest when the first cruise missiles finally arrived. In 1984 the focus of the peace movement shifted to Cruisewatch, a 'highly effective network of people organised to track and harass deployment exercises from the Greenham base' (Hinton, 1989: 193). Efforts were also made to launch private prosecutions against Mrs Thatcher for the alleged crime of threatening to kill under section 16 of the Offences Against the Person Act 1861. In 1985 CND made the proposed new cruise missile base at Molesworth in Cambridgeshire the target for their Easter protests. Three marches starting in Leicester, Stevenage, and Cambridge on Good Friday converged on Molesworth on Easter Sunday. The police responded by erecting road-blocks limiting access to the area. They issued passes to local inhabitants and representatives of the media. *The Times* reported that 'the police decided by late evening that enough vehicles had arrived to prevent any further cars approaching the base. Even press passes issued by Cambridge police did not allow access closer than about three miles from the base.'[19] The legality of these road-blocks was not tested in court; the police claimed to be relying both on the Road Traffic Act and on the breach of the peace power as it had been developed during the miners' strike (see below). Yet it is hard to see what violence the police foresaw as direct and immediate. The weekend of protest was very peaceful. Ten arrests were made on Easter Saturday, with eight of those detained being charged and bailed on condition that they did not come within 15 miles of the Molesworth base.[20]

In 1985 a new form of protest reached its height. Centred in East Anglia, the Snowball Campaign involved a symbolic cutting of the perimeter fence at air-force bases around the country. The idea was that the number of people engaged in this activity would increase dramatically with every action, thereby demonstrating the depth of feeling against nuclear weapons. The movement attracted widespread support from peace campaigners. Over the weekend of 21/2 September 1985, for example, 60 protesters were arrested for wire-cutting at Molesworth and a further 55 were arrested or reported for the same action at RAF Sculthorpe. CND claimed that sixteen air bases were affected by a co-ordinated action over the two days.[21] The authorities responded to this new aggravation in two ways. First, new by-laws were promulgated. At Greenham Common, for example, it was declared a criminal offence to 'enter, pass through or over or remain in or over' the area of the base. At Fylingdales, to 'remain in' the area of the air base 'after having been directed to leave' by an official was designated a breach of by-law 3(k). In due course, these new laws were applied against the protesters who appeared to be on strong ground when challenging their convictions, since, in their haste to bring these laws into operation, the drafters had apparently acted *ultra vires*. Section 14 of the Military Lands Act 1892 set out the general enabling power, but then went on to provide 'that no bylaws promulgated under this section shall authorise the Secretary of State to take away or prejudicially affect any right of common'.

[19] *The Times*, 8 Apr. 1985.
[20] *The Times*, 8 Apr. 1985.
[21] *The Times*, 23 Sept. 1985.

The Divisional Court found that the by-laws did in fact adversely impinge upon just such rights.[22] Yet in giving the judgment of the Divisional Court, Schiemann J. contrived to avoid the conclusion that the by-laws were as a result void and the convictions made under them of no effect. He observed that the protesters did not enjoy the rights of common that had been affected, and on this basis he decided to modify the by-laws so that they could continue to apply to all the world except the commoners themselves. As the protesters were not commoners, the by-laws would apply to them. This judicial tinkering was justified because the court was 'sure that the altered decision represent[ed] that which the decision-maker would have enacted had he appreciated the limitation on his powers'. It was 'abundantly clear that the byelaw maker, if he had appreciated the limitation on his powers, would both at Greenham Common and at Fylingdales nevertheless have gone on to make the bylaws in such a way that the proviso to section 14(1) was given effect but all the world save commoners would still have been within their ambit'. The Court made no reference to any presumption that the criminal law should be construed strictly in favour of a defendant. The by-laws were lawful not because of what they said but rather because of what they would have said if they had been drafted lawfully.

The second tactic employed by the authorities related specifically to the Snowball campaign and involved dealing with the symbolic fence-cutting as the offence of criminal damage. This led to a vast number of prosecutions, usually in the magistrates' court, because the authorities were quite careful about alleging that less damage had occurred than would give the protesters the option of having a jury trial, something for which most of them would have very happily volunteered. The protesters argued that they had a 'lawful excuse' for what they did. A partial definition of this phrase appears in section 5 of the Criminal Damage Act 1971. Such an excuse exists if an accused 'damaged . . . the property in

---

[22] *DPP* v. *Hutchinson; R.* v. *Secretary of State for Defence, ex parte Parker; R.* v. *Defence Secretary, ex parte Hayman* [1989] 1 All ER 1060. The relevant by-laws were: Royal Air Force Greenham Common By-laws 1985 (SI 1985/485), By-law 2(b); Royal Air Force Fylingdales By-laws 1987 (SI 1987/1069).

question . . . in order to protect property belonging to himself or another . . . and at the time of the act . . . alleged to constitute the offence he believed—(i) that the property . . . was in immediate need of protection; and (ii) that the means of protection adopted . . . were . . . reasonable having regard to all the circumstances'. A later subsection was emphatic that it was 'immaterial whether a belief [was] justified or not if it [was] honestly held'. The way this defence was used can be seen from the following submission, made by a defendant charged with the possession of a hacksaw blade with intent to do criminal damage to the perimeter fence of the US naval base at Brawdy:

[T]he purpose of the United States base was to monitor the movements of Soviet submarines; in the event of hostilities breaking out, the base would be the subject of a nuclear strike, with resulting devastation in the area, including to the property of the applicant, her friends and neighbours. Her property was some forty miles from the base. Alternatively, the Soviets might select the site at Brawdy as a target for a sudden nuclear strike in order to demonstrate that they were able to protect their submarines in the Atlantic and so maintain the nuclear threat which the presence of such posed to the United States. If enough people cut the perimeter wire, the Americans might conclude that the safety and integrity of their base could not be securely maintained. Consequently, they might remove the base, thereby removing the reason for a nuclear attack.[23]

One of the purposes behind the action was, therefore, the protection of property, and it was motivated by a belief in the immediate need to act. Since the good faith and honesty of the protesters were admitted by all concerned, this seemed to bring them within the statutory defence regardless of whether their beliefs were reasonable or whether they were universally held. This defence caused some difficulty for the Court of Appeal when two cases raised it in quick succession in the summer and autumn of 1988. The judges responded by saying that the 'purpose' of the accused was something which could be defined objectively. On the facts before them, and contrary to what the defendants actually maintained, their purpose did not include the desire to protect property as required by the section. This reasoning fails to meet the logical objection, identified some years earlier by Lord

[23] *R. v. Hill and Hall* [1989] Crim. Law Rev. 136.

Devlin, that a 'purpose must exist in the mind. It cannot exist anywhere else.'[24] A leading commentator on the criminal law, Professor J. C. Smith, has drawn attention to a situation where a farmer shoots dead an alsatian dog. He may have acted in this way because the dog was worrying sheep, or because he wanted to annoy the dog's owner, or simply because he despises all alsatians. We cannot tell which it was by merely looking at the facts; we have to ask what his purpose actually was. Professor Smith thought the reasoning employed in the CND cases to be 'indefensible'. It made a 'mockery of the oft-proclaimed principle that statutes are to be construed in favour of the defendant'.[25]

In the second case, the Court of Appeal is reported as having concluded that there was no evidence of 'a need of protection from immediate danger'.[26] The statute requires, however, not a threat of immediate danger, but rather an immediate need to act to protect. The two are not the same. Suppose that a slate falls from our roof, leaving the attic exposed. The weather forecast is good and rain is not expected for the next few days. Notwithstanding this, we have an immediate need to protect our property from the moment the slate falls. No one would say that the need only becomes immediate when rain is imminent; the need is immediate from the start because rain is certain to fall some time. The protesters were equally convinced of their belief in the inevitability of nuclear war; this gave rise to their honest perception of what was immediately needed to protect their property. The court does not appear to have dealt directly with this argument. Yet this was not the only aspect of this and the other case to cause concern. Another point relates to the fact that, in the first case,[27] the jury acquitted the defendants of one charge and convicted them of another. Both charges arose out of the same facts. The only issue before the court concerned the defence of lawful excuse. This meant that the jury must have accepted the defence in relation to one charge but not in relation to the other. This may have been a just compromise, but it was clearly illogical. The normal rule in such circumstances is for the

---

[24] *Chandler* v. *DPP* [1964] AC 763, at p. 804.
[25] See Professor Smith's commentary on the two cases: *R.* v. *Ashford and Smith* [1988] Crim. Law Rev. 682 and *R.* v. *Hill and Hall* [1989] Crim. Law Rev. 136.
[26] *R.* v. *Hill and Hall.*   [27] *R.* v. *Ashford and Smith.*

convictions to be set aside: 'no reasonable jury who had applied their mind properly to the facts in the case could have arrived at the conclusion, and once one assumes that they are an unreasonable jury, or they could not have reasonably come to the conclusion, then the convictions cannot stand.'[28] The Court of Appeal, however, thought the acquittals wrong and declared that it was not going to 'compound the error' by quashing the convictions. Professor Smith has remarked that 'an acquittal is an acquittal' and the 'Court was bound to assume that [the jury was] right'. It had no jurisdiction to undermine the jury verdict in this way.

Policing the Miners' Strike

The miners' strike which lasted from March 1984 to March 1985 was not the only example of industrial conflict in Britain in the past two decades, but it was easily the longest and the most violent. Though to some extent exaggerated by the press, the disorder that surrounded it was far greater than anything occasioned by earlier industrial confrontations at locations such as Saltley, Grunwick, and Warrington. The police worked over fourteen million hours' overtime, at an estimated cost of £140 million (Wallington, 1985: 152). In England and Wales, 1,392 police officers were injured, 85 of them seriously. In Scotland, 94 officers were injured, though only one was detained in hospital. Official figures are not available on the number of pickets injured, but there were at least a couple of fatalities and it is the opinion of some observers that, in the major conflicts of the dispute, casualties amongst the pickets greatly exceeded those of the police (Wallington, 1985: 149). The failure of the strikers to achieve their aims was the result of a variety of factors, but to the fore amongst these was the way in which the police and the law were employed against them.

1. New policing strategies
The commitment of large numbers of police officers to the task of keeping the pits open made it impossible for the National Union

[28] R. v. Stone, unreported 13 Dec. 1954 (Court of Criminal Appeal) quoted in R. v. Hunt [1968] 2 QB 433, at p. 438 by Parker LCJ.

of Mineworkers to achieve a total shut-down in domestic coal production. Police determination to control the volume and the effect of picketing made movement around the country and demonstrations at collieries extremely difficult; 'much secondary picketing was prevented from taking place, effectively or at all, by police action rather than the intervention of the civil courts, and it is this factor that is at the heart of complaints that the police broke the strike, or were used to break it' (Wallington, 1985: 148). When the pickets tried to prevent the importation of coal into the country, or its movement into major steelworks like Port Talbot and Ravenscraig, they once more found lines of constables in their way. The miners' strike was a platform for the exercise of new police tactics to deal with disorder. These had gradually developed in the preceding ten years, and were displayed on British streets on a consistent basis for the first time during this dispute.

The first tactic related to the national co-ordination of policing strategy. Police forces in this country are local forces accountable to local police authorities, except in London where the police authority is the Home Secretary. Britain does not have a national police force under the control and direction of a central government department, any such notion having been rejected by the Royal Commission on the Police in 1962. Nevertheless, with the acquiescence of successive Home Secretaries, but without the support of Parliament, we have seen a growing centralization of police conduct in recent years. This is based upon the National Reporting Centre which operates from Scotland Yard. Set up in 1972, the NRC is not a permanent body and is only activated in times of crisis—as during the miners' strike, from which two developments of particular importance emerged. The first is that the NRC co-ordinates strategy and the deployment of officers on a national basis in consultation with the Home Office, which may well have keen political interests in the matter to hand. Secondly, in the co-ordination of this strategy, it is believed that the NRC gives policing orders to local forces, thereby overruling the operational discretion of these local forces. This is a far cry from the procedures under the Police Act 1964, where mutual aid may be provided by one force to another, but only after a request from the latter.

A second feature of public order policing highlighted by the miners' strike was the use of élite groups of police officers within each police force. These groups are trained for a more aggressive role in crowd control, and represent a significant move away from the traditional approach to public order policing which was based on containment and the use of minimum force. The modern origin of this approach is the Special Patrol Group (SPG) which was formed in London in 1965 to act as a mobile anti-crime group to help local police forces to deal with the rising rate of urban crime. The SPG was, however, highly controversial and widely criticized for its behaviour at demonstrations in particular. Indeed, in 1981, Lord Scarman expressed concern about 'too inward-looking and self-conscious an *esprit de corps* developing in the Group'. Nevertheless, the SPG still exists, albeit reorganized and with a new name (the Territorial Support Group). Moreover, similar groups exist in the provinces, often bearing different names. In Manchester, for example, a permanent Tactical Aid Group of seventy-four specially trained officers was set up in 1976. Like the SPG, the TAGs have the reputation for robust policing at demonstrations. In addition to these élite groups, in both London and the provinces there exist Police Support Units of ordinary police officers who have had riot training and who may be pulled off normal duties to help with demonstrations and assemblies. It is these PSUs which are now placed at the disposal of the NRC. During the miners' strike, for example it appears that the NRC could deploy some 13,000 police officers in a total of 416 PSUs.

But the miners' strike did not only reveal that élite groups of police officers were operating to some extent under national co-ordination and control. Both the NRC and the SPG and its equivalents had been known about for some time. More sensational was the information produced inadvertently about the Public Order Manual of Tactical Options and Related Matters, a document prepared by the Association of Chief Police Officers (ACPO). The techniques referred to in the revised manual appear to have been developed particularly after the inner-city riots of 1981. The contents are secret and have been seen in their entirety by very few officers below the rank of Assistant Chief Constable. (Even the Shadow Home Secretary has been denied access.) Parts of the contents of the manual only came to light as a result of criminal trials following an incident at Orgreave during the strike, at which some of the techniques were implemented for the first time. Defence barristers for people charged with riot asked police officers in court to justify their behaviour at Orgreave— the details of which had appeared on television screens across the country. One of the police officers responded by referring to the 'new manual', parts of which were then read out in court. The techniques it deals with appear to have been imported from Hong Kong. There are references to long-shield formations, short-shield units, and horses. The first are designed to present a formidable appearance in front of a crowd; the second are sent into a crowd to disperse and/or incapacitate people with truncheons; and the third are used to create a fear and scatter effect.

Not all of the manual has been disclosed or published, and it has been suggested that the unpublished parts cover the use of plastic bullets, CS gas, and other anti-crowd techniques (Northam, 1985). Yet, as might be gathered from the secret nature of the procedures, none of this has any formal parliamentary approval, and there is no formal parliamentary accountability or scrutiny of these rather sinister developments. So we see the emergence without any express authority of an *ad hoc* national police force, co-ordinating the use of highly trained riot police and operating aggressive and uncompromising new tactics. The practical reality of modern police organization and its response bears absolutely no relation to the rather quaint legal structure within which the police are supposed to be contained. This is not to deny that the opportunity has been made available to question these developments or to call a halt to them. In *R.* v. *Secretary of State for the Home Department, ex parte Northumbria Police Authority*,[29] the police authority sought judicial review to compel the Home Secretary to withdraw a circular issuing plastic bullets and CS gas to local police forces. The authority was opposed to the use of the equipment by its force and was 'very concerned that such weapons should not be used to quell public demonstrations or riots because of the likelihood of serious personal injury or death thereby resulting to individuals'.

[29] [1988] 2 WLR 590.

The application failed in the Court of Appeal. There were two grounds. First, it was unsuccessful on the correct interpretation of the relevant statute, the Police Act 1964. This was surprising in view of the fact that, under this Act, it is the local authorities who are empowered to provide and maintain such buildings, vehicles, apparatus, and equipment as may be required for the police purposes of their area. The Court of Appeal, however, upheld the Home Office argument that the local authorities did not have exclusive power in this respect. Remarkably, the Court relied on section 41, which is concerned mainly with the provision by the Home Office of such things as police colleges and forensic science laboratories. To say that this was creative statutory interpretation would be a gross understatement. Yet this was not the only source of Home Office power to supply the hardware which the local police authority did not want to have. The Court of Appeal also declared that the Crown had 'a prerogative power to keep the peace'. This power devolved to the Home Secretary who was entitled to 'do all that [was] reasonably necessary to preserve the peace of the realm'. This prerogative was exercisable in times of quiet as well as of emergency and it was in no way fettered or reduced by the enactment of legislation like the Police Act.

The power comes as something of a surprise. The judges extrapolated it from the fact that constables hold office under the Crown and are sworn to keep the peace. It does not feature in the textbooks on the subject (apart from a sentence in one book about which the judges made an immense fuss). The cases relied upon were fairly eccentric, one a hitherto uncited judgment dating from 1855 and the other an obscure decision about the taxation of police stations in 1883. Nourse LJ thought it worth mentioning Lord Blackburn's comment, based on Blackstone, that 'the sheriff also was bound to raise the hue and cry, and call out the posse comitatus of the county whenever it was necessary for any police purposes; in so doing he was acting for the Crown'. The fact that almost nobody had heard of this prerogative turned out to one of the judges to be a point in its favour:

I have already expressed the view that the scarcity of references in the books to the prerogative of keeping the peace within the realm does not disprove that it exists. Rather it may point to an unspoken assumption that it does.

The supposed dogma that no new prerogatives may be created hardly matters when there are endless old ones such as this waiting to be discovered. The problem now, of course, is to determine just how far it extends. If there is no restriction on CS gas or plastic bullets (and by November 1987, twenty forces had been issued with plastic bullets),[30] there is presumably no restriction on water cannon and live ammunition. And all with the seal of judicial approval without any formal power granted by Parliament. It is curious how easily we allow liberty to be eroded.

2. The expanding frontiers of the law

The *Northumbria* case shows just how flexible the law can be. The success of the policing operation during the miners' strike was not due to new laws passed by Parliament to give the authorities greater powers. No state of emergency was ever called. Instead, the police relied upon the wide range of old laws that were already in place. The scale of their utilization of traditional law was remarkable, both in the exploitation of the rules of criminal procedure and in the development of the pre-existing substantive law. On the procedural side, 9,808 people were arrested in connection with the strike in England and Wales, but nearly one in five of these were not charged with any offence. Of those who did eventually end up in court, the acquittal rate by March 1985 was 24 per cent (Wallington, 1985: 150). In Scotland, 1,483 people were arrested and charged, but as many as 33 per cent of these were not proceeded against by the Procurator-fiscal. In Strathclyde alone, nearly three out of every five cases were not pursued to court, a statistic which provides 'considerable support for the view that a policy of mass arrests was pursued by the police in that area' (Wallington, 1985: 150).

Most of the charges in both jurisdictions were relatively minor. The overwhelming majority of Scottish cases related to one of four offences: conduct likely or intended to cause a breach of the peace, obstruction of a police officer in the execution of his or her duty, criminal damage or breach of bail conditions (Wallington, 1985: 150). The same four offences were prominent south of the

[30] See Mr Douglas Hogg's parliamentary written answer at 123 HC Debs. (WA) 57 (23 Nov. 1987).

border, though there the police revealed a propensity for more serious charges, including, by the end of the strike, 509 of unlawful assembly and 139 of riot. (Many of these prosecutions were later to collapse.) The authorities in England and Wales also brought over 600 charges under the Conspiracy and Protection of Property Act 1875 for 'watching and besetting' premises, including the homes of working miners; this was the first significant use of this section in living memory. When cases came to court, the police often dropped charges in return for binding-over orders, issued under an even more ancient statute, the Justices of the Peace Act 1361. This did not require proof of any wrongdoing and involved the defendant undertaking, on pain of a financial penalty, either to keep the peace or to be of good behaviour, depending on how the matter was treated by the magistrates. During the strike, there were allegations that the police used binding-over orders in cases which they knew could never result in convictions but in which they wanted to avail themselves of the opportunity for the imposition of bail conditions which they knew such a charge would give them (Christian, 1985: 133).

Conditions on the granting of bail may be imposed by the magistrates' court on defendants against whom charges are pending. During the strike, the police found them to be a useful device with which to restrict the freedom of movement of pickets. This was so, despite the fact that many of the charges were minor and could not result in terms of imprisonment, and regardless of how the cases turned out if indeed they were ever proceeded with. The conditions typically restricted the defendant to peaceful picketing at his or her usual place of employment, but they could be wider than this, embracing curfews and residency requirements such as the stipulation on one occasion that a defendant reside in Wick (Wallington, 1985: 156). The effect of this policy has been described by one writer in the following terms:

The blanket imposition of bail conditions on striking miners had dramatic effects both on the individual concerned and on the ability of the N.U.M. to mount effective pickets. A number of miners went to prison for breach of bail conditions. . . . At Mansfield a 20 year-old miner went to prison even though unconvicted of any offence for alleged breach of bail conditions. Yet on both occasions he had been in the vicinity of his own pit; unsurprisingly because his house was only fifty yards from it. His 17 year-old brother who was not a miner was also sent to prison after the police claimed that he would 'support his brother' if released. Nearly two weeks later the police admitted that this was not sufficient reason for refusing bail. Both brothers had never been in any kind of trouble before. Their treatment caused three hundred miners to demonstrate spontaneously outside Lincoln Prison for their release.

Women too were imprisoned for breach of bail conditions. One woman from Ollerton was imprisoned in Risley Remand Centre after joining a picket line in breach of a bail condition prohibiting her from doing so. The conditional bail had been granted after she had been arrested for shouting 'scab' at working miners. (Christian, 1985: 129)

Magistrates became so familiar with this procedure that, in some courts, the 'usual conditions' came to be attached to the granting of bail to striking miners in a way that seemed both autocratic and inevitable. In Mansfield, for example, there were cases in which the clerk had put the conditions on the bail form even before the defendant's solicitor had concluded his application for unconditional bail. The legality of such a procedure was upheld in the Divisional Court.[31] The Lord Chief Justice, Lord Lane, admitted that it did a bench of magistrates no 'credit if their clerk continues to affix standard conditions to bail forms even while applications are being made for unconditional bail'. However, the 'fact that the outcome of the application was correctly anticipated [did] not vitiate the decision'. The Bail Act 1976 required that each applicant for bail be individually assessed in order to ascertain whether there was a real risk of a further offence. This reflected Parliament's concern that such persons, presumed still to be innocent of any crime, should be further deprived of their liberty only in narrow and defined circumstances. The Divisional Court thought it 'clear to everyone, and to the justices in particular, that any suggestion of peaceful picketing was a colourable pretence and that it was a question of picketing by intimidation and threat'. The justices were, therefore, right to conclude that the conditions they imposed had been necessary and lawful. Lord Lane did, however, express concern on behalf of the court that to some people, 'putting into the dock together

[31] R. v. Mansfield Justices, ex parte Sharkey [1985] QB 613.

defendants who [had] been arrested on different occasions or at different places makes it difficult to avoid the appearance of "group justice"'. The practice was one 'to be discouraged', though the Court sympathized with the magistrates' 'uphill task of dealing with literally hundreds of cases over and above their normal list'.

The police did not only employ the law of criminal procedure in their tactical battle against the striking miners. The vagueness of the substantive law also gave them opportunities. Nowhere was this more clearly seen than in relation to their old power to do whatever was necessary to prevent reasonably anticipated breaches of the peace. Wallington notes that road-blocks 'were widely used, especially within and on access roads to Nottinghamshire, but also elsewhere—notably (for a few days in March 1984) at the south entrance to the Dartford tunnel. In Nottinghamshire no less than 164,508 "presumed pickets" were turned back during the first 27 weeks of the strike' (Wallington, 1985: 154). Since the start of 1986, the Police and Criminal Evidence Act 1984 has authorized 'road checks' under certain conditions. During the strike, the policy was justified by reference first to a section in the Road Traffic Act 1972 which allows a police officer in uniform to stop vehicles and secondly to the common law breach of the peace power. The police treated those who refused to turn back as being vulnerable to the charge of obstruction of the police in the execution of their duty, contrary to section 51(3) of the Police Act 1964. This practice was upheld in the High Court, where Skinner J. accepted that, in the case before him, the police 'honestly and reasonably form[ed] the opinion that there [was] a real risk of a breach of the peace in the sense that it [was] in close proximity both in place and time'.[32] This is despite the fact that according to the law report the police officers did not know to which specific pits the pickets were travelling and that some of the evidence of violence on which the police officers relied was that which they had gathered from press and television reports.

It is regrettable that the court in this case did not display any principled commitment to the idea of freedom of movement or evinced any anxiety that such an ancient liberty was being

[32] *Moss* v. *McLachlan* [1985] IRLR 76.

seriously eroded. Instead, there was the now familiar preoccupation with the police officer's perception of impending violence. This is all the more unrealistic in light of the fact that the judgment here was only theoretically that of the police officer 'on the spot'. In reality, road-blocking was part of a broad police strategy, decided upon at a high level, aimed at preventing 'flying pickets' travelling from county to county lending support to striking miners. This is clear from the Attorney-General's statement in Parliament that the practice in its widest form was lawful: a curious (though not unprecedented) anticipation of a judicial decision by the Government's senior law officer and a member of the executive (Adeney and Lloyd, 1986: 104). The affair thus highlights the unreality of the common-law rule which continues to concentrate on the independent judgment of a police officer who is in fact simply obeying instructions which are issued as part of a general policy not necessarily susceptible of being influenced by the specific facts of particular cases. The affair also highlights the major lesson of the strike: the law was flexible enough, and the courts were deferential enough, to allow the police almost unrestrained freedom of manœuvre. Wallington (1985: 159) put it in the following way:

The police were given whatever resources they needed to preserve law and order and access to the pits. This enabled them to make the choice to preserve order by containment or prevention of picketing. With fewer resources it might in some cases have been necessary, and would certainly have been lawful, to preserve the peace by preventing individual returning miners from attempting to pass through picket lines. Resources enabled a choice to be made as to whose activities were to be curtailed, even (certainly in the case of the operation of a blanket turn-back policy) whose lawful activities were to be curtailed. Those critics of the police who argue that they took a partisan position can at least point to legal authority that would have justified a different approach. It is scarcely conceivable in the political climate of the time that the alternative would have been adopted as a matter of policy, but that it was avoided at the cost of serious reductions in the level of policing in much of the country suggests a conscious choice.

The Public Order Act 1986

The policing of CND rallies and the miners' strike could hardly be said from the Government's point of view to have failed, and certainly the police did not suffer for want of legal powers. Although some specific legislation was later to emerge, on free speech in the universities and football identity cards, for example, the breadth of what was already in place made complaints about the inadequacy of the law difficult to sustain. Thus, during the disorder of the first part of the 1980s, the authorities utilized the 1936 Act procedure to ban many more marches than they had done before: in 1981 alone, there were 42 banning orders, and the figures for the following years were also high: 13, 9, and 11 in 1982, 1983, and 1984 respectively (Home Office, 1985b: 23). A government review 'revealed no yawning gaps' and admitted that no 'amount of tightening of the law, short of draconian measures which would be quite unacceptable, can guarantee the prevention of all disorder'. The problem confronting the police when disorder had broken out was 'essentially one of enforcement' (Home Office, 1985b: 2). If anything, the problem after the miners' strike was that, in a fast-moving sequence of events, the police had accumulated altogether too much power.

1. The use and refinement of existing powers

The legal and operational precedents set by the strike were being followed and expanded by the police almost as soon as the dispute was over. In particular, there have been several complaints of heavy-handed policing of demonstrations, of which three examples may be given here. The first two relate to students. In 1985 considerable disquiet was caused by the methods used by Greater Manchester Police to deal with protesters during the visit of the then Home Secretary, Leon Brittan, to Manchester University. The way in which the police had cleared a way through to the front door of the building at which Mr Brittan was to speak was particularly controversial. The local City Council set up a committee of inquiry to investigate the policing arrangements for the visit and complaints were made to the Police Complaints

Authority. A student protest against education loans which took place three years later in central London also ran into trouble. Of the 17,000 demonstrators involved, 1,000 broke away from the agreed route of the march and gathered on the south side of Westminster Bridge, where they were prevented from crossing by a large group of officers. After a couple of hours, during which some sticks and other items were thrown at the police and insults were shouted, a mounted police line was drawn up behind the police cordon and a row of police vans. On command, the vans raced to the side of the road, the cordon parted, and the demonstrators found themselves facing a mounted police charge at full gallop. The protesters scattered and a number, estimated by the National Union of Students at over 100, were injured. At least 69 arrests were made, and charges were brought against 50 of these. The alleged offences included one of riot and another of 'assaulting a police horse'. The total police strength on the day was: 36 police vans, 1,500 officers, 2 boats, 1 helicopter, and 47 horses. The Home Secretary described the dispersal of the crowd by mounted officers as 'a controlled action . . . not a charge'.[33]

A major and long-running source of disorder since the conclusion of the miners' strike was the industrial dispute with Mr Rupert Murdoch's News International Group, centred on its new printing plant at Wapping in East London. During a demonstration to mark the first anniversary of the group's move to its new location, 300 people, including over 160 police officers, were injured in battles between 1,400 police and at least 7,000 demonstrators. A number of police officers face charges relating to their alleged misbehaviour on that night, after complaints involving more than 100 officers were referred to the Police Complaints Authority. At the time of writing, the first batch of prosecutions had collapsed in the magistrates' court, on account of the long delay in launching the prosecutions against those involved. Many police officers were angry that the cases had been brought at all, since the methods employed by the defendant constables were said to have involved no more than what was set out in the Home Office-approved Tactical Options Manual. One police spokesman was reported as saying shortly after the

[33] 142 HC Debs. 174–6 (WA) (29 Nov. 1988).

hearings that 'complaints were inevitable when officers "got involved" with demonstrators'.[34]

Apart from these changes in police tactics, some of the new legal powers of the police which emerged during the miners' strike have been developed in interesting ways. We have already seen how the road-blocking and binding-over powers were employed against protesters at RAF Molesworth in 1985. According to press reports, road-blocking now plays a regular part in police efforts to control the movement of fans on their way to football matches. The power is often used in Northern Ireland. On one occasion, the RUC stopped a bus containing members of a Protestant apprentice boys band, 30 miles from the largely Catholic town where it was their intention to march. After confiscating their musical instruments, the police allowed them to proceed and they went on to parade—much more quietly than they would have liked. The action of the RUC was upheld in court. Even though the fear of violence may have been justified in this case, the 30-mile zone and the fact that the disorder was expected to emanate from other than the marchers make the implications of the case disturbing, even in the context of Northern Ireland.[35] Bail conditions appear also to have become a standard practice in public order cases. Animal rights activists have been bailed on condition that they do not attend any hunt meetings in England or Wales.[36] In a letter to the *Independent*, a representative of the Irish Freedom Movement alleged that, at the annual anti-internment march in London on 6 August 1988, there were over thirty arrests, with the charges ranging from threatening behaviour to affray and some accused being 'granted bail only on condition that they did not attend political meetings or marches'.[37]

Quite apart from the development of new police tactics and the emergence of new common-law public order powers, the open-ended and vague nature of the traditional law has continued the erratic erosion of freedom for those whose views, attitudes, or behaviour is out of the mainstream. Occasional evidence of this percolates through into the newspapers and, now and again, the

[34] *Independent*, 18 May 1989.
[35] *Re Atkinson's Application* [1987] 8 NILR 6.
[36] *R. v. Bournemouth Justices, ex parte Cross* (1989) 89 Cr. App. R. 90.
[37] *Independent*, 12 Sept. 1988.

law reports. Thus, in November 1987, twenty-six Greenpeace supporters were arrested outside a conference on North Sea pollution in London; their alleged offence was obstruction of the highway. Amongst those detained was a Belgian Member of the European Parliament who had earlier disclosed to the newspapers plans for a 3 km-wide 'waste island' off Zeebrugge.[38] In a reported case the same year,[39] Lorraine Agu and Malcolm Hirst were members of a group of animal rights supporters who were demonstrating slogans and distributing leaflets about animal rights on a spacious pedestrian precinct in Bradford. This activity was close to a couple of shops which sold animal furs. The police arrested Agu and four others for conduct likely to cause a breach of the peace. When Hirst and another four members of the group protested to the police about this, they too were arrested, for conduct likely to breach the peace and for obstruction. The reported facts of the case reveal no hint of any threat to the peace. Agu and Hirst were later charged with obstruction of the highway, and the breach of the peace allegation, which was the basis of Agu's arrest, was quietly forgotten. They were convicted in the magistrates' court, but appealed successfully to the Divisional Court on the ground that the question whether their obstruction had been reasonable had not been adequately considered.

This case provides a rare glimpse into police practice and raises serious questions about the use made by the police of their arrest powers. It also suggests the possibility that demonstrators fall foul of the law in the magistrates' court in ways which may never afterwards be given thoughtful re-examination at a more senior judicial level. The vast majority of defendants, even politically motivated ones, have not the energy, and may not have the means, to launch long and expensive appeals. In one extraordinary case in 1987, the defendant was charged and convicted of an offence, called abusing a constable in the execution of his office, contrary to the Justices of the Peace Act 1361. Legal aid to appeal was denied. Counsel took the case on for nothing and, on appeal, the Divisional Court found that the crime did not exist. How

---

[38] *Independent*, 25 Nov. 1987.

[39] *Hirst and Agu* v. *Chief Constable of West Yorkshire* (1987) 85 Cr. App. R. 143.

many unlucky convicts lack the services of a generous counsel?[40] Yet this has not been the only old law turned to by the police. An ominous dimension in recent years has been the use of public order legislation as a means with which to repress the expression of sexual preferences. In a recent case, section 54(13) of the Metropolitan Police Act 1839 was used successfully against two men who were kissing and cuddling at a bus stop in Oxford Street at 1.55 a.m.[41] Their amorous activity attracted the attention of two passing couples and the two males in this group were beginning to respond in an ugly way when the police arrived. The two male lovers were arrested and their convictions were upheld in the High Court. Their conduct amounted to insulting behaviour (it insulted the women!) which may have occasioned a breach of the peace (the partners of the women might have beaten up the two male lovers).

2. The new preventive powers of the 1986 Act.

Notwithstanding these wide and expanding powers, the Home Office review of public order legislation led to the enactment of the Public Order Act 1986. This was justified because the existing law was 'complex and fragmented'. There were 'important points where the law [could] helpfully be extended and clarified' and these related mainly to 'improving the opportunities for the police to try to prevent disorder or disruption before it occurs' (Home Office, 1985*b*: 2). According to the then Home Secretary, Mr Leon Brittan, the Act was intended to 'bring up to date the age-old balance between fundamental but sometimes competing rights in our society'. These are fine sentiments. It is unfortunate that they are not met by the Act. In the first place, if the law was complex and fragmented before 1986, it is even more so now. For what the 1986 Act does in large measure is to add to the extensive list of police public order powers. And it does so without taking away or redrawing the boundaries of the controversial powers discussed in this chapter. Secondly, to the extent that the Act brings up to date the balance between the liberty of the individual

[40] *Nawrot and Shaler* v. *DPP* [1988] Crim. Law Rev. 107.
[41] *Masterson* v. *Holden* [1986] 1 WLR 1017.

and the state, it does so by tilting the balance even more squarely in favour of the latter.

Essentially the Act addresses three areas: it extends the preventive powers of the police; it extends the public order offence which had been contained in section 5 of the 1936 Act; and it makes provision for the serious public order offences such as riot and unlawful assembly which are beyond the scope of this chapter. So far as the police preventive powers are concerned, we saw earlier that section 3 of the Public Order Act 1936 dealt only with processions and permitted the imposition of conditions and outright bans only when the police apprehended 'serious public disorder'. The new Act continues to require such a fear as a precondition for a total ban. The rest of the law has been modified in three important respects. First, subject to a very few exceptions, the police must now be given written notice of all public processions at least six days before they are due to take place. Notice requirements had already existed in some local areas but this provision applies throughout England and Wales. It is not a licensing power. Giving notice is not the same as asking permission; but the knowledge thereby gained by the police provides a useful backdrop against which to exercise their other powers. The second change the Act makes is that it permits the imposition of conditions on public assemblies as well as on processions; in other words on meetings as well as on marches. These restrictions come into play where there is 'an assembly of 20 or more persons in a public place which is wholly or partly open to the air'. As the case-law on reasonably anticipated breaches of the peace makes perfectly clear, the police already had the power to control meetings, regardless of how many people were attending them. In the vast majority of situations considered by the White Paper to be covered by this section, the police already had the power—indeed the duty—to act under the common law.

What novelty this new power has lies in a very specific area which has no direct connection with disorder. This is the third change introduced by the Act. The criteria on the basis of which conditions may be imposed on either meetings or processions include but extend beyond the apprehension of serious public disorder. Under sections 12 and 14, any of the following is now also sufficient, the sole precondition being that the police 'reasonably believe' that one or other of them may occur as a result of the protest:

(*a*) serious damage to property;
(*b*) serious disruption to the life of the community;
(*c*) the intimidation of others 'with a view to compelling them not to do an act they have a right to do, or to do an act they have a right not to do' (as long as such intimidation is the purpose behind the protest).

If one of these criteria is fulfilled to the police officer's satisfaction, then such conditions on a procession may be imposed '*as appear to him* [emphasis added] to be necessary to prevent such disorder, damage, disruption or intimidation, including conditions as to the route of the procession'. The officer may prohibit it 'from entering any public place specified in the directions'. If it is a meeting, then the conditions may relate 'to the place at which the assembly may be (or continue to be) held, its maximum duration, or the maximum number of persons who may constitute it'. These powers may be exercised in advance or on the spot, by a police constable who stumbles upon the preparations for a protest. There is a power of arrest without warrant. Disobeying police instructions issued under the Act is a criminal offence for which it is possible to be sent to jail. Judicial review may be a possibility in the case of processions, though it is unlikely to be effective, and the circumstances may often be such that there is no time to seek any judicial ruling.

It is quite clear that the imposition of conditions may be as effective as an outright ban. A CND march around an empty common is less effective, if causing less inconvenience, than one down a High Street. A meeting about South Africa is less meaningful at Waterloo Bridge than in front of the country's embassy in Trafalgar Square, especially if the number is cut to 20 after 2,000 turn up. It is no answer to say that such unreasonableness will not occur. It already has. In one case in 1987, a vibrant and vocal, though entirely peaceful, demonstration outside the entrance to South Africa House was ordered to retreat to Duncannon Street, so as not to 'intimidate' guests arriving for a reception at the embassy. The chief inspector present called in the

Territorial Support Group to reinforce his condition, issued under the Public Order Act. Lorna Reid, who refused to retreat, was arrested and charged with an offence under the Act. She was acquitted when the magistrate concluded that the police view, that intimidation could be equated with discomfort, was an error of law: an element of compulsion was also required.[42] The vagueness of the criteria in the Act was the source of the police error in this case. We may expect more careful exposition of the police view of facts in the future. The case is best viewed in the context of an extraordinary police campaign waged against the permanent picket outside South Africa House in the summer of 1987. In May and June of that year, 172 arrests were made. The charges brought included a 'variety of public order and other offences, including criminal damage, assault on the police occasioning actual bodily harm, breach of bail conditions and obstruction'.[43]

The criteria in the Act are not at all precise. Intimidation, aimed at mass picketing and racist marching, may be reasonably clear, but what is 'serious disruption to the life of the community'? The Home Secretary thought that this criterion could be used to 'limit the resulting congestion of traffic, to prevent a bridge being blocked, for example, or to stop a city centre being brought to a standstill'. The White Paper gave a few hints by the examples it used. Thus, it noted that in 'the diplomatic quarter of London residents have occasionally complained about the disruption caused by demonstrations outside neighbouring embassies: if the disruption was shown to be serious the police could limit the numbers or duration of a demonstration, or move it further away' (Home Office, 1985b: 33). Another set of events identified by some police forces as a problem were 'marches being held through shopping centres on Saturdays, or through city centres in the rush hour' (Home Office, 1985b: 27). But the basic issue of definition remains unresolved. The Act is content to leave the question to the courts, but, given the immediate impact of this type of decision, recourse to the judiciary is more theoretical than real.

[42] *Police* v. *Reid (Lorna)* [1987] Crim. Law Rev. 702.

[43] This information is gleaned from two parliamentary written answers by the relevant Minister, Douglas Hogg, at 119 HC Debs. (WA) 212 (9 July 1987) and 120 HC Debs. (WA) 58 (20 July 1987).

Without more guidance, the section puts both the police officer and the demonstrator on the spot. How large is a community? Is Oxford Street one, or inner London, or the whole Metropolitan area? All we know is that disruption is unconnected with violence or damage to property. It must involve, as Mr Hurd has suggested, the causing of inconvenience to drivers, to shoppers, to pedestrians, to others who—on that day at least—desire, consciously or unconsciously, to uphold the status quo. Peaceful demonstrators seek attention. The way to get it is to be obviously present, in impressive numbers, in an important place, with flair and style. To an extent, some inconvenience is the inevitable consequence of a successful protest. There is a clash of interests here. The Act passes to the police the opportunity to favour the predictable habits of the majority over the peaceful, law-abiding, protests of the few. It threatens to permit only those demonstrations that are so convenient that they become invisible. The yardstick of legitimacy must never become the propensity to fail; if it does the streets may be used for other forms of protest by those who find all peaceful routes to change barred to them.

3. The new public order offences of the 1986 Act

If we turn to the new public order offences in sections 4 and 5 of the 1986 Act, we find that section 4 re-enacts in a more precise form the old 'insulting behaviour' section under the 1936 Act which we have already discussed in an earlier part of this chapter. The concept of 'unlawful violence' has replaced the vaguer notion of 'breach of the peace' and the offending behaviour required by the section has now to be directed at another person; it is not enough for the conduct to exist in a world of its own, as seemed to have been suggested by the case concerning the prosecution of the two male lovers, discussed above. Section 5 is altogether different in its approach. It is new, very broad, and extremely controversial. Subsection 1 reads as follows:

A person is guilty of an offence if he—

    (a) uses threatening, abusive or insulting words or behaviour, or disorderly behaviour, or

    (b) displays any writing, sign or other visible representation which is threatening, abusive or insulting, within the hearing or sight of a person likely to be caused harassment, alarm or distress thereby.

The Government has said that the purpose of this section is to control conduct like

> rowdy behaviour in the streets late at night which alarms local residents; someone turning out the lights in a crowded dance hall, in a way likely to cause panic; groups of youths persistently shouting abuse and obscenities or pestering people waiting to catch public transport or to enter a hall or cinema; hooligans on housing estates causing disturbances in the common parts of blocks of flats, blockading entrances, throwing things down the stairs, banging on doors, peering in at windows and knocking over dustbins. (Home Office, 1985b: 18)

No doubt, such offenders will occasionally be caught by section 5. Perhaps it is right to employ the full weight of the criminal law to punish them. But these are not the only people potentially affected. Lord Scarman has said that the provision extends 'the bounds of criminality further than we can accept'. Consider the facts. 'Threatening, abusive and insulting' words, signs, or behaviour are manageable concepts, familiar to us from section 4. There they are qualified by the requirement for a connection with violence or the fear of violence. Here all that is required is that they be *likely* to cause harassment, alarm, or distress. This is very vague. What is it that is being threatened, if it is neither violence nor the fear of violence? Perhaps all conduct that is likely to cause harassment, alarm, or distress is, as a result, also threatening? If so, then the word is redundant and the section even broader than it appears. The determination of what is 'abusive' and 'insulting' leaves a lot to the discretion of the magistrates: vulgarity to some may be a powerful expression of opinion to others. Where violence gave us a crucial yardstick in section 4, 'harassment, alarm or distress' (any one of them being enough) gives the police open-ended room for manœuvre in section 5. The Act has in fact been employed to curb what the police described as a 'craze for obscene T-shirts and hats' in Skegness and Mablethorpe. One of the purposes of peaceful protest is often to alarm or distress (or even mildly to harass) so as ultimately to inform. This is where the more ominous side of the new power emerges. A poster containing an unflattering depiction of Mrs Thatcher, with the caption, 'On your knees to Madam M' has led to a prosecution under section 5. (The magistrates acquitted.) Consider a group of students outside the Department of Education, with distorted caricatures of the Minister and slogans about his ineffectiveness; or animal rights activists distributing graphic illustrations of animal experiments to passers-by on a shopping precinct; or activists chanting 'black power' as guests enter South Africa House. All are vulnerable, because all are capable of being described as likely to cause harassment, alarm, or distress.

Nor is it a complete answer to persuade the police officer or magistrate that such behaviour is not threatening, or abusive, or insulting. Section 5 also criminalizes 'disorderly behaviour' likely to cause harassment, alarm, or distress. This disorderliness is never violent—or it would be caught by section 4 or some other branch of the criminal law. So what does the phrase mean? The Act gives no clues. Like those other 'plain English words', 'threatening, abusive and insulting', the law leaves its meaning to the robust good sense of the magistrates. The temptation is to say that that which is not orderly is disorderly. Conduct which alarms, distresses, or harasses is never 'orderly' as such; so is it by definition always disorderly? If so, the phrase adds nothing. The dictionary suggests a definition in terms of 'violating moral order, constituted authority, or recognised rule'. It is likely that the section will be used to criminalize the unusual. The father of a family following a nudist way of life has been convicted for being seen with his family, unclothed, in the grounds of his own home. In a letter to the *Independent*, a representative of the Irish Freedom Movement stated that a poster produced by that organization, 'depicting four young Irishmen throwing stones at a British Army Saracen, and proclaiming "Ireland: 20 years of resistance"', had led to charges under section 5.[44] Rowdy and boisterous Cambridge undergraduates may not be disorderly; but are Rastafarians or punks in exactly the same situation? Individuality and flair, the 'shock of the new', are more alarming than dull conventionality. In section 5, we now have a mechanism for punishing non-violent nonconformity for the crime of being itself.

[44] *Independent*, 12 Sept. 1988.

Other aspects of the provision compound the iniquity of bestowing such power upon the police. There is a power of arrest after a warning has been ignored. In what it said was a gesture towards the 'weak' and the 'vulnerable', the Government decided that it was not necessary that anyone should have to be harassed, distressed, or alarmed; it was enough merely that one of these eventualities should be 'likely' to happen. The White Paper had earlier dismissed such a proposal on the ground that it would give rise to 'justifiable objections to a wide extension of the criminal law which might catch conduct not deserving of criminal sanctions' (Home Office, 1985*b*: 19). Now, however, there does not have to be any victim of a section 5 offence, only a person present who might have been offended. No one other than a police officer has to give evidence. The courts have broadened this even further by saying that it is not necessary for the persons alarmed to feel alarm for themselves; it is enough if they feel it for someone else.[45] In a later case,[46] the Divisional Court added to this by saying that a police officer 'can be a person who is likely to be caused harassment', under the section. This will not happen often because 'frequently, words and behaviour with which every police officer will be wearily familiar will have little emotional impact on them save that of boredom', but every case depends on its own facts. The magistrates will have to decide how much anxiety and alarm these trained law enforcement officers are to be expected to take. As a result, the position will contrast sharply with the approach adopted by the US Supreme Court in *Coates* v. *City of Cincinnati*,[47] where five pickets were convicted under an ordinance which made it an offence for three or more persons to assemble on a sidewalk 'and there conduct themselves in a manner annoying to persons passing by'. The US Supreme Court declared the law unconstitutionally vague and an infringement of the American right of free assembly. The prohibition contained 'an obvious invitation to discriminatory enforcement against those whose association together is "annoying" because their ideas, their lifestyle, or their physical appearance is resented by the majority of their fellow citizens'. Such an ordinance was not

[45] *Lodge* v. *DPP*, *The Times*, 26 Oct. 1988.
[46] *DPP* v. *Orum* [1989] 1 WLR 88.
[47] 402 US 611 (1971).

permitted because its 'violation may entirely depend upon whether or not a policeman is annoyed' (Stewart J.).

Conclusion: Stonehenge

The complex web of statute and common-law restrictions on freedom of assembly can have devastating results when utilized to the full by the police. We saw this in the way that picketing was effectively curbed during the miners' strike. Another example comes from the now annual confrontation between Wiltshire police and various travelling people over access to Stonehenge at the summer solstice. The origins of this dispute lie in a free festival which was held at the Stones on an annual basis for ten years from 1974 to 1984. It lasted between a week and a month and invariably included the solstice on 21 June. In its last year, the numbers involved over 30,000 and the authorities, fearing damage to the ancient monument, decided that restrictions had to be imposed on the use of the site in future years. In particular, it was agreed that access to the Stones should be dramatically curtailed, and that it should be closed completely from 20–2 June. As the 1985 solstice approached, the whole weight of the law was mustered in support of this change of policy. English Heritage, who are responsible for Stonehenge, and the National Trust, who own 1,400 acres around it, secured 'precautionary injunctions' against named persons forbidding them from trespassing on to their property. Wiltshire County Council closed certain roads around the site relying upon a power under the Road Traffic Regulation Act 1984 which allowed such action where (as the Council alleged here) there was a 'danger to the public'. The police supplemented this by setting up their own road-blocks on other routes, at which they warned travellers not to proceed and threatened to arrest them for obstruction if they did. They claimed this power under the breach of the peace law, as it had been interpreted by the courts in the Nottinghamshire miners' case.

The situation that developed when the travellers finally arrived was described in an NCCL report into the affair:

On 31st May, a convoy of 140 vehicles, escorted by the police, moved into Wiltshire and camped at Savernake Forest near Marlborough. Police, including a helicopter, surrounded the camp. On 1st June the convoy set off south down the A338 accompanied by the police, the helicopter, and the Earl of Cardigan, whose family owns Savernake Forest and leases it to the Forestry Commission. On arriving near Parkhouse the convoy was met by a police road block. Some members of the convoy tried to move away on the A303 to be confronted by another road block. The trapped convoy, surrounded by police, moved into an adjacent field. The police, in visored helmets, and carrying riot shields, followed and a pitched battle between the convoy and the police ensued. Moving away from the police, some convoy vehicles drove on to the next field which was planted with beans. The 'Battle of the Beanfield' was well reported. The police followed each vehicle until it stopped or crashed. Television cameras saw the occupants of the vehicles, including children, being removed from what are their travelling homes. The Earl of Cardigan who witnessed the scene said:

'I shall never forget the screams of one woman who was holding up her little baby in a bus with smashed windows. She screamed and screamed at them to stop, but five seconds later 50 men with truncheons and shields just boiled into that bus. It was mayhem, no other word for it.'

Over 500 members of the convoy were arrested and charged with unlawful assembly, obstruction of the police and obstruction of the highway. (NCCL, 1986: 4, 5)

The same combination of civil and criminal law and police hostility greeted the travellers when they returned to the area for the summer solstice in 1986. By now, however, the issue had reached the centre of the political stage. The Home Secretary, Mr Hurd, described the convoy as 'a band of medieval brigands who have no respect for law and order and the rights of others'. The Prime Minister wondered 'how to deal with people who accept all the advantages and benefits of a free society but refuse to rise to their responsibilities'.[48] The summer's pursuit of the convoy culminated in Operation Daybreak on the morning of 9 June. In a dawn raid, and after having sealed off all approach roads, 440 police encircled and evicted some 400 adults and 100 children from a disused Second World War airfield in the New Forest. No less than 64 arrests were made and 129 vehicles were impounded. The convoy put up no resistance. In the summers since 1986, the

[48] 98 HC Debs. 1082–3 (5 June 1986).

police have been able to call upon their new powers in the Public Order Act and, in particular, on section 39 which created a limited offence of criminal trespass and which was enacted with the travellers in mind. In June 1987, the *Independent* reported that '[t]he threat of section 14 of the Public Order Act 1986 swept a hippy convoy off a Wiltshire hillside yesterday and dumped it back on the road in fragments'. The convoy had been gathered on Salisbury Plain. 'The disruption was minimal because there [were] no houses nearby. Wiltshire police said it was a public right of way, the hippies were not trespassing on anyone's land and there was only "minimal damage" to the immediate surroundings'.[49] The paper's editorial described the section as 'a nasty piece of work' which gave the police 'a considerable measure of arbitrary and unchallengeable judgement'. Using it against the hippies was like relying on 'an earthmover to crack a nut'.

In 1989 Stonehenge was closed completely for the summer solstice. This decision, which was unsuccessfully challenged in Europe,[50] was described by Mr Rollo Maughfling, the archdruid of the Glastonbury order, as 'like closing Westminster Abbey at Christmas. It is a gross violation of religious freedom'.[51] Despite such sentiments, the authorities showed no qualms in enforcing the outright closure. In addition to the now predictable trespass actions, road-closures, road-blocks, obstruction charges, and restrictive bail conditions, the local Council agreed to a police request for a ban under the Public Order Act 1986 on all processions (one of the very few exceptions was for funeral cortèges) within a 4-mile range of Stonehenge. The police stated that the ban was essentially a preventive measure, to avoid a confrontation. This seemed to imply that its purpose was to prevent a fight between the travellers and the police—a curious basis, to say the least, for such a severe restriction on the right to assemble. Paradoxically, it was the enforcement of this 'exclusion zone' around Stonehenge that caused the trouble the police said

---

[50] *Chappell* v. *United Kingdom* (1988) 10 EHRR 510. The case, based on the two freedoms of religion and assembly, was held manifestly ill-founded by the Commission and never reached the Court.

[51] *Guardian*, 3 Mar. 1989.

they had hoped to avoid. On the night of 21/2 June, groups of travellers numbering in total about 500 people gathered at various places within 4 miles of Stonehenge. The police broke up these crowds and arrested over 250 of the travellers for breach of the banning order. One small group was forced back into the centre of the village of Amesbury by a series of short police charges. No damage was done by any of the travellers and the police action came in for some criticism from local townspeople. The whole exercise involved the use of 800 officers, two helicopters with searchlights, snatch squads, mounted police, and a private security firm. The police were reported to have been 'pleased with the operation'.[52] Over the years, the authorities seem to have lost a sense of proportion about the danger posed by the travellers. They seem to have been punished as much because they are different as because of any physical danger that they pose to a pagan monument that has already survived for thousands of years. They remind us that unpopular minorities in Britain are more likely to be condemned than protected by the law.

[52] This account is taken from the *Independent* and *Guardian* newspapers of 22 June 1989.

5

The National Security State

QUESTIONS of national security and governmental secrecy have not been fetishes peculiar to the Thatcher administrations. It is easy to forget that two American journalists, Philip Agee and Mark Hosenball, were deported in 1977 by Mr Merlyn Rees, then Home Secretary, on the ground that their departure would be conducive to the public good in the interests of national security. It is also easy to forget that it was during the life of the last Labour Government that attempts were made to ban the publication of the Crossman diaries and that criminal prosecutions were instituted against Crispin Aubrey, John Berry, and Duncan Campbell in connection with an interview given by Berry about his work with SIGINT, a governmental service dealing with the interception and analysis of radio communications. Yet while all British Governments this century have been obsessed by questions of secrecy and security, the last ten years have seen these obsessions carried to remarkable lengths. Indeed, it has been suggested that 'Mrs Thatcher is believed within Whitehall to take a close personal interest in the working of the intelligence community. She chairs the Ministerial Steering Committee on Intelligence (MIS) which supervises the community and fixes its budget priorities' (Andrew, 1986: 701). In this chapter we examine some of the major national security controversies in which the Thatcher Government has been engaged. It will soon be apparent that in several instances the Government and the Prime Minister were helped rather than hindered by Her Majesty's judges.

GCHQ

Since the early years of this century it has been generally accepted by successive administrations that the government should set an example as a model employer. Civil servants have thus enjoyed favourable terms and conditions of employment, assisted no doubt by various forms of official encouragement for strong and independent trade unionism. Since 1979, however, a noticeable change has become evident in Whitehall. In 1981 the Government terminated a 1925 agreement whereby a dispute could be referred by either the Government or the civil service unions to binding arbitration. This was done without giving the six months' notice required by the agreement. Also, since 1981 steps have been taken to undermine the right of freedom of expression previously enjoyed by civil servants. Thus, 'there have been cases where civil servants have been threatened with disciplinary action or dismissal because of articles which they have written in their trade union journals' (Corby, 1986: 165). The same author—the assistant general-secretary of the Association of First Division Civil Servants—pointed out that civil servants have also been threatened with disciplinary action for contacting MPs on matters affecting their employment.

In addition to these developments, the cloak of national security has been used to tighten the restrictions on those engaged in government employment. Since the end of the last war procedures have been in operation to purge from the service (for security reasons) anyone who is or who has recently been a member of the Communist Party of Great Britain or who is sympathetic to communism. In April 1985 this was extended to include a member of or a person sympathetic to a subversive group 'whose aims are to undermine or overthrow parliamentary democracy by political, industrial or violent means' (Corby, 1986: 172). The extension of the purge procedures—without consultation—was particularly insensitive in view of the controversy still surrounding the most hotly disputed decision of the Prime Minister in respect of Her Majesty's servants. This was the decision—announced by Sir Geoffrey Howe to the House of Commons on 25 January 1984—that staff employed at GCHQ were no longer permitted to be members of an existing trade union, but would be free to join only a Government-approved departmental staff association. Staff would also lose their protection from acts of anti-union discrimination.[1]

GCHQ is a civilian operated branch of government connected to the security services, providing signals intelligence for the Government. The activity is based mainly at Cheltenham where there are some 4,000 employees, there being an additional 3,000 employees engaged at smaller establishments elsewhere in Britain. Ever since 1947, when the service became operational in its present form, the staff had been permitted and indeed were encouraged to join the civil service trade unions, and by December 1982 over half the staff were paid-up trade unionists. As relations between these unions and the Thatcher Government turned sour, the employees participated in various forms of industrial action—strikes, works to rule, and overtime bans—so that between February 1979 and April 1981 some 10,000 working days had been lost by trade-union action at GCHQ. Rather than address the problems of which such action was a symptom, the Government responded by denying the unions the right to organize in this vulnerable soft underbelly of Crown employment. One reason why it was not done until 1984 was the reluctance of the Government to admit to the existence of the establishment. It was temporarily impaled on the horns of its own dilemma: either maintain the secret which everyone knew and risk further disruption; or seek to eliminate the disruption by acknowledging the existence of GCHQ.

The announcement, when made, was met with widespread condemnation, and was hardly assuaged by the offer of £1,000 to each employee, in recognition of the loss of the rights previously enjoyed. Even this was devalued by the subsequent realization that the sum was subject to income tax.[2] Nevertheless, the staff had little choice. Those unwilling to accept the new conditions unilaterally imposed were to be given the opportunity of a transfer elsewhere within the civil service. If such a transfer were not possible the staff involved would be prematurely retired. In the end most of the staff accepted the new terms (with some of the

[1] 52 HC Debs. 917 (25 Jan. 1984).
[2] *Hamblett* v. *Godfrey (Inspector of Taxes)* [1987] 1 All ER 916.

so-called 'refusenicks' being transferred and thirteen being dismissed, the last dismissals taking place on 13 April 1989),[3] the Government proving itself to be impervious to compromise. The unions had proposed a no-disruption agreement which would preserve the individual right to freedom of association while also providing adequate safeguards for the Government. Despite the fact that a similar position seemed to have been supported by the House of Commons Select Committee on Employment in a report issued in February 1984,[4] this was rejected by the administration which took the view that such an agreement would not provide adequate guarantees that conflicting pressures would not cause difficulties in the future.

Faced with such intransigence, the unions had little choice but to seek a legal remedy. One avenue pursued was under international law by making a complaint to the International Labour Organisation based in Geneva, and operating now under the auspices of the United Nations. The ILO was established in the wake of the First World War in an ultimately vain attempt to secure a lasting peace. The principal function of the Organisation is to prescribe and enforce minimum labour standards on national governments, though its enforcement powers are very limited in the sense that there is no procedure for the making of binding orders. It succeeds only because national governments are willing to submit to international pressure. In this instance the unions relied on perhaps the most fundamental of all ILO Conventions, namely Convention 87 which was adopted in 1948. This deals with Freedom of Association and provides by Article 2:

Workers and employers, without distinction whatsoever, shall have the right to establish and, subject only to the rules of the organisation concerned, to join organisations of their own choosing without previous authorisation.

Based on this provision the complaint of the GCHQ unions thus appeared irrefutable. The Government, however, drew attention to a complementary convention, namely Convention 151 on the Right to Organise in the Public Service. Although this provides by Article 4:

[3] *Guardian*, 13 Apr. 1989.
[4] HC 238 (1983–4).

1. Public employees shall enjoy adequate protection against acts of anti-union discrimination in respect of their employment.
2. Such protection shall apply more particularly in respect of acts calculated to (a) make the employment of public employees subject to the condition that they shall not join or shall relinquish membership of a public employees' organisation; (b) cause the dismissal of or otherwise prejudice a public employee by reason of membership of a public employees' organisation or because of participation in the normal activities of such an organisation.

it also provides in Article 1(2) that

The extent to which the guarantees provided for in this Convention shall apply to high-level employees whose functions are normally considered as policy-making or managerial, or to employees whose duties are of a highly confidential nature, shall be determined by national laws or regulations.

The Government thus argued that it acted lawfully under ILO Conventions, and that Article 1(2) of the Convention 151, dealing specifically with the public service, had displaced the more general provisions of Convention 87.

This approach was rejected by the Freedom of Association Committee of the ILO.[5] Quite apart from the fact that Convention 87 is regarded as a form of 'higher law' with which all states are expected to comply, Article 1(1) of Convention 151 provides expressly that that Convention applies to all persons employed by public authorities only 'to the extent that more favourable provisions in other international labour Conventions are not applicable to them'. The matter is thus determined conclusively in favour of the GCHQ unions by the fact that Convention 87 provides freedom of association guarantees from which civilian personnel engaged in security work are not excluded. The committee—which is set up to deal with complaints—reported on 1 June 1984 that the Government's conduct was not consistent with the requirements of Convention 87. Although the decision was ratified by the governing body of the ILO, the Government nevertheless refused to take any steps towards restoring the rights thus held to have been violated. As already pointed out, it could not be compelled to do so. Much more serious, however, was the

[5] ILO Official Bulletin, 67 (1984), series B, no. 2, 234th Report, pp. 112–20.

decision delivered six weeks later by Glidewell J. in the Queens Bench Division of the High Court.[6] Quite independently of the complaints to the ILO, the affected unions had sought judicial review of the Government's decision in the English courts. In a path-breaking judgment, Glidewell J. held for the unions because of the Government's failure to comply with the legal requirement that in certain circumstances interested parties (in this case the civil service unions) should be consulted before governmental decisions are taken to their prejudice (in this case the withdrawal of the right to represent their members).

Although the Government could ignore the ILO, a decision of the High Court was much more serious, the unions having obtained a declaration that the instruction issued to vary the conditions of service was invalid. The Government was not in the mood to submit and so the long process of appeal was engaged, with the Government succeeding before both the Court of Appeal[7] and the House of Lords, the decision of the latter being delivered on 22 November 1984. The unions were always on a sticky wicket (despite the decision of Glidewell J. to move into uncharted waters) for the fact was that the decision to exclude them had been taken under the Royal Prerogative. The doctrine of the rule of law means that government must normally have legal authority for everything that it does.[8] In Britain the executive has two sources of legal authority: statute and Royal Prerogative, the latter being the common-law powers of the Crown recognized by the courts. Although these are now exceptional, they are nevertheless very important, dealing with a wide range of government activity, including the conduct of foreign affairs and the disposition of the armed forces, as well as the regulation of employment conditions in the civil service.

Traditionally, the power of the courts to review government decisions under the prerogative has been quite limited. First, they could determine whether a particular prerogative power claimed by government in fact existed. So in a famous case in 1765 two King's Messengers were sued for having unlawfully broken and entered the home of John Entick and having seized his papers.[9]

---

[6] [1984] IRLR 309.   [7] [1984] IRLR 353.

[8] Cf. *Malone* v. *Metropolitan Police Commissioner* [1979] 2 All 620.

[9] *Entick* v. *Carrington* (1765) 2 Wils. 275.

This was done under the authority of a warrant issued by the Home Secretary on behalf of whom it was argued that he had a prerogative power to issue such warrants where the interests of state security so required. It was held, however, that the search was illegal, there being no such power. It was for the judges and not the government to determine whether or not a common-law power in fact exists. This is clearly a decision of first importance for it meant that no government could be the arbiter of its own power. And in addition to their role in determining the existence of a particular prerogative power the courts could also determine its scope. This is illustrated by a case in 1965 when the House of Lords held that there was a prerogative power to take and destroy private property in times of war (to prevent it falling into enemy hands) but that the Crown had to pay compensation to those whose property was affected in this way.[10] The Government was thus held liable to compensate the Burmah Oil Company to the tune of £31 million for destruction of its installations, a step which had been taken during the Second World War to prevent them falling into the hands of the invading Japanese army.[11]

Yet although there was thus an established power to determine the existence and extent of prerogative power, the courts had consistently refused to review the manner of its exercise. So even if prerogative power was used in a manifestly unreasonable way, no judicial relief was available. The great breakthrough of the House of Lords decision in the GCHQ case was the fact that in boldly discarding the constraints of well-settled law, a majority in the House of Lords held that all power of government is in principle subject to judicial review.[12] What was important, said a majority of their Lordships, was the nature of the power and not its source. But although the decision on this point was of great constitutional significance, its impact was limited by the House of Lords on two grounds. First, it was made clear that not all prerogative powers are subject to judicial review as to the manner of their exercise. The courts will only intervene if the issue in question is justiciable, that is to say, if it deals with a matter that

[10] *Burmah Oil Co. Ltd* v. *Lord Advocate* [1965] AC 75.

[11] The decision was, however, effectively reversed by the retrospective War Damage Act 1965.

[12] *Council of Civil Service Unions* v. *Minister for the Civil Service* [1985] AC 374.

is capable of adjudication in a court of law. Most of the prerogative powers were in fact said to be non-justiciable so that this great breakthrough in principle may have rather limited impact in practice. Still, it was apparently accepted that the prerogative power to regulate the conditions of service in government employment was justiciable and thus subject to judicial review. This is clearly of great importance to civil servants in view of their precarious legal position. Yet despite its obvious relevance to the instant case, the unions still lost.

Having established that the prerogative is reviewable if the power is justiciable, that this instant power was justiciable, and that the Prime Minister had acted improperly in failing to consult with the unions before introducing the new arrangements, the unions then remarkably stumbled at a final hurdle. This was the Government's defence that the decision had been taken for reasons of national security and so could not be challenged by the courts. As we saw in Chapter 3 the exclusion of judicial review for this reason is not particularly novel: the courts typically permit the rule of law to be subordinated to the external and internal security interests of the state.[13] It is true that the mere assertion by the Government that they had acted on security grounds was not enough. The Lords confirmed that there must be evidence that national security was in fact a reason for the decision. A majority of the Lords also confirmed, however, that the courts will go no further, and will not question whether the steps taken are in fact necessary for reasons of national security. What is necessary is a matter on which the Government must have the last word. In 1964 one law Lord had said that 'Men can exaggerate the extent of their interests and so can the Crown'.[14] But in the GCHQ case only Lord Scarman seemed alert to this point in what was on this question a disappointing performance by their Lordships. So although state security does not permit the creation of new prerogative powers, it does prevent review of existing ones. National security was thus used as a pretext to justify illegal conduct. The courts had come to the rescue of the Government. The ghost of John Entick was well and truly buried.

---

[13] See esp. *Liversidge* v. *Anderson* [1942] AC 206.
[14] *Chandler* v. *DPP* [1964] AC 763.

Revival of the Official Secrets Acts

A second issue which highlighted the growing obsession with security matters was the revival of the Official Secrets Acts and the announcement of reforms designed to enhance their utility (Home Office, 1988a). The main statute in this area was the Official Secrets Act 1911, a statute which had been amended on several occasions, most recently in 1939, before its partial repeal and replacement in 1989. The 1911 Act was not in fact the first British statute to address the question of official secrecy though it was by far the most comprehensive and the most tightly drawn. Earlier legislation of 1889 was thought to be inadequate to cope with the largely imaginary German spy scare in the period immediately before the First World War and so was replaced—at the instance of the head of the security service newly created in 1909—by the more sweeping and comprehensive provisions of the 1911 Act.

Dealing with 'penalties for spying', section 1 of the 1911 Act contains a number of offences. Essentially, however, it is an offence for any person 'for any purpose prejudicial to the safety or interests of the state' to be in the vicinity of a military establishment or to obtain or communicate to any other person any document or information 'which is calculated to be or might be or is intended to be directly or indirectly useful to an enemy'. Despite the generally held view that it is rather uncontroversial, section 1 is much more widely used than is sometimes imagined. We have already seen how it was deployed to deal with the activities of CND which in the 1960s involved the occupation of US military establishments. And as we suggested in Chapter 4, it is conceivable that section 1 could have been used successfully against demonstrators in the 1980s, such as the women at Greenham Common and the anti-nuclear protesters at the US bases at Molesworth in Cambridgeshire and Faslane in Scotland.

But if section 1 has the potential for considerable controversy, such potential was easily fulfilled by section 2, one of the most notorious and most condemned sections of an Act of Parliament ever. Section 2 applied to any person having in his or her possession any information which he or she obtained while holding a position under Her Majesty. It applied also to anyone possessing information by virtue of holding a contract from the Crown or by virtue of being employed by a Crown contractor. A number of offences were created by the section, but the principal offence was for such a person to communicate the information in question unless authorized to do so, or unless the accused had given the information to a person to whom it was his or her duty in the interests of the state to communicate the information. The section was thus one of staggering scope. It applied to all civil servants by making it a criminal offence to communicate any information, no matter how trivial and no matter to whom, unless there was authority. And some civil servants, it seemed, had no authority, express or implied, to reveal anything, even to their spouses or partners.

Very few of the prosecutions under section 2 have been reported in the Law Reports. Those which have, however, indicate nicely the extraordinary scope of the section. In 1919 a clerk in the War Office passed on information relating to contracts between the War Office and government contractors. Although the information was not secret, and although national security was hardly compromised, still the offence had been committed and the clerk was convicted.[15] Despite the title of the Act, it was not necessary for the securing of a conviction under section 2 that the information be secret! A more recent case, involving a senior official at the Central Office of Information, is equally instructive. Over a period of years the well-meaning Miss Fell had lent confidential information to an employee of the Yugoslavian embassy in London in order to influence him in favour of British policies. Although she had no intention of doing anything to prejudice the safety of the state, the Court of Criminal Appeal held, nevertheless, that the offence was absolute and was committed whatever the document contained and regardless of the motive with which it was communicated.[16]

Yet despite the recent controversy, section 2 was not widely used in the twenty-five-year period after the Second World War. Thus, from 1945 to 1971 (covering the cold-war period) only 23 prosecutions were brought involving 34 defendants of whom 27

[15] *R.* v. *Crisp* (1919) 83 JP 121.
[16] *R.* v. *Fell* [1963] Crim. Law Rev. 207.

were convicted. For the most part the Attorney-General exercised restraint in bringing prosecutions. More than one-third of prosecutions involved the leaking of police and prison information. In all, only two cases involved journalists. By the 1970s, section 2 had largely fallen into disuse. In 1971 it was roundly condemned from the Bench by Caulfield J. who urged that it should be 'pensioned off' in the course of an unsuccessful prosecution after the *Sunday Telegraph* had published a confidential report by the defence adviser at the British High Commission in Lagos. More significantly perhaps, a departmental committee under the chairmanship of Lord Franks completed a detailed investigation of section 2 and recommended that it should be replaced by legislation more narrowly and more appropriately written. We return to the Franks Report in Chapter 6.

Since 1978, however, the use of section 2 has revived significantly. Information provided to the House of Commons by successive Attorneys-General demonstrates that between then and December 1986 no fewer than 29 people were prosecuted under Section 2, with at least another 5 prosecutions pending at the time. There were thus as many prosecutions in these nine years as there were in the twenty-five post-war years, during which the cold war was at its height! Arguably, some of the prosecutions were unexceptionable (such as those of the police officer who gave information about local crimes to representatives of burglar alarm companies; and the civil servant who gave personal information to a political candidate about his rivals), though it is questionable whether the Official Secrets Act was the most appropriate vehicle for dealing with many of these cases. But it is arguable also that several of the prosecutions were designed not to protect national security but to protect the Government from future political embarrassment, a point not lost on Lord Scarman in legal proceedings relating to one of the incidents. The cases in question are those involving Miss Sarah Tisdall, a clerk in the personal office of Sir Geoffrey Howe, the then Foreign Secretary, and, some time later, Mr Clive Ponting, who was engaged in a senior position at the Ministry of Defence. In the end, however, the latter case in particular caused more political embarrassment than it was ever likely to prevent.

On 22 October 1983 Miss Tisdall delivered to the *Guardian* a photocopy of a secret document entitled 'Deliveries of Cruise Missiles to R.A.F. Greenham Common—Parliamentary and Public Statements'. The document was addressed by the Defence Minister, Michael Heseltine, to the Prime Minister, with copies being sent also to the Home Secretary and the Foreign Secretary, as well as to others. Miss Tisdall made photocopies of this and another minute, and 'After doing her best with a felt pen to render indecipherable the marginal markings on the documents which would enable them to be identified as the copies . . . that had been directed to the Foreign Secretary',[17] she took them to the *Guardian* where she gave them (in an envelope) to an attendant on the door. The *Guardian* then published articles based upon the documents, and on 31 October 1983 published one of them verbatim. This demonstrated clearly that the Government was uneasy about the delivery of the missiles and that a statement to Parliament would be made after and not before their arrival 'in order to concentrate as much attention as possible on the Government's position before the Opposition and the "peace movement" had an opportunity to react'. It was also stated that 'there can be no question of revealing the timetable for equipment deliveries in advance'.

Following these publications, an internal investigation was conducted to find the source of the leak. When initial inquiries proved unfruitful, the Treasury Solicitor wrote to the *Guardian* asking for delivery of the documents, which the newspaper was willing to do only on the condition that all marginal marks were removed to protect the identity of the still anonymous Miss Tisdall. The offer was refused when matters took an unsavoury twist with the Government instituting proceedings for delivery of the unmutilated documents. Surprisingly perhaps, by this stage the *Guardian* had neither destroyed the documents (as the *Independent* did later with the *Spycatcher* manuscript) nor taken steps unilaterally to remove all incriminating marks. As a result, on 15 December 1983 Scott J. was able to order that the documents should be given back, a decision affirmed by the Court of Appeal on the following day. Forensic tests then enabled Tisdall to be identified as a prime suspect. Following her

[17] *Guardian Newspapers Ltd.* v. *Secretary of State for Defence* [1984] 3 All ER 601.

confession on 9 January 1984, she was successfully prosecuted under section 2 and imprisoned.

A crucial feature of the Tisdall prosecution is the role played by the courts in helping her to be identified for the purposes of prosecution. The Government was not entitled as a matter of course to the return of the documents, since the newspaper was theoretically protected by section 10 of the Contempt of Court Act 1981. Although the Act was passed to deal with the *Sunday Times* thalidomide case, the opportunity was taken to use the measure as a vehicle for other reforms in the general area of contempt of court. Section 10 addresses the serious problem of whether newspapers or broadcasters should be compelled to disclose their sources in legal proceedings or whether journalists should enjoy a privilege in this respect, as is the case in certain circumstances in the United States. Cases arising out of the Vassall spy inquiry in the 1960s,[18] and subsequent decisions involving first a senior reporter with the *Scottish Daily Record*,[19] and secondly Granada television,[20] made it clear that there was no such privilege or immunity in English law, or in Scots law either for that matter. In the *Granada* case Lord Wilberforce said that all the authorities 'came down firmly against immunity for the press or for journalists'.

Section 10 of the 1981 Act provides that no court may require a person to disclose the source of information contained in a publication unless it is established to the satisfaction of the court in question that disclosure is 'necessary in the interests of justice or national security or for the prevention of disorder or crime'. The Tisdall case was clearly the big test for the efficacy of this section, with the courts being asked to intervene in a major matter of public interest. In the event, however, section 10 did little to prevent Miss Tisdall from being identified, with the decisions of Scott J. and the Court of Appeal being upheld albeit by a closely divided House of Lords. The fact that the Lords appeal was not heard until July 1984 was of rather academic interest to Tisdall who was by then behind bars. It would have been ironical, to say the least, if a majority of their Lordships had

---

[18] *Attorney-General* v. *Mulholland and Foster* [1963] 2 QB 477.
[19] *HM Advocate* v. *Airs* 1975 SLT 177.
[20] *British Steel Corporation* v. *Granada Television Ltd.* [1981] AC 1096.

decided that the lower court had been wrong in ordering delivery up of the documents. But they did not, in the process construing the section in a manner which was a gift to the executive and which left the section offering very little protection to journalists in national security cases.

It is true that the House of Lords initially read the section widely so that it could be used to prevent the recovery of documents where this would have the effect of revealing a source. Their lordships rejected the suggestion made in the courts below that the section only protects the journalist who refuses to answer questions in the court room when directed to do so by the judge. Here, however, the progress ended with the majority accepting the Crown's case for return, based on paragraph 6 of its affidavit, which read as follows:

The fact that a document marked 'Secret' addressed by the Secretary of State for Defence to the Prime Minister on 20th October 1983 which was concerned with a matter of great significance in relation to the defence of the United Kingdom and the North Atlantic Treaty Organisation had, by the 31st October 1983, found its way into the possession of a national newspaper, is of the gravest importance to the continued maintenance of national security. It also represents a threat to the United Kingdom's relations with her allies, who cannot be expected to continue to entrust Her Majesty's Government with secret information which may be liable to unauthorised disclosure, even though its circulation is restricted to the innermost circles of government. Thus the identity of the person or persons who disclosed or assisted in the disclosure of the above mentioned document to the Defendant must be established in order that national security should be preserved.

The House of Lords divided 3 : 2 in holding that this was enough to establish that it was necessary in the interests of national security that the documents be returned.

In so holding the majority suggested strongly that the Crown needs only to claim national security in order to establish the need for disclosure, or, in this case, recovery of the documents. Concern about this is evident from the dissenting speeches of Lords Fraser and Scarman. The latter concluded that the evidence fell far short of what was needed to establish that disclosure was necessary in the interests of national security. So far as the affidavit was concerned, this was sworn by the principal establishment officer of the Ministry of Defence who was described as having certain responsibilities concerned with the security of records. In Lord Scarman's view such undefined responsibilities did not offer any clue as to whether the officer was in any position to make a judgment on questions of national security. But if he was, it was not enough to assert that a document was secret: its contents from a national security point of view were innocuous, and it could well have been marked secret because 'it would have been politically embarrassing for the Government if Parliament or the public were to learn of what was in the Government's mind as to the publicity to be given to this politically sensitive matter before a parliamentary statement was made'.[21]

Shortly before the *Guardian* case was argued in the House of Lords, and several months before its decision was delivered, there occurred another leak of official information even more devastating than Sarah Tisdall's. On 16 July 1984 Clive Ponting sent to Tam Dalyell, the MP for Linlithgow, two Ministry of Defence documents relating to parliamentary enquiries about the sinking of the Argentine vessel, the *General Belgrano*, during the Falklands conflict.[22] The first document, which was unclassified, was a draft reply written by Ponting, in his departmental capacity, to questions asked in Parliament by Dalyell of the Minister of Defence. The second was a minute marked confidential, but later declassified, indicating that certain answers should not be given to questions which might be asked about changes in the Rules of Engagement by the House of Commons Select Committee on Foreign Affairs. According to the press, at the time the documents were leaked Mr Dalyell 'had been fighting a long and increasingly lonely battle to expose what he believes to be serious government mis-statements about the sinking of the Belgrano'.

For his part, Mr Ponting was a man of some distinction. Aged thirty-eight, he was head of Defence Secretariat (DS)5 which

---

[21] The protection for journalists was further undermined several years later in a case involving Jeremy Warner, a financial journalist. See *Re an Inquiry under the Company Securities (Insider Dealing) Act 1985* [1988] 1 All ER 203.

[22] The account of the Ponting case is drawn principally from *The Times*, Jan.–Apr. 1985.

involved working with naval staff on day-to-day activities of the fleet, particularly in relation to political and policy matters. Earlier work in the civil service had led to Ponting being awarded an OBE and allegedly also led to his being favoured for promotion following the direct intervention of the Prime Minister whom he had impressed by a presentation made to the Cabinet on departmental economies. Although it is unclear whether he removed all incriminating markings from the documents before sending them to Dalyell, Ponting is reported as having subsequently confessed to an internal investigation and having stated that 'I did this because I believe that ministers within this department were not prepared to answer legitimate questions from a member of Parliament about a question of considerable public concern, simply in order to protect their own political position'. In giving evidence at his trial for an offence under section 2 Ponting repeated his allegation that he had felt obliged to tell Parliament how it had been misled by Ministers and how Ministers had planned to mislead the Foreign Affairs Select Committee. It was said at the trial that Ministers were concerned not to do anything which might show previous statements to be incorrect.

The trial, once it got going, was a truly remarkable affair. First, it was conceded on day one that 'It is not suggested that disclosure in fact damaged national security. The case involves an alleged breach of confidentiality.' This rightly gave rise to questions as to why the criminal law should be used in this way and why it was not sufficient to deal with the breach of duty by dismissal—as would be the fate of any other employee. Secondly, and perhaps even more surprising, were the revelations that the jury had been vetted—despite the fact that there were no national security issues raised! Jury-vetting is a process which is designed to exclude from service certain categories of dangerously independent minded persons. Under the guidelines issued by the Attorney-General, jury-vetting will take place in cases involving terrorism, or in national security cases, including cases under the Official Secrets Acts, if part of the evidence is to be heard in camera. In this case the prosecution had applied for some of the evidence to be heard in camera. The request was granted, with the judge exercising powers in section 8 of the Official Secrets Act 1920 which is a major departure from the general rule that 'the English system of administering justice does require that it be done in public'.[23]

Over sixty potential jurors had been vetted in this case by the Special Branch, which reassuringly does not engage in any personal visitations of potential jurors, but which conducts its business from its own files and from searches of criminal records.[24] The Special Branch (and possibly the security service) is asked to determine whether each potential juror is known for 'political beliefs . . . so biased as to go beyond normally reflecting the broad spectrum of views and interests in the community to reflect the extreme views of sectarian interest or pressure group to a degree which might interfere with his fair assessment of the facts of the case or lead him to exert improper pressure on his fellow jurors'. The sinister feature of these 'guidelines' of course is the implicit admission that files are kept on people active out of the mainstream of party politics. What chance a member of CND serving on the jury in the Ponting trial? Yet it seems that a Labour member of Islington council sat on the jury, despite the council having passed a resolution urging the charge to be dropped. It is not clear if this demonstrates the relative tolerance or absolute incompetence of those engaged in the vetting process.

In this context the muzzling of Channel 4 and Mr Tam Dalyell by the judge seems very small beer. Exercising powers contained in section 4(2) of the Contempt of Court Act 1981, McCowan J. ordered Channel 4 not to recreate each evening the day's proceedings, though he appeared not to take exception to the employment of newscasters to read excerpts from the day's events.[25] Dalyell was summoned during the course of the trial to be told that he might be jailed if he made public statements about the case out of court. If he was unable to control himself, scolded McCowan J., 'I may be driven to put you where you have no option'. Dalyell promised to behave, though only after protesting that his comments had been expressed in Scotland and that he should be held to account in a Scottish court with the rep-

---

[23] *Attorney-General* v. *Leveller Magazine Ltd.* [1979] AC 440.

[24] The procedure for jury-vetting is now to be found at [1988] 3 All ER 1086.

[25] The Court of Appeal exercised a similar power to prevent Channel 4 covering the daily proceedings of the Court in the Birmingham Six bombing case: see *Attorney-General* v. *Channel 4 Television Co. Ltd.* [1988] Crim. Law Rev. 237.

resentation of Scottish lawyers. A Sunday newspaper also found itself in hot water by reporting details of what had taken place during the in camera proceedings. Although he had not issued an order directing that details of these proceedings should not be published, McCowan J. was later to lament that even the greenest reporter on the smallest of regional newspapers would know that such publications could not be tolerated.

Meanwhile the main event was proceeding apace. There was little doubt that Ponting had communicated information acquired in his position as a servant of Her Majesty to an unauthorized person. For despite his status, Dalyell was not a person to whom Ponting was authorized to communicate the documents in question. Ponting's defence then was that Dalyell was a person to whom it was his duty in the interests of the state to communicate the information. This defence had only rarely been raised, and apparently had never succeeded. Ponting's liberty for perhaps two years thus hung by a slender thread. Some big guns were, however, rolled out in his defence. Mr Merlyn Rees, a former Home Secretary, put a civil servant's truth and accountability to Parliament above all else. Professor H. W. R. Wade of Cambridge University claimed that 'the Government of the country could not run as it does now if Parliament was consistantly fed with wrong information'. He said that if a civil servant was convinced that truthful information was not being given 'it might be in the public interest for him to give his information direct to Parliament'. In his summing-up to the jury, however, McCowan J. gave such considerations fairly short shrift.

McCowan J. dealt with Ponting's defence that it was his duty in the interests of the state to communicate the information to Dalyell by saying that the term 'duty' in section 2 meant 'official duty'. In this case, Ponting's duties clearly did not extend to giving out confidential information to hostile MPs. So far as the words 'in the interest of the state' were concerned, he directed that 'these words mean the policies of the state as they were in July 1984 . . . and not the interests of the state as Mr Ponting, Mr Dalyell, you or I might think they ought to have been'. He continued by saying that the 'policies of the state mean the policies laid down by those recognised organs of government and authority', that is to say the Government which currently enjoys the confidence of the House of Commons. Yet despite this direction (described by *The Times* as uncomfortably reminiscent of a chilling direction of the Court of Appeal in 1916), the jury took less than three hours to return a verdict of not guilty, to the obvious embarrassment of the Government. The decision had major repercussions, with *The Times* pointing out that the jury had acted in sublime disregard of the oppressive spirit which formulated section 2, and had left the machinery for the protection of government confidentiality in disarray. Further evidence of this was highlighted by the impotence of the Government in the light of Cathy Massiter's allegations, which we have already encountered.

It is true that in the same month that the jury delivered the Ponting verdict, Channel 4 decided to withdraw the *20/20 Vision* programme which would broadcast the Massiter allegations. This was done because of the fear that it might involve a violation of the Official Secrets Act 1911. The programme was, however, later cleared by the Attorney-General and the broadcast was eventually made. The Ponting case did not, however, bury the Official Secrets Act completely. A new use for the Act was found during the so-called Zircon affair.[26] On 19 January 1987 it was reported that a film in the BBC documentary series *The Secret Society* had been withdrawn by the BBC on the ground that its broadcast might cause a threat to national security. In the film it would be claimed that the Ministry of Defence had secretly launched a £500 million electronic surveillance project without informing Parliament, despite a firm undertaking that any defence projects valued at more than £250 million had to be disclosed to the House of Commons Public Accounts Committee. In taking steps to ban the film, the BBC denied that there had been any government pressure. The Government had, however, apparently known about the series in which the film was to be shown for several months and had intervened at least to the extent that discussions had taken place between a senior civil servant at the Ministry of Defence and the BBC. Following the announcement that the programme was to be withdrawn, Duncan Campbell (the

[26] The account of the Zircon affair is drawn principally from *The Times*, Jan.–Apr. 1987.

journalist who had made it) arranged for the film to be shown in the House of Commons (in defiance of a BBC instruction) in order to demonstrate to Members of Parliament that there was in fact no risk to national security. It was arranged that the film would be shown in Committee Room 6 at the House of Commons on Thursday, 22 January 1987.

But, according to press reports, 22 January was to become a day of 'unprecedented legal and constitutional action', accompanied by 'panic' in government circles. First the Attorney-General tried unsuccessfully to obtain an injunction to prevent the MPs from seeing the banned film. Apparently it took Kennedy J. no more than one minute to reject the application on the ground that it was for Parliament to regulate its own proceedings. In the words of the editor of *Public Law*—a leading academic journal—'What is notable in the matter is not the judge's decision—a refusal of the application was the only conceivable outcome, if a massive clash of jurisdiction between the High Court and the Commons was to be avoided—but that the Attorney-General, Sir Michael Havers, Q.C., should have thought it worthwhile or legitimate to make the application' (Bradley, 1987a: 2). Thus, according to the leading British textbook on constitutional law, the House of Commons 'has the right to control its own proceedings and to regulate its internal affairs without interference by the courts' (Wade and Bradley, 1985: 217). It is perhaps easy to understand why in this incident 'the Attorney-General would be best advised to rely on his own ineptitude if he is to escape more serious criticism' (Bradley 1987a: 2). The failure to obtain the injunction did not, however, end the matter. Following a personal briefing on the national security implications from the Attorney-General, the Speaker intervened to ban the showing of the film in the House of Commons.

As might be expected this caused an uproar, the Speaker's intervention in the view of some being unprecedented and in the view of others unconstitutional. It is the duty of the Speaker to defend rather than undermine the ancient privileges of Parliament which would be seriously threatened if 'arguments about national security are to be accepted as valid excuses for the control of the House of Commons by the Government'. The heat was taken out of this issue when, following a debate in the Commons on the

Speaker's ruling, the matter was referred to the Committee on Privileges for consideration. Elsewhere, however, matters were only beginning to warm up. On 21 January an injunction had been obtained against Duncan Campbell 'preventing him from talking or writing about the contents of the film'. At the same time a threatening letter was sent by hand by the Government Solicitor to all national newspaper editors seeking an assurance by noon the following day that nothing relating to the subject-matter of the injunction would be published. Failure to comply was understood by one national newspaper to mean either that proceedings for contempt of court would be instituted for aiding and abetting a breach of the injunction against Campbell or that the newspaper would be prosecuted under the Official Secrets Act. But, to the irritation of the Government, Mr Campbell could not be found to serve the injunction with the result that it was too late to stop the *New Statesman* from making a splash with the contents of the film.

It was only after the magazine appeared that Campbell was served with the court order. Full details were revealed, and the Prime Minister was furious. 'Unfortunately,' she is reported as having said, 'there seem to be people with more interest in trying to ferret out and reveal information of use to our enemies, rather than preserving the defence interest of this country, and thus the freedom which we all enjoy.' On another occasion she is reported as having found it 'very significant' that the matter had been published by a 'left-wing magazine'. But having thus slipped the net of prior restraint, Duncan Campbell and the *New Statesman* found themselves the targets of state retribution. On the night of Friday, 23 January, warrants were granted to search the premises of Mr Campbell, apparently in connection with offences under the Official Secrets Act. Seven Special Branch officers arrived and entered the premises, while a separate team searched the offices of the *New Statesman* under the incredulous eyes of its new editor, Mr John Lloyd, who had just moved into the job from the *Financial Times*. The home of a researcher working on the programme was also searched. The condemnation of this behaviour was as justified as it was predictable. Mr Campbell reminded the nation that these were the tactics of Eastern Europe and South Africa. A Member of Parliament remarked chillingly, 'It's the knock on the door in the night.'

It was widely felt that the police action was vindictive, Campbell stating that it was an attempt to placate Mrs Thatcher's embarrassment, and Lloyd commenting that it was a clear indication that the Government would not tolerate open enquiry and stories which embarrassed them. But matters were to take an even more sinister twist. Although it was still not known what the police were looking for, the search was extended when, the following weekend, ten officers from the Strathclyde and Metropolitan police forces swooped upon the Scottish office of the BBC in a twenty-eight-hour raid. Remarkably it took three attempts before an acceptable search warrant could be obtained, and even that was probably unlawful. The warrant was issued under section 9 of the Official Secrets Act 1911, a section of quite extraordinary scope. It provides that where there is reasonable ground to suspect that an offence under the Act has been or is about to be committed, a justice of the peace may grant a search warrant authorizing any constable named in the warrant to enter at any time any premises or place named in the warrant, if necessary by force. The constable is empowered to search the premises or place (and every person found therein) and to seize any articles, notes, or documents or anything of a like nature which he may find on the premises.

The first warrant was successfully challenged by the BBC on the ground that it was too general. It is a well-established rule of Scots law, as it is of English law, that search warrants must be framed with reasonable specificity.[27] A second warrant was equally invalid on the ground that it applied to the address of a flat used by Campbell when he stayed in Glasgow and not to the Corporation's offices in Hamilton Drive, Glasgow! A third warrant was obtained and regarded as lawful for the purposes of the search, though as was pointed out forcefully by the Professor of Scots Law at the University of Edinburgh it too was almost certainly invalid with the result that the whole procedure was unlawful. The warrant was granted by a sheriff, a Scottish judicial officer, whereas the Act requires the warrant to be issued by a justice of the peace. Although a 'number of Acts of Parliament which confer powers and duties on Scottish justices of the peace go on to provide expressly that for the purposes of that particular

[27] *Bell* v. *Black* (1865) 5 Irv. 57.

Act, "justice" shall be read as including "sheriff"' the Official Secrets Act contains no such provision (Black, 1987: 138). Nevertheless the police used the warrant to remove documents, as well as 200 containers of film and video, including discarded clips. These filled several police vans. Once again there was outrage though much of this missed the point that the discredited Official Secrets Act was not being tested against a jury, it was being used simply as a means of state harassment of those who dared to question.

One notable defender of the BBC claimed that state officials were not entitled to go on a fishing expedition to ransack offices and look wherever they wanted. The state has to be answerable to the rule of law. Such principled postures were beginning to look increasingly naïve in modern Britain. For his part Mr Roy Jenkins asked just what was the supreme objective for which the Government was 'prepared to look as though they were running a second-rate police state, infused equally with illiberalism and incompetence'. Several other critics were also to contend that the Government was dragging Britain towards a police state. As might be expected the affair was the subject of a stormy emergency debate in Parliament and was condemned by the European Parliament. The new Chairman of the BBC wrote to both the Home Secretary and the Scottish Secretary that he had followed the events with 'mounting dismay' and that he was bound to protest 'vigorously' about the conduct of the police. The BBC could rightly feel aggrieved. They did after all refuse to show the film. Moreover, the search warrant by which the raid took place was in such general terms that it authorized the removal of the other five films in the series, to which no objection had apparently been taken!

In view of the uproar and dismay, the Government not unnaturally sought to distance itself from the police conduct. The claim that there had been no ministerial involvement in seeking the search warrant was not uncontroversial. In the end, however, the matter fizzled out, the Official Secrets Act having served its purpose of intimidation. The injunctions against Campbell were discharged, the Speaker lifted his ban on the showing of the film in Parliament, and it was eventually transmitted by the BBC some two years later. Significantly, no charges were brought in connection with the incident, though the Special Branch did advise that Campbell be prosecuted under the Official Secrets Act.[28] An interesting footnote to the affair is that while the issue was centre-stage in February 1987 private viewings of pirate copies of the film had been arranged at different locations throughout the country, including Edinburgh, Glasgow, and London. The BBC moved on several occasions to obtain injunctions to prevent such shows, standing on its copyright in the material in question. Equally significantly, the Freedom Association reportedly took legal action, not to facilitate the showing of the film, but to issue private writs against Campbell and seven others after the showing of the film at Conway Hall in London, on the ground of an alleged breach of the Official Secrets Act.

Spycatcher

Despite the Zircon affair, the Massiter incident demonstrated clearly the extent to which the Official Secrets Act had been discredited by the Ponting case. That case, perhaps more than any other, was an important inducement for the Government to move more quickly on the question of reform of the Official Secrets Act, though as we shall see the so-called reform is likely to authorize as much if not more (rather than less) authoritarian conduct by the executive. No doubt also critical in expediting the process of reform was the *Spycatcher* case in which millions of pounds were spent by the British Government to publicize the memoirs of a former British security service agent living in Tasmania, memoirs which it has to be said the Government would rather have suppressed. This is despite the fact that much of the information was stale and available in other sources, even if it was sensational.

The MI5 agent involved, Mr Peter Wright, had acknowledged on several occasions that he was bound by the Official Secrets Acts and he had given undertakings that he would not divulge

[28] An announcement of the decision to broadcast was made in the press on 2 July 1988. It was also stated that the BBC had been advised that the film did not breach national security after all, despite earlier allegations that 'serious damage' would be caused by endangering the 'continuation of American co-operation'. The Foreign Office now only 'regretted' the BBC's decision.

information acquired in the course of his duties unless authorized to do so. But notwithstanding this vow of silence he provided a frank and explicit account of his work as a security officer, claiming for example that MI5 had been involved in the burglary and bugging of political parties and trade unions; that the British security service had been implicated in an attempt to assassinate the Egyptian President, Nasser; and that MI5 had taken part in attempts to discredit and destabilize the democratically elected Labour Government of Mr Harold Wilson. More embarrassing, perhaps, was the allegation that a former head of MI5, Sir Roger Hollis, was a Soviet double agent. These disclosures were all the more controversial because they were made at a time when the work of the security service was being called into question. In particular, concern was beginning to be expressed about its lack of accountability, it being subject to no effective scrutiny or control by the legislative, judicial, or indeed even the executive branches of government, a point to which we return in Chapter 6.

There was no reason why the Thatcher Government should have been embarrassed by Wright's revelations or indeed why it should have wished to draw worldwide attention to them by seeking to suppress the book in at least four jurisdictions. But it did, despite the fact that the Official Secrets Act could not be used in view of Wright's location far removed from the jurisdiction of the English courts. Unable to use the 1911 Act, the Government turned to the civil law action of breach of confidence as a means of restraining publication, a course of action which we encountered in Chapter 3 in our discussion of the *Malone* case.[29] Until 1976 it appears that breach of confidence had been used only in regard to private and personal rights, including trade secrets and marital secrets. A major development of great significance in 1976, however, was a decision of the Lord Chief Justice to sweep 'public rights into the confidentiality net', a step which was described by counsel at the time as 'frightening and dangerous'. The case in question involved an attempt (albeit ultimately unsuccessful) by the then Labour Government to restrain by injunction the publication of Mr Richard Crossman's diaries, Crossman having been a Cabinet Minister. Although there was no

[29] *Malone* v. *Metropolitan Police Commissioner* [1979] 2 All ER 620.

precedent for the application of breach of confidence to governmental information, the Lord Chief Justice responded simply by saying that he could see no reason 'why the courts should be powerless to restrain the publication of public secrets'.[30] Of some importance subsequently to Peter Wright and his publishers is the fact that in 1980 the High Court of Australia agreed with the Lord Chief Justice, albeit that in that case too the circumstances were not such as to justify the granting of an injunction.[31]

1. The trial in Sydney

The *Spycatcher* litigation covered a period of more than three years. On 10 September 1985 an ex parte injunction was obtained by the Attorney-General in New South Wales restraining the publication of the book in Australia by Heinemann. Thereafter the Crown accepted undertakings from Wright and his publisher that they would not publish the book pending the trial, as a result of which the injunctions were not continued. Before the trial of the matter in New South Wales, however, in June 1986 the *Observer* and the *Guardian* published outlines of the allegations that were going to be made in the Australian proceedings whereupon they were restrained by a temporary injunction granted ex parte by MacPherson J. from disclosing or publishing information obtained by Wright in his capacity as a member of the security service. And following a move by the newspapers to have the injunctions discharged they were continued by Millett J. on 11 July 1986, though varied to permit, first, quotations from earlier broadcasts by Mr Wright to which no exception had been taken, and secondly, the publication of any information allowed to be published by the Supreme Court of New South Wales. The order was varied further on 25 July following an appeal by the newspapers to the Court of Appeal.[32] Although the injunctions were maintained, the newspapers were now also permitted to report parliamentary proceedings as well as judicial proceedings concerning the case.

[30] *Attorney-General* v. *Jonathan Cape Ltd.* [1976] QB 752.
[31] *Commonwealth of Australia* v. *John Fairfax and Sons Ltd.* (1980) 32 ALR 485.
[32] *Attorney-General* v. *Observer Newspapers Ltd.* (1986) 136 NLJ 799.

With two British newspapers muzzled by temporary injunctions, the focus of attention shifted back to Sydney where the trial before Powell J. started on 17 November 1986. From the perspective of the Government, that trial was a disaster. The seriousness with which it viewed the matter was reflected in the fact that Sir Robert Armstrong, the Cabinet Secretary, was sent all the way to Australia to bat for England. For the away team, however, his contribution was perhaps less effective than were the subsequent contributions of the test side. Our most senior civil servant was given a very uncomfortable time by a young Sydney lawyer, Mr Malcolm Turnbull, in a trial which immortalized the phrase 'economical with the truth'. Equally embarrassing for the Government (which in the meantime had failed in the Irish courts to restrain the publication of the memoirs of a wartime security agent),[33] was the decision in favour of the defence, Powell J. taking the view that the material in the book was already in the public domain and was thus no longer confidential. But to the extent that some of this information retained its confidential quality, he still refused relief on the ground that publication would not cause sufficient detriment to the British Government. The need to maintain a leakproof front could hardly be a basis for an injunction when the security service had for years 'leaked like a sieve'.[34]

Judgment was given by Powell J. on 13 March 1987 but still there was no publication, with the defendant undertaking not to publish pending an appeal to the New South Wales Court of Appeal. The appeal was dismissed on 24 September 1987.[35] The court divided 2 : 1, with the majority deciding essentially on different grounds. One of the judges relied mainly on principles derived from international law, holding that the action was in substance designed to enforce the Official Secrets Act when in fact the penal statutes of one country are not enforceable in the courts of a foreign sovereign power. The other judge making up

---

[33] *Attorney-General for England and Wales* v. *Brandon Book Publishers Ltd.* [1987] ILRM 135.

[34] *Attorney-General (UK)* v. *Heinemann Publishers Australia Pty. Ltd.* (1987) 8 NSWLR 341.

[35] *Attorney-General (UK)* v. *Heinemann Publishers Australia Pty. Ltd.* (1987) 75 ALR 353.

the majority dismissed the appeal on the ground that the injunction could be imposed only if it was in the British public interest to do so but that the Australian courts were not competent to make judgments of what is in the public interest of a foreign country. The dissent of Street CJ was in fact the only discordant note amongst the eleven Australian judges who gave judgment in this case. On another appeal by the British Government, the High Court of Australia decided 7 : 0 in favour of Wright and his publishers in a decision handed down on 2 June 1988.[36] In so doing the Court decided mainly on international law grounds, thereby side-stepping the problems which had confronted Powell J. Essentially the case was decided according to the principle that 'domestic courts will not enforce a foreign penal or public law'. So ended the proceedings in Australia during the course of which the New Zealand courts[37] also rejected an application from the Crown for relief against Wright.[38]

2. New restrictions in London

Back in London with the Australian proceedings continuing, the *Independent* of 27 April 1987 carried an article containing verbatim passages from the Wright book, while on the same day the *London Evening Standard* and the *London Daily News* quoted from the same passages. The three newspapers had thus done what the *Observer* and the *Guardian* had been restrained from doing by the Millett injunctions of July 1986. Thereupon the Attorney-General moved against these three newspapers for contempt of court, even though they had not been the subject of the restraining order. The Court of Appeal held on 15 July 1987, reversing Sir Nicolas Browne-Wilkinson, that a publication, made in the knowledge of an outstanding injunction against another party and which if made by that other party would be in

---

[36] *Attorney-General (UK)* v. *Heinemann Publishers Australia Pty. Ltd.* (1988) 78 ALR 449.

[37] *Attorney-General for the UK* v. *Wellington Newspapers Ltd.* [1988] 1 NZLR 129.

[38] The Hong Kong Court of Appeal in contrast granted an order restraining publication of extracts of the book by the *South China Morning Post: Attorney-General in and for the UK* v. *South China Morning Post Ltd.* [1988] 1 HKLR 143.

breach thereof, constitutes a criminal contempt of court.[39] In making this extraordinary and unprecedented extension of the contempt power, the Court of Appeal thus rejected the arguments of counsel for the defendants that such a decision would run counter to the whole basis of English law that orders given by courts only bind the parties who are involved in the proceedings. Suddenly it was a crime, punishable by imprisonment following a trial without a jury, to mention Peter Wright's allegations anywhere in the British media. The Government quickly acquired a taste for this power which was later used to prevent the widespread reporting of a confidential document relating to the purchase of Harrods by the el-Fayed brothers.[40]

At about the same time that leave was granted to bring the contempt proceedings against the *Independent* and the other newspapers (29 April 1987), both the *Guardian* and the *Observer* gave notice to discharge or vary the temporary injunctions which had been issued in 1986. Shortly thereafter (on 12 July 1987) the *Sunday Times* began a serialization of the book to coincide with its publication in the United States. On 13 July 1987 the Attorney-General felt moved to apply for an order that Times Newspapers Ltd. and its editor Mr Andrew Neil be respectively fined and committed to prison for contempt of court. The two issues were taken together by the courts on the ground that if the order against the *Observer* and the *Guardian* were discharged, the claim against the *Sunday Times* on the ground of contempt of court must also fail. The newspapers succeeded again before the Vice-Chancellor, Sir Nicolas Browne-Wilkinson, who was influenced by the changing circumstances since 1986 and in particular by the fact that since the full text of the book was available to anyone in the country with the money to get it (by having it sent from the United States), 'a large part of the purpose of the Attorney General's proceedings in this case has now been defeated'. The victory was, however, short-lived, with an appeal by the Attorney-General being upheld by both the Court of Appeal (unanimously) and by the House of Lords (in a 3 : 2 decision over a powerful dissent by Lord Bridge of Harwich) on 30 July 1987.[41]

---

[39] *Attorney-General* v. *Newspaper Publishing plc* [1987] 3 All ER 276.
[40] *Independent*, 1 Apr. 1989.
[41] *Attorney-General* v. *Guardian Newspaper Ltd.* [1987] 3 All ER 316.

In sustaining the temporary injunctions (and indeed in amending them to prevent the publication of material disclosed in open court, thereby making them more restrictive than they had ever been) the House of Lords was persuaded that publication of matters contained in *Spycatcher* would be a breach of the duty of the confidentiality owed by Wright to the Crown and that such publication would 'do great harm to the British Security Service'. The newspapers had argued, however, that publication of the book in the United States constituted decisive grounds for discharging the injunctions, for two reasons. First, now that the information had become public knowledge any duty of non-disclosure ceased to be legally binding; and secondly, continuation of the injunctions would be futile in the sense that damage had already been done to the security service and there was no further damage which could be done. In other words, although publication would be a breach of Wright's duty of confidentiality, there was now no public interest to be served in restricting the publication. Both arguments were, however, rejected on very debatable grounds. For example, the first was met by the claim by Lord Brandon that if the newspapers could now publish, Wright himself would be free to return to the UK and publish his memoirs 'without any legal restraint'. This is a surprising piece of reasoning. If Wright had returned to the UK he would surely have been prosecuted under section 2 of the Official Secrets Act 1911.

The dissenting speeches were delivered by Lord Bridge of Harwich and Lord Oliver of Aylmerton, with the former being notable for its acerbic tone, and all the more notable still for the fact that its author had been Chairman of the Security Commission. It will be recalled that Mr Roy Jenkins had accused Lord Bridge of appearing to be a poodle of the executive following his investigation into the Massiter allegations. On this occasion, however, the poodle barked and, as already pointed out, Mr Jenkins wrote to *The Times* unreservedly to withdraw his earlier remarks. Lord Bridge's starting-point in the *Spycatcher* case was the fact that the book was now freely available: 'The fact is that the intelligence and security services of any country in the world can buy the book . . . and read what is in it. The fact is that any citizen of this country can buy the book in America and bring it home with him or order the book from America and receive a copy by post.' Faced with this reality, it was too late for injunctions to protect sensitive and classified information and it was too late for the injunction to restore the confidence of those friendly countries whose faith in the British security services had been undermined by the disclosure. In his view there was no remaining public interest to be served in sustaining the injunctions which could justify 'the massive encroachment of freedom of speech' which the confirmation of the Millett injunctions necessarily involved.

By far the most significant parts of Lord Bridge's speech were reserved for the end. First, he turned on his judicial colleagues in the House of Lords:

What of the other side of the coin and the encroachment on freedom of speech? Having no written constitution, we have no equivalent in our law to the First Amendment to the Constitution of the United States of America. Some think that puts freedom of speech on too lofty a pedestal. Perhaps they are right. We have not adopted as part of our law the European Convention on Human Rights to which this country is a signatory. Many think that we should. I have hitherto not been of that persuasion, in large part because I have had confidence in the capacity of the common law to safeguard the fundamental freedoms essential to a free society including the right to freedom of speech which is specifically safeguarded by art. 10 of the convention. My confidence is seriously undermined by your Lordships' decision. . . . I can see nothing whatever, either in law or on the merits, to be said for the maintenance of a total ban on discussion in the press of this country of matters of undoubted public interest and concern which the rest of the world now knows all about and can discuss freely. Still less can I approve your Lordships' decision to throw in for good measure a restriction on reporting court proceedings in Australia which the Attorney General had never even asked for.

Then he turned his sights on the Government:

Freedom of speech is always the first casualty under a totalitarian regime. Such a regime cannot afford to allow the free circulation of information and ideas among its citizens. Censorship is the indispensable tool to regulate what the public may and what they may not know. The present attempt to insulate the public in this country from information which is freely available elsewhere is a significant step down that very dangerous road. The maintenance of the ban, as more and more copies of the book

Spycatcher enter this country and circulate here, will seem more and more ridiculous. If the government are determined to fight to maintain the ban to the end, they will face inevitable condemnation and humiliation by the European Court of Human Rights in Strasbourg. Long before that they will have been condemned at the bar of public opinion in the free world.

And he concluded with an invitation—to the Prime Minister herself?—of a kind quite unprecedented in the modern law reports:

But there is another alternative. The government will surely want to reappraise the whole *Spycatcher* situation in the light of the views expressed in the courts below and in this House. I dare to hope that they will bring to that reappraisal qualities of vision and of statesmanship sufficient to recognise that their wafer thin victory in this litigation has been gained at a price which no government committed to upholding the values of a free society can afford to pay.

3. The application for permanent injunctions

Such a reappraisal did not take place and the trial for permanent injunctions against the British newspapers eventually opened in the High Court on 23 November 1987, by which time of course the Government had lost for a second time in Sydney. In a judgment delivered on 21 December (before which fresh controversy had been created by an injunction restraining a series of radio programmes entitled *My Country Right or Wrong* concerning the work of the security service),[42] Scott J. expressed the view that the absolute protection being sought for the security service by the Government 'could not be achieved this side of the Iron Curtain'.[43] Scott J. held first that Wright had acted in breach of confidence and that he and his agents could be restrained from publishing in the UK. Security officers must carry secrets with them to the grave. Although the material was no longer secret, still Wright and his agents could be restrained on the basis that he must not now be allowed to profit from his own wrong. This duty of silence was subject to three exceptions. The first was where the

---

[42] In granting the injunction, Owen J. applied the principles laid down by the majority in the House of Lords in *Attorney-General* v. *Guardian Newspapers Ltd.* [1987] 3 All ER 316.

[43] *Attorney-General* v. *Guardian Newspapers Ltd (No. 2)* [1988] 3 All ER 545.

material and information disclosed was trivial; the second was where there was authorization (and here Scott J. held, surprisingly in the light of earlier case-law, that the unreasonable refusal to given authorization would be subject to judicial review[44]); and the third was where the disclosure revealed an iniquity, examples in this case being the plans to assassinate Nasser and the attempts to destabilize the Wilson Government. Otherwise an agent must not disclose. It has to be said, however, that if agents do disclose even in accordance with these permitted exceptions, they do so at some personal risk. These are exceptions only to liability for breach of confidence. Even the disclosure of an iniquity was potentially a breach of the Official Secrets Act carrying a two-year sentence.

The actions in the English courts were not, however, brought against Wright and his agents, but against the press—a point which should not be forgotten. Scott J. held that although the newspapers were also under a duty not to disclose confidential information which they had acquired, unlike the agents themselves the press could publish if it was in the public interest to do so and there were no countervailing public interest considerations which outweighed the public interest in publication. In holding for the *Observer* and the *Guardian*, Scott J. took the view that the articles of 22 and 23 June 1986 did not violate any duty of confidentiality. The articles simply gave a fair report of the forthcoming Australian trial together with some of the allegations which would be made. In this case the public interest in press freedom was held to outweigh the public interest in suppressing the information. The position was different, however, in the case of the *Sunday Times*, which the judge held had acted in breach of its duty of confidentiality. In holding that the public interest in disclosure did not override the requirements of national security, Scott J. said of its editor, Mr Andrew Neil:

neither he nor any member of his editorial staff gave any critical assessment as to what parts of *Spycatcher* raised issues of 'important matters of public interest' on which the public should 'form a judgment for themselves,' and what parts were simply unauthorised disclosures of confidential information. The contents of the extracts published on 12 July 1987 include a good deal of material that could not be represented as

---

[44] Cf. *US* v. *Marchetti* 466 F. 2d 1309 (1972).

raising any issue on which the public should be invited to judge or in respect of which the public interest to be served by disclosure could be thought to outweigh the interests of national security.

The *Sunday Times* was thus held liable to account for its profits made from the publication of 12 July.

Perhaps the crucial point about the decision, however, was that the Crown's application for a permanent injunction failed. The Crown's case for the injunction was based on a number of by now quite unconvincing considerations. Thus, it was argued that unauthorized disclosure would damage the trust which members of the security service should have in each other, that unless restraints are imposed other officers may break faith and go public, other countries will lose confidence in the British security service, the confidence of informers who rely on their identities being kept secret will be damaged, and, remarkably, detriment 'will flow from the publication of information about the methodology, and personnel and organisation' of the security service. The court held for the defendants, however, mainly because of the worldwide dissemination of the book. Anyone with the money and the know-how could easily obtain a copy of the book. And, said Scott J., 'a duty of confidence that operates to keep away from the mass of the people information which is freely available to the more sophisticated or better off is not, I think, a duty that a court of equity would be likely to construct'. So what were the implications? First, it meant that the press were now free to disclose and report on the information contained in the book. Secondly, people were free to import and sell the book; and, thirdly, libraries (which had already been caught by injunctions) were free to stock and lend it. On the other hand, however, Wright could not publish the book in this country.

February 1988 was a bad month for the Government. It lost before the Scottish court in its attempt to restrain the press reporting of information disclosed by Mr Anthony Cavendish, another retired security officer.[45] More troubling perhaps was that the Court of Appeal in England and Wales rejected its fruitless appeal from the decision of Scott J. in the *Spycatcher* case.[46] But

---

[45] *Lord Advocate* v. *The Scotsman Publications*, 1988 SLT 490.
[46] *Attorney-General* v. *Guardian Newspapers Ltd.* (*No. 2*).

although the Court of Appeal upheld Scott J. it did so despite what was perhaps the most remarkable feature to emerge from the entire litigation. Of some public concern are the remarks expressed by Sir John Donaldson, who, as Master of the Rolls, is the senior member of the Court of Appeal, a mantle which he inherited from Lord Denning. Two points in particular may be mentioned here. The first is the suggestion that it was appropriate in some circumstances for the security service to commit criminal offences. Indeed, the Master of the Rolls went so far as to suggest that it was 'absurd' to claim that every breach of the law by the security service amounted to a 'wrongdoing'! Thus,

Let us suppose that the service has information which suggests that a spy may be operating from particular premises. It needs to have confirmation. It may well consider that, if he proves to be a spy, the interests of the nation are better served by letting him continue with his activities under surveillance . . . What is the Service expected to do? A secret search of the premises is the obvious answer.

This possible criminal activity, dismissed merely as 'covert invasions of privacy', was likened to the emergency services who break the law by speeding to the site of an emergency. Happily, however, he could never conceive of physical violence coming into the category of excusable criminal conduct. Nevertheless such comments so publicly expressed so soon after the tercentenary of the Bill of Rights by one of our most senior judges is somewhat surprising. Quite apart from the fact that the victims of this criminal activity may turn out to be innocent and that a 'covert invasion of privacy' suddenly becomes 'burglary' when committed by an unemployed youth in search of money for food, the comments sit uneasily with constitutional principle.

One of the hallmarks of a democratic and civilized society is that government is conducted in accordance with the rule of law. One of the hallmarks of a totalitarian society is that state officials have unrestrained power. Dicey, no radical by a long chalk, pointed out in a passage well known to all first year students of constitutional law that the rule of law 'excludes the idea of any exemption of officials or others from the duty of obedience to the law which governs other citizens or from the jurisdiction of the ordinary tribunals' (Dicey, 1959: 202–3). There is little recognition of this in the passages quoted above, though the principle expressed by Dicey is perhaps the most fundamental of all the liberal values. It was the triumph of this principle which occurred when John Entick successfully claimed that the government does not have the authority to determine the scope of its own power even when questions of state security are at stake.[47] Here is further evidence that that battle will have to be fought and won again. This is not to deny that the security service needs special powers to conduct its surveillance work. But, as is now the case, such powers should be exercised in accordance with legislation approved by Parliament, and the legislation should require officers to show cause why the exercise of such powers are necessary in the circumstances of any particular case. It is not for state officers to carry out such tasks without legal authority and without any accountability. And it is certainly not fitting for one of our most senior judges to be seen to condone a violation of the first principle of the British Constitution. Otherwise, why stop with the security service? On what principled ground can the right to commit criminal offences be confined? Should not every public official be free to commit any criminal offence (short of physical violence—*sed quaere*) if this is necessary for the security of the state, however that may be defined by the government of the day?

The second cause for concern is the attitude to the role of the press in a modern liberal democracy. When the *Sunday Times* published its serialization of *Spycatcher* on 12 July it was fully aware that it would be restrained by injunction if the Government got wind of the plan. So in order to throw the Government off the scent the first edition (some 76,000 copies) was published without the *Spycatcher* extracts. Later editions, however, did contain the extracts, and by the time they came to the Government's attention, it was too late for any action to be taken to restrain the publication. In fact 1.25 million copies were printed with the extracts, and the sales of the *Sunday Times* were slightly above average. Yet despite his claim that he would yield to no one in his belief that the existence of a free press 'is an essential element in maintaining parliamentary democracy and the British way of life

[47] *Entick* v. *Carrington* (1765) 2 Wils. 275.

as we know it', Sir John Donaldson proceeded to admonish the editor of the *Sunday Times* for having adopted this stratagem, even though it was done precisely because the press would have been muzzled by the Government had he not done so. Rather than applaud Mr Neil for his ingenuity in ensuring that both Parliament and the people were informed of the *Spycatcher* allegations, Sir John charged, 'Quite apart from whether it has any consequences in law it was disreputable and irresponsible conduct, unworthy of him and his newspaper.' Contrast with this the Pentagon Papers case where in the US Supreme Court it was said from the Bench that 'far from deserving condemnation for their courageous reporting' the newspapers in that case should be 'commended for serving the purpose that the Founding Fathers saw so clearly'.[48]

Sir John Donaldson's unyielding faith in press freedom did not only prevent him from condemning those who exercise this freedom. In a quite remarkable passage he also proposed the introduction of measures which would strike a blow at the freedom of the press quite unprecedented in modern Britain. At the present time the British press submits to what is known as the D-notice system whereby D-notices are sent by the Services, Press, and Broadcasting Committee to editors requesting a ban on specified subjects relating to national security. To this form of censorship the press not only submits but actively participates. The Committee which issues the notices has more representatives of the press than it has civil servants. Yet as was demonstrated by the *My Country Right or Wrong* affair, approval by the Committee is no guarantee against harassment; and even if a matter has been approved by the Committee it is possible that publication could still lead to prosecution under the Official Secrets Act. Apparently not content even with this degree of censorship, Sir John Donaldson stated in concluding his *Spycatcher* judgment:

Finally, Parliament may wish to reconsider the D notice machinery. It has worked well in the past, but if any part of the media is not only going to ignore it, but also to resort to subterfuges to prevent any adjudication by the courts, the time may have come to think again. Subject to any revision of the Official Secrets Acts, which may be an alternative

[48] *New York Times* v. *US* 403 US 713 (1971).

approach, what, as it seems to me, may now be required is some right in the Home Secretary to issue instructions equivalent to a D notice, but having the force of an ex parte injunction, the media being entitled to appeal to the courts or to some special tribunal to have it set aside or modified, the proceedings necessarily being held in camera.

If this proposal were implemented, it is difficult to see how it would sit properly with any conception of the separation of powers. It would be most unusual for the judicial function to be exercised by a Minister of the Crown in this way particularly on a matter of such importance in which the Government has a clear and direct interest.

Yet despite the strong words of the Master of the Rolls, the Court of Appeal found a majority on all points to agree with Scott J., the first-instance judge. The House of Lords reached a similar conclusion on 13 October 1988 following yet another fruitless but expensive appeal by the Government.[49] The availability of the book in the United States in particular was fatal to the Government's claim about the vital necessity for continuing secrecy. This result was, however, obtained despite a rather disappointing performance by some of the judges involved. Thus the most striking feature of the speeches of the Lords was not the way in which the law was developed or applied, but the gratuitous insults directed at some of the major participants in the dispute. Lord Keith set Mr Wright very firmly in his sights. After saying that he regarded the *Spycatcher* case 'as having established that members and former members of the security service do have a lifelong obligation of confidence owed to the Crown', Lord Keith continued by saying that 'Those who breach it, such as Mr Wright, are guilty of treachery just as heinous as that of some of the spies he excoriates in his book.' In less emotive tones, Lord Jauncey of Tullichettle said that the action of Mr Wright 'reeked of turpitude'. Yet neither of them said a word about the turpitude which Mr Wright claims to have exposed. It would appear that the court was more offended by the whistle-blower than by the treachery of those who allegedly sought actively to undermine the democratic process.

The second notable target for the condemnation of their

---

[49] *Attorney-General* v. *Guardian Newspapers Ltd.* (*No. 2*).

Lordships was (again) the editor of the *Sunday Times*, with his tactics for publication coming under particular scrutiny. Lord Keith referred to him as having employed 'peculiarly sneaky methods' to avoid a restraining injunction; Lord Brightman accused him of having engaged in 'a deceit to hoodwink the government'. Mr Neil stood condemned *despite* the fact that 'there can be no question but that the Crown, had it learned of the intended publication in the *Sunday Times*, would have been entitled to an injunction to restrain it'. For his part Lord Griffiths agreed that 'if Sir Roger Hollis was a spy or if MI6 plotted to kill President Nasser or if a cabal in MI5 had plotted the overthrow of the Wilson government it reveals a very serious state of affairs requiring immediate and effective action to identify and deal with all those concerned with such activities'. So far so good. The impact of this was lessened, however, by the subsequent remark that Lord Griffiths was unable to agree that 'if a member of the service made such an allegation to a journalist that it would necessarily be in the public interest that it should immediately be published in a newspaper'. The ideal solution, he said, would be for the editor to inform the Treasury Solicitor that he was in possession of such information and proposed to publish it. And in a passage which might well stick in the gorges of those who decided the Pentagon Papers case (see above), he said that 'This would enable the government to apply for an injunction so that a judge could decide whether the balance came down in favour of preserving secrecy or publication'! In other words, the ideal solution was censorship of the media by judges. But, for reasons unspecified, Lord Griffiths suspected it was too much to hope that newspaper editors would voluntarily submit to this system of censorship. Nevertheless, he was not short of advice for the press. Thus, where allegations had been made, 'even if the editor concluded that there were serious reasons for believing that the information might be true, he should pause long before publishing it rather than taking it to the responsible minister so that it could be investigated and dealt with without causing unnecessary public disquiet and possibly unjustified loss of confidence in the security services'.

In this case Lord Griffiths had no doubt that it would have been the duty of an editor in the first instance to report the allegations about Hollis, Nasser, and the Wilson plot to the appropriate minister and only then to consider publication in his newspaper if convinced that no effective action had been taken. What Lord Griffiths does not say is that having alerted the responsible minister who chooses to do nothing, the editor is exposing his or her newspaper to litigation in the way that the *Guardian* was treated in the Tisdall case. More significantly and more seriously, the newspaper will also have alerted the Government which would be well placed to take legal action to prevent any publication should its lethargy convince the editor that no effective response has been made. The Government may also be in a position to threaten the use of criminal sanctions, a threat which it will be all the more able to carry out since the replacement of section 2 of the Official Secrets Act 1911 with the much more precise terms of the Official Secrets Act 1989, which we encounter in the next chapter. But remarkable though all of this may be, perhaps the most distressing feature is the apparent assumption behind it all that the press should in some way act as an agent of the Government or should act in the interests of the state, however they should be defined. Newspapers are not, and should not be required to become, ferrets accountable and answerable to the Treasury Solicitor. The function of the press in a democratic society is to inform, scrutinize, and criticize, independently of government. These functions would be irretrievably undermined if a newspaper editor was to run cap in hand to the Treasury Solicitor for permission to publish, regardless of the subject-matter of the story in question.

So although the newspapers finally won their battle in the House of Lords, the victory was far from emphatic. True, it was held that the *Observer* and the *Guardian* had not acted in breach of confidence by their articles of June 1986. True also that no permanent injunctions were granted to restrain future publication by the press of the Wright allegations and that no general injunction was issued restraining the future publication of information derived from Wright or other members or ex-members of the security service. But it is also true that the *Sunday Times* was held to have acted in breach of its duty of confidentiality for the serialization on 12 July 1987 and that the Attorney-General was entitled to an account of profits. And perhaps even more significant is the fact that their Lordships confirmed the existence of a lifelong civil duty of confidence on the part of security service officers, with a corresponding duty owed by the press. These duties are subject to very exceptional qualifications, with the trivia defence admitted by Scott J. having been wiped out by the Lords, and with the public interest defence having been restricted. But *Spycatcher* is significant not only for developing the legal obligations of security service personnel and the press or for the apparent frustration of a judicial branch unable to apply the developing principles to protect the Government from an allegedly treacherous individual. *Spycatcher* is significant also for having been one of the greatest laxatives ever known to the constipated process of national security law reform. We now move in Chapter 6 to consider how this process turned out.

6

A New Framework for National Security and Official Secrecy

THE *Spycatcher* affair both revealed and created a true crisis of confidence in the security services of this country. Taken together with allegations by people such as Mr Anthony Cavendish and others, it at least gave rise to concern about the lack of accountability of the service, the principles governing which were laid down in a Directive issued by the Home Secretary in 1952. But not being a legal body there was no way of ensuring that the service complied with these principles. So while Lord Denning could proclaim that the security service was not 'to be used so as to pry into any man's private conduct, or business affairs: or even into his political opinions, except in so far as they are subversive, that is, they would contemplate the overthrow of the Government by unlawful means' (Denning, 1963), there was no parliamentary or legal accountability to ensure that these boundaries were not breached.[1] Similarly, while Lord Denning could assert that 'it would be intolerable to us to have anything in the nature of a Gestapo or Secret Police to snoop into all that we do', there was a political and legal vacuum to be filled to ensure that the service did not assume this role. The need to respond to *Spycatcher* provided the Government with a rare opportunity to address this

---

[1] The only way the service could be controlled was indirectly through the courts supervising the political decisions which were made on evidence provided by its officers. But the courts were unwilling to interfere. See *R*. v. *Halliday* [1917] AC 260; *Liversidge* v. *Anderson* [1942] AC 260; and *R*. v. *Secretary of State for the Home Department, ex parte Hosenball* [1977] 3 All ER 452.

problem. But although a number of initiatives have been taken to create a new framework for national security and official secrecy, it is seriously open to question whether the response has been adequate.

The Staff Counsellor

The first significant response to *Spycatcher* was the creation of a staff counsellor for the security and intelligence services.[2] In a parliamentary written answer, the Prime Minister said on 2 November 1987 that the counsellor:

will be available to be consulted by any member of the security and intelligence services who has anxieties relating to the work of his or her service which it has not been possible to allay through the ordinary processes of management–staff relations. He will have access to all relevant documents and to any level of management in each service. He will be able to make recommendations to the head of the service concerned. He will also have access to the Secretary of the Cabinet if he wishes and will have the right to make recommendations to him. He will report as appropriate to the heads of the services and will report not less frequently than once a year to me and to my right hon. Friends the Foreign and Commonwealth Secretary and the Home Secretary as appropriate on his activities and on the working of the system.

The Prime Minister also announced that the first person to hold this position would be Sir Philip Woodfield, a man who has spent much of his working life as a senior civil servant in the Home Office, and in the Northern Ireland Office, with a spell as private secretary to the Prime Minister from 1961–5.

This development is disappointing to the extent that it reinforces the tendency towards secrecy rather than towards the public accountability of the service. No matter how serious the complaints or concerns of individual officers, there is still no right to bring such issues to the attention of the public. The fact is that this new arrangement is reinforced by the terms of the Official Secrets Act 1989 whereby it is an offence to disclose any information about

---

[2] This may also have been a response to the serious personnel management defects within the security service which had been identified by the Security Commission in its investigation of the Michael Bettaney affair in 1985.

the activities of the security service. So if the staff counsellor arrangement fails in any individual case, or if the matter is of such significance that it ought in principle to be brought to the attention of the citizens of the Realm whom the service is designed to defend, disclosure will be nevertheless a criminal offence. This is despite what was said by Scott J. in the *Spycatcher* case that it is not an answer to say that an

allegation has been investigated and been found to be groundless. Where that is the case, public belief in the allegation will, no doubt, be reduced. Nor is it . . . necessarily an answer to say that the allegation should not have been made public but should have been reported to some proper investigating authority. In relation to some, perhaps many, allegations made by insiders, that may be the only proper course open to the press. *But the importance to the public of this country of the allegation that members of MI5 endeavoured to undermine and destroy public confidence in a democratically elected government makes the public the proper recipient of the information.*[3] (Emphasis added)

The powers of the staff counsellor were extended on 21 December 1988 by an announcement from the Home Office.[4] It was stated that serving members or former members of the security service would have the opportunity to refer to the counsellor any departmental refusal for an official or former official to publish his or her memoirs. Hitherto, if any member or former member of the security services wished to write material about his or her work, he or she would first talk to a senior official about the plans for publication. Apparently all serving members know to whom they should turn to talk about such matters, and all retired staff have a point of contact with the relevant service. Indeed 'No member of the services is unclear where he or she should turn if he or she wishes to seek clearance.' It was further explained that if authorization cannot be given—because publication will jeopardize national security directly or indirectly—a member or former member of the security services who is dissatisfied may turn to the staff counsellor, who may put the dissatisfied officer in touch with the relevant Secretary of State or the Prime Minister. This hardly seems satisfactory. For the fact is that under the published procedures the staff counsellor will not offer

[3] *Attorney-General* v. *Guardian Newspapers Ltd. (No. 2)* [1988] 3 All ER 545.
[4] 144 HC Debs. 537–8 (21 Dec. 1988).

an independent scrutiny of the decision not to grant clearance, but rather will simply facilitate the process of ministerial review of a departmental decision. It is hardly surprising that not all Members of Parliament were convinced that this system 'gives the sort of cast-iron assurances that someone who wishes to publish has redress'. As one Conservative member asked rhetorically: 'should the sole arbiter of these matters be the former Department of a particular employee? Would it not be possible to have [an independent] publication review board?'

It is perhaps possible in principle that the decision to refuse publication clearance could be subject to judicial review. So much was suggested by Scott J. in the course of the *Spycatcher* litigation,[5] and it may well be necessary in view of the announcement by the Home Secretary that authorization will be rare and will be given only in exceptional circumstances. Whether in practice this would amount to very much is, however, a rather different matter. At best the aggrieved officer will have to satisfy the court that the departmental decision was 'so outrageous in its defiance of logic . . . that no sensible person who had applied his mind to the question to be decided could have arrived at it'.[6] Given the deference of the judiciary to the executive branch on matters of national security, this may be a very tall order.[7] Yet unless a department can be required by judicial review to give clearance for publication, it will be an offence to publish the disputed material just as it is an offence for a serving security officer to reveal any information without lawful authority. Under the Official Secrets Act 1989 it is an offence for a person who is or who has been a member of the security and intelligence services to disclose any information, document, or other article relating to security or intelligence which is in his or her possession by virtue of having been a member of any of those services. And this is to say nothing of the reports that a new contract of employment was being considered by officials at the Cabinet Office and in the Attorney-General's office which was to include a clause warning

---

[5] *Attorney-General* v. *Guardian Newspapers Ltd. (No. 2)*.

[6] *R.* v. *Secretary of State for the Home Department, ex parte Ruddock* [1987] 2 All ER 518.

[7] Cf. *US* v. *Marchetti* 466 F. 2d 1309 (1972) and *Snepp* v. *US* 444 US 507 (1980).

intelligence officers that 'they will forfeit their pension rights if they forfeit their lifelong duty of confidentiality'.[8]

In addition to the criticism of this kind, an even more fundamental objection to the institution of the staff counsellor is that it was done by executive fiat without any parliamentary approval. What is more, the counsellor is not accountable in any sense to Parliament, with the Government having rejected an amendment to its Security Service Bill 1989, proposed by one of its own back-benchers, which would have placed the position on a statutory base and which would have required the counsellor to submit an annual report to the Prime Minister who would be required to lay a copy of it before each House of Parliament. In introducing this amendment, Mr Jonathan Aitken was especially concerned to have the position regulated by statute, noting that 'Some of us do not necessarily approve of Government by written answer'—a reference to the fact that the introduction of the post was announced by a Commons written answer by the Prime Minister. Speakers in support of the amendment emphasized the need for accountability and for information to be provided to Parliament on an annual basis. For its part, however, the Government opposed the amendment, with the Home Office minister explaining that the system was already in place and working well, and did not need to be underpinned by legislation. The security service staff were well aware of the counsellor's existence and of the arrangements for consulting him. But as might be expected this hardly satisfied the Government's critics, one of whom lamented that he did not 'know how much detail we have about Sir Phillip's activities, or about how many members of the service have been to see him, or about what his functions have been. We shall have to take it on trust that everything is going perfectly.'[9]

---

[8] *The Times*, 4 July 1988.
[9] An attempt was also made during the passage of the Official Secrets Act 1989 to introduce a statutory procedure for the review of publications.

The Security Service Act 1989

The second major initiative taken in the post-*Spycatcher* era was the enactment of the Security Service Act 1989.[10] Again, however, rather than leading to the liberalization of the security system, it gives considerable statutory powers to the executive without any effective method of scrutiny and accountability. It is true that the Act makes great progress to the extent that it puts MI5 on a statutory basis for the first time. Thus, section 1 provides that there shall continue to be a security service under the authority of the Secretary of State. It must be pointed out, however, that the statutory base is a very narrow one, on which there is no room for MI6, the other branch of the secret security services of this country.

But although MI5 is thus placed on a statutory basis, any benefit that this brings is lost by the sheer breadth of its statutory functions. Thus, section 1, drafted in very wide terms, also provides that the function of the service 'shall be the protection of national security and, in particular, its protection against threats from espionage, terrorism and sabotage, from the activities of agents of foreign powers and from actions intended to overthrow or undermine parliamentary democracy by political, industrial or violent means'. Also under section 1, it is the function of the service 'to safeguard the economic well-being of the United Kingdom against threats posed by the actions or intentions of persons outside the British Islands'. Indeed such was the concern of the Opposition with these provisions, that they complained that the legislation 'gives the security services the right to do whatever they choose'. Mr Hattersley could not 'imagine any circumstance that is not covered' by the subsection. A matter of particular concern is the fact that an individual or body may be placed under surveillance even though he or she may be engaged

---

[10] Much of what follows is drawn from the parliamentary debates on the Security Service Bill which may be found at 143 HC Debs. 1112 (15 Dec. 1988) (2nd Reading); 145 HC Debs. 180 (17 Jan.) (Committee); 145 HC Debs. 743 (23 Jan.) (Report and 3rd Reading); 504 HL Debs. 859 (27 Feb.) (2nd Reading); 505 HL Debs. 581 (21 Mar.) (Committee); 506 HL Debs. 874 (20 Apr., 27 Apr.) (Report and 3rd Reading).

in perfectly lawful political activity which is not intended to serve any foreign interest. The government refused to accept an amendment based on the Canadian legislation,[11] which would have excluded from the lawful surveillance of the security service those engaged in 'lawful advocacy, protest or dissent'. The fact that the service must not be used to further the interests of any political party does not even begin to address this very significant problem, particularly as it was pointed out in the House of Lords that MI5 is free to act *contrary* to the interests of a political party.

Apart from thus defining the functions of the service in very wide terms, the 1989 Act also equips it with new legal powers. One of the most embarrassing features of the *Spycatcher* case was the allegation that MI5 was burgling its way through London. Even more embarrassing perhaps was the apparent judicial tolerance, not to say endoresement, of such conduct. Any threat to the rule of law thereby revealed has been addressed, not by stopping the practice, but by giving legal authority for it in the shape of burglar warrants. The procedure is modelled closely on that governing warrants for the interception of communications. But given that the new procedure involves an interference with property it is all the more remarkable particularly in light of the rather cavalier disregard of the need for any effective safeguards. On an application by the security service, the Home Secretary may issue a warrant authorizing the taking of such action as is specified in the warrant in respect of any property so specified. These words should be looked at carefully. They authorize the Home Secretary to permit any form of interference with any property. This he may do if he thinks it necessary to obtain information which is likely to be of substantial value in assisting the service to discharge any of its functions and which 'cannot reasonably be obtained by other means'.

The contrast here with the legislation in Canada governing the Canadian Security Intelligence Service (CSIS) is profound. Although burglar warrants are authorized there too, these may be granted only on the authority of a judge. An application for such a warrant may be made by the service only with the approval of the Solicitor-General of Canada. Judicial authorization as opposed to

---

[11] The relevant Canadian legislation, to which reference is made in this section, is the *Canadian Security Intelligence Service Act*, 1984.

political authorization is not purely a matter of form. Apart from providing a more independent control of whether the conditions for granting a warrant have been met, it also provides an independent means of ensuring that the warrant was granted to promote the statutory functions of the service. It would thus help to ensure that these statutory functions were interpreted and determined in accordance with law. Yet an amendment requiring judicial authorization of warrants was rejected by the Government, arguably for the very reasons that it should have been endorsed. Thus, Mr John Patten said:

it is essential to be able to deal with applications for warrants as quickly as possible. If we adopted some scheme for judicial intervention . . . argument would be on the basis of written papers. The judge might have no previous understanding of or experience in Security Service issues. He will have to make a first judgment on issues that have never been before him . . . Secretaries of State will at least—it is an important at least— have had considerable briefing on the Security Service and how it works. The judge will have had no previous experience in the consideration of Security Service work, or knowledge of the policy or background to the work.

Later in the same speech, Mr Patten was to claim that the 'judiciary should not become involved in the day-to-day operational decisions of the Security Service' and that 'to take decisions about warrants requires an appreciation of the overall objectives of the Security Service and the considerations relating to the well-being and security of this country'. Goodness knows how the security services in Canada and other countries manage to operate effectively against such odds!

This, however, is not the only defect of the warrant procedure. Unlike in the 1989 Act, the Canadian procedures require the application to be accompanied by a sworn statement (in Britain the application need not even be in writing) which states

(a) the facts relied on to justify the belief that a warrant is necessary to investigate a threat to national security;

(b) that other investigative procedures have been tried and failed or why it appears that they would be unlikely to succeed.

And unlike Britain where the new Act authorizes the taking of any action in respect of any property, the Canadian legislation restricts a warrant to authorize entry, search, seizure, or installation where this is done for the purpose of obtaining 'any information, record, document or thing'. Another major difference with the British procedure is that the Canadian legislation requires a warrant to specify:

(a) the type of information, records, documents, or things authorized to be obtained;

(b) the identity of the person who has possession of the information, records, documents, or things to be obtained;

(c) the persons or classes of persons to whom the warrant is directed;

(d) a general description of the place where the warrant may be executed;

(e) the period for which the warrant is in force; and

(f) such terms and conditions as the judge considers advisable in the public interest.

The 1989 Act, in contrast, permits warrants to be granted 'authorising the taking of such action as is specified in the warrant'.

The 1989 Act is indeed a remarkable piece of legislation. Drafted by the Home Office, it allows the Home Secretary to determine the scope of his own legislation. A third major cause for concern about the Act then—apart from the wide definition of the functions of the service and the lack of any safeguards in the very significant power to issue warrants for the interference with private property—is the failure adequately to confront the need for accountability and review of the activities of the service. It is true that the Act offers two gestures in this direction, but neither is adequate on its own or indeed in combination with the other. Both are in fact modelled very closely on the 'safeguards' in the Interception of Communications Act 1985 which seems to have been the inspiration generally for the Security Service Act. The first 'safeguard' is the provision for the appointment by the Prime Minister of a law lord (active or retired) to act as the Security Service Commissioner. Among the duties which he or she will be required to perform is that to keep under review the exercise by the Home Secretary of his powers to grant warrants for the interference with private property. This means that in principle the Commissioner could seek to ensure that warrants were granted only to the extent that they were necessary to assist the service to discharge its functions. In practice, however, this form of scrutiny and review is fraught with difficulty. First, and most obviously, the Commissioner operates at too late a stage in the proceedings to be genuinely effective. There is, for example, no review at the time a warrant is issued so that any intervention (which in any event may well be fortuitous) will necessarily occur after a warrant has been improperly or illegally issued. Secondly, the Commissioner has only the power to keep matters under review: he or she has no power to require a Minister to desist from any practices which are improper. This means for example that if the Commissioner believes the Minister to be exceeding his or her powers—say by keeping under surveillance an organization which poses no threat to national security—there are no executive measures which may be taken to stop the practice. It is true that the Commissioner must make an annual report on the discharge of his or her functions to the Prime Minister. But therein lies a third problem. The Prime Minister need not lay before Parliament a copy of any part of this report if it appears to him or her that publication would be prejudicial to the continued discharge of the functions of the service.

The second 'safeguard' against abuse is also seriously limited. This is the creation of a tribunal—similar to the Interception of Communications Tribunal—to investigate complaints. Under the Act, the Tribunal shall consist of between three and five members, each of whom must be a legal practitioner of at least ten years' standing. Appointment is by the Prime Minister for five-year periods, this being renewable. So like the telephone-tapping Tribunal there is no security of tenure. It is true that a member of the Tribunal cannot be removed from office without the approval of both Houses of Parliament. But anyone who fails to provide service which is not politically satisfactory could well find that he or she is no longer required. Yet the problems with the Tribunal are not confined to the fact that it is appointed and reappointed by the Prime Minister. Questions must also be asked about its rather limited powers. It is true that any person 'may complain to the Tribunal if he is aggrieved by anything which he believes the Service has done in relation to him or to any property of his'. But in at least one of the three types of complaint with which it may deal, what is given with one hand is taken away with the other. Thus, one of the grounds for investigation is that the complainant has been the subject of inquiries by the service. If such a complaint is made, the Tribunal shall consider whether the service had reasonable grounds to institute or continue enquiries against the complainant in the discharge of its functions. The Tribunal has, however, no power to determine whether the service acted reasonably in deciding whether to institute or to continue enquiries about 'a category of persons'. The Tribunal thus has no power to determine whether it is reasonable to conclude that groups like CND, the Communist Party, or the Labour Party pose any threat to national security. And indeed the Act goes even further by providing expressly that 'the Tribunal shall regard the Service as having reasonable grounds for deciding to institute or continue inquiries about the complainant if the Tribunal consider that the Service had reasonable grounds for believing him to be a member of that category'.

It is difficult to see what possible justification there can be for the exclusion of any right to complain about the exercise of this power by the security service. But whatever the reason, the drafting of the Act is such that it is difficult to see what the Tribunal could do in the performance of its first investigative function. Indeed, the same is true, though perhaps less so, in the case of the other two functions of the Tribunal, one of which is to consider complaints that the service has disclosed information about the complainant to a prospective employer. It is astonishing to note that the Tribunal is not empowered to question whether the service acted properly in disclosing the information. Rather, having found that the information has been disclosed, the Tribunal may only determine whether the Service had reasonable grounds for believing the information to be true. So there is no power to investigate the malicious, unreasonable, or discriminatory use of the truth (or indeed of that which reasonably but wrongly is believed to be true). That the need for such power of investigation exists is illustrated by the case of Isabel Hilton who was denied a job by the BBC after a negative MI5 vetting. Her sin, it seems, was to be the secretary, for eight months or so, of the innocuous Scotland–China Association. Yet if the most important function is denied the Tribunal under its second investigative power, the limits on its third function further confirm that its members would be ill-advised to give up any full-time jobs that they hold at the time of their appointment. The Tribunal has no power to deal with but may only refer to the Commissioner any complaint about the improper issuing of burglar warrants, and in determining whether the warrant was properly issued or renewed the Commissioner shall utilize 'the principles applied by a court on an application for judicial review'. The relevant principles are those which were laid down in the Joan Ruddock telephone-tapping case where, as we saw, the judge asked whether the decision of the Home Secretary in granting the warrant was 'so outrageous in its defiance of logic or accepted moral standards that no sensible person who applied his mind to the question to be decided could have arrived at it'.[12] In the area of national security, given the tradition of judicial restraint in this field, it seems unlikely that the Tribunal and the Commissioner will disturb many of the decisions of the service which might not be tolerated by a more demanding standard of scrutiny.

As a result of its very limited powers it is highly improbable that the Tribunal will be called upon frequently to take any of the remedial measures (including compensation) authorized by the Act. But not only has the Government again appointed a Tribunal with very little or no effective powers, it has also insulated the Tribunal (and the Commissioner) from judicial review in the ordinary courts. The Act mirrors the Interception of Communications Act 1985 by including what was until then unprecedented, namely a clause empowering the Tribunal and (on this occasion) the Commissioner to define the limits of their own powers. Thus the Act provides that 'The decisions of the Tribunal and the Commissioner . . . (including decisions as to their jurisdictions) shall not be subject to appeal or liable to be questioned in any court.' This means that if the Tribunal or the Commissioner take an ultra-cautious approach either to the already very conservative principles of judicial review, or to the disposal of complaints which are held to be well founded (there are no limits on the power to award compensation), there is nothing which the

[12] R. v. Home Secretary, ex parte Ruddock.

aggrieved complainant may do. On the other hand, in the unlikely event of the Government being troubled by an over-enthusiastic use of these powers, it is of course free not to renew the appointments of the individuals in question. Yet despite the Government's best efforts, judicial review of the security service and its use of the 1989 Act may not be completely excluded. In view of the fact that neither the Tribunal nor the Commissioner has jurisdiction to deal with complaints that a body of persons is subject to surveillance by the service, it would be open to an organization or an individual to seek judicial review of any such decision on the ground that it is not permitted by the (admittedly wide) powers of the service under the Act, or that it is an unreasonable use of these powers. It may indeed be noted that the collection of information and intelligence about individuals is not authorized by legislation—as it is in Canada. This must give rise to serious questions about whether the security service is complying with Article 8 of the ECHR in the sense that part of what it does is still not prescribed by law. As the Malone case made clear in the context of telephone-tapping, it is no longer sufficient or appropriate for the Government to claim that that which is not prohibited by law is permitted by law and therefore prescribed by law.

But back to judicial review of the decision to place under surveillance. Although in principle this is a power which may well be reviewable, the barriers to success were clearly illustrated in a decision of the High Court of Australia reported in 1982. The Australian Security and Intelligence Agency (ASIO) is governed by legislation which defines its functions as follows:

(a) to obtain, correlate and evaluate intelligence relevant to security;

(b) for purposes relevant to security and not otherwise, to communicate any such intelligence to such persons, and in such manner, as are appropriate to those purposes; and

(c) to advise Ministers and authorities of the Commonwealth in respect of matters relating to security, in so far as those matters are relevant to their functions and responsibilities.

The plaintiff organization in *Church of Scientology* v. *Woodward*[13] will be well known to students of English law. Described as

[13] (1982) 43 ALR 587.

'a religious organisation engaged in the practice, promotion, propagation, teaching and application of the Scientology Religion',[14] it complained that it had been the subject of ASIO surveillance even though the obtaining and evaluation of information about its activities could not have been relevant to security within the meaning of the Act, this phrase having been defined as the protection of the people from espionage, sabotage, subversion, terrorism, and active measures of foreign intervention. The question before the court was one of principle, namely whether the activities of ASIO could be the subject of judicial review or whether the governing legislation when taken as a whole displayed a clear legislative intention to shield the organization from such scrutiny. Surprisingly perhaps, by a majority the High Court of Australia (reversing the first instance judge) held that judicial review was available in principle, being influenced in this decision by prominent policy considerations. Thus Murphy J. asserted that the need for control over ASIO 'is demonstrated by the history of such organizations here and overseas. Characteristically from time-to-time they exceed, and misuse, their powers.' He also claimed that experience had shown that for 'a free society to exist intelligence organizations must be subject to administrative supervision and amenable to legal process'. Given these concerns of the majority (rarely, if ever, articulated by a British court, though the anxieties here are no less real), it was unsurprising that they should find unattractive the submission that, save for bad faith, a decision by the organization 'to engage in a particular activity is not open to review merely because a mistake is made as to whether that activity is within its charter'.

In so holding the majority was undaunted by the prospect that 'the revelation of security intelligence in legal proceedings would be detrimental to national security'. It did not follow from the national security dimension of the case that 'ASIO's activities should be completely free from judicial review'. Nevertheless, the Court had no illusions as to the impact of its decision, it being clear that there would be major obstacles to the bringing of a successful action in practice. The first is the standard of review which the court would apply. Thus, while 'the difficulties

[14] (1980) 31 ALR 609 at 610.

inherent in questions of national security do not affect the justiciability of the issues', 'they are of major importance in determining the sufficiency of evidence bearing on those issues'. In order to succeed in a case of this kind the plaintiff would have to show that there was 'no reasonable basis for concluding that the actions in question have a real connection with security'. So far as Mason J. was concerned, this would be 'a formidable task'. A second and equally serious set of barriers were 'the restrictions imposed upon discovery in aid of proving, and upon the admission of evidence in proof of, what is and what is not relevant to security'. One reason why judicial review was held to be available in a national security context was that to conclude otherwise 'would be to ignore the protection which is given by the doctrine of Crown privilege to information the disclosure of which is prejudicial to national security'. But while Crown privilege was thus used on the one hand not to exclude judicial review, it is clear on the other hand that it would effectively kill off any such action at a very early stage. As Mason J. also pointed out, 'Crown privilege will almost certainly exclude from consideration some evidence that is material and would otherwise assist the court'. Brennan J. was even more forthright, commenting that 'discovery would not be given against the Director-General save in a most exceptional case'. He continued, drawing heavily on English authority in the following terms:

The secrecy of the work of an intelligence organization which is to counter espionage, sabotage, etc is essential to national security, and the public interest in national security will seldom yield to the public interest in the administration of civil justice (*R*. v. *Lewes Justices; Ex parte Home Secretary*). Indeed, even if the plaintiff were in possession of evidence relevant to the activities of the Organization and the matters in respect of which those activities were being pursued, the evidence might be inadmissible. In *D*. v. *National Society for the Prevention of Cruelty to Children*, Lord Simon of Glaisdale observed: 'So the law says that, important as it is to the administration of justice that all relevant evidence should be adduced to the court, such evidence must be withheld if, on the balance of public interest, the peril of its adduction to national security outweighs its benefit to the forensic process . . .'

Although it is disappointing that the majority should have qualified their decision in such a restrictive way, there is no reason to believe that the English courts would behave any differently. Assuming that they too hold the powers of MI5 to be justiciable, the standard of review would be that of Taylor J. in the *Ruddock* case (not dissimilar to the approach of Mason J.) while the problem of discovery would be just as acute in Australia as it is in England, bearing in mind too that the authorities cited by Brennan J. were decisions of the House of Lords. When all is said and done then, the Security Service Act is a rather disturbing document. It places the security service on a statutory footing, but gives it very wide statutory functions and fails to constrain the service with any meaningful system of accountability. There is effectively no review of the decision to place a body of persons under surveillance, despite Article 8 of the European Convention on Human Rights with regard to which it has been stated judicially that 'in view of the risk that a system of secret surveillance for the protection of national security poses of undermining or even destroying democracy on the ground of defending it, the Court must be satisfied that there exist adequate and effective guarantees against abuse'.[15] The Court would look long and hard to find any such guarantees in the 1989 Act. But it is not only the decision to place under surveillance which is a cause for concern. Equally troubling is the lack of any effective review or accountability of how any information is used or as to how it is obtained. There is, for example, no commitment that security service officers will be prosecuted if they burgle without a warrant. Not that they should ever need to, with the executive act of burglary being authorized by the executive branch of government subject to minimalist standards of scrutiny by a tribunal which is not permitted to publish reasons for its decisions. At the very best, there is no cause for the optimism or the complacency of the Home Office which appears to think that it is enough to introduce a bill to place the security service on a statutory footing without seeming to understand that the contents of such a bill are just as important.

Yet while the Government may be complacent and indifferent, it can hardly claim that its attention has not been drawn to the absence of any effective system of accountability or control. Even

---

[15] *Leander* v. *Sweden* (1987) 9 EHRR 433.

a former MI5 official joined the debate by contending that change was necessary in the arrangements for the scrutiny of the service. In Committee a number of amendments were tabled from both its own benches and from the Opposition side in an attempt to strengthen the supervision and scrutiny of the service. One proposal, from the Tory back-bencher Richard Shepherd, was based on the legislation in Canada which provides for the creation of a Security Intelligence Review Committee (Mr Shepherd had proposed a Security Service Review Committee). The Committee of between three and five Privy Councillors is appointed by the Queen's representative in Canada after consultations between the Prime Minister of Canada and the leader in the House of Commons of each political party having at least twelve members in that House. Members of the Review Committee are appointed for renewable periods of five years and have the function of reviewing generally the performance by the service of its duties and functions. The Committee may also deal with any complaints made by any person with respect to any act or thing done by the service. The advantages of this system over that contained in the 1989 Act are obvious: appointment to the review body is not dominated by the Prime Minister, and its powers of review are wide and unconstrained. These points were not, however, very fully brought out in debate and the amendment was quickly dismissed by the Home Secretary. The Home Office was more concerned, it seems, to respond to the amendment from the Labour benches which was for the creation of a Commons Select Committee, also to review generally the performance by the service of its duties and functions under the Act. There is nothing particularly pernicious about this proposal, particularly when it is considered that in the United States legislative scrutiny has operated for more than a decade. There are intelligence committees of both the Senate and the House of Representatives, each with fifteen members and each with a large staff. It is also the case that since 1986 there has been scrutiny by a joint parliamentary committee of the Australian security service, ASIO.[16]

The amendment had been moved by Mr Hattersley first to remove much of the party political controversy that currently

---

[16] See Australian Security Intelligence Organisation Amendment Act 1986.

surrounds MI5's work; secondly to remove the fear that MI5 operates illegally, unlawfully, or improperly; and thirdly to increase the efficiency of the service by putting it in touch with the real world. More important perhaps was Hattersley's contention that 'to ensure sensible, acceptable and democratic control, the House needs something more than just the supervision of one Minister'. Indeed, the revelation in the debate on these amendments about the weakness of the existing system of political control of the service by the Home Secretary indicated that the need for this amendment was even greater than had been imagined. It is well established that neither the Prime Minister nor the Home Secretary will answer questions in the House about the operations of the service, but it is nevertheless a shock to learn that

One of the problems for a Home Secretary or a Foreign Secretary is that information available about problems in MI5 and MI6 is not communicated to new Ministers. Therefore, when it came to appointing a new head of MI5, in which the Home Secretary and the Prime Minister play a part, we were not informed, but we now discover that in 1972 there was a great concern in the Home Office about what was going on in MI5. The new Home Secretary was not told.

It seems hard to argue with Mr Merlyn Rees in his assessment that information about the service should be available on a long-term basis and should straddle governments. But this alone would hardly be sufficient particularly in view of claims made in the House of Commons by Jonathan Aitken and Rupert Allason respectively that 'even people as close as the Cabinet Secretary have for many years past had no awareness, or no adequate awareness, of what is going on in the security services' and that

Until fairly recent times the attitude of the Home Secretary has been 'I do not wish to know about these things'. When Security Service officers have had to conduct some clandestine entry they have obtained permission, but have done so through the Permanent Under-Secretary. I know that on at least one occasion the Home Secretary was consulted, but that was on the basis that he could more or less deny that he knew what was going to happen if anything went wrong.

Yet even if there is no substance in any of these allegations, a close working knowledge by the Home Secretary and senior civil servants is hardly an acceptable substitute for independent scrutiny and accountability. But in a passage which reads like support for the amendment rather than opposition to it, the Home Secretary complained that

The Select Committee which [Mr Hattersley] proposes would be able to examine any aspect relating to the Security Service. The amendment suggests that the very existence of the Security Service would depend on that examination. The Select Committee proposed by the Opposition would be able, at any time and in any way, to question all the actions undertaken by the Security Service. All its individual operations and all its most sensitive and secret techniques, all its information, all its expenditure and management decisions would be open to investigation. In practice . . . next to nothing could be kept from the Select Committee.

It soon transpired that the concern of the Home Office was that 'the service and the nation' would be undermined 'as a result of information passing into the Select Committee's hands'. Presumably the fear was of the misuse of confidential information by Members of Parliament who it seems are not to be trusted. Yet this point had been anticipated convincingly by several speakers. It was demonstrated that Departments of State appear to be much less watertight and leakproof than Commons' Committees. Secondly, it was pointed out that existing Select Committees—on Defence and Foreign Affairs—already deal with sensitive material without any untoward consequences. And, thirdly, it was claimed that 'parallel systems allowing members of legislatures to investigate security matters and to maintain overall supervision of security services operate successfully in other democracies without any leakage of essential information'. But the Home Office was inflexible. The Government was unwilling to surrender the autonomy of the security service and was unwilling to lose its ultimate control over the system of scrutiny. The last word should perhaps be left with Jonathan Aitken, a critic from the Government's side of the House:

Britain is now the only democracy in the English-speaking world that has no form of independent oversight of its security services. Today we are advancing arguments that one day are bound to triumph. In the light of experience, it is unacceptable for the Home Secretary of the day to continue to demand that he and he alone, with the assistance of the Prime Minister, should monitor and supervise our security services.

The Official Secrets Act 1989

A third major consequence of the *Spycatcher* case has been the implementation at long last of proposals to replace the much criticized and badly discredited section 2 of the Official Secrets Act 1911. Regardless of the factors which led to this reform, and regardless of whether it is an adequate measure, the Government must be credited for having taken a step which began as long ago as 1971, the year that Lord Franks of Headington was appointed by Mr Edward Heath's Government to chair a committee (which included William Deedes, Merlyn Rees, Ian Trethowan, and Brian Walden) to review the operation of section 2 of the Official Secrets Act 1911 and to make recommendations. The committee had its origins in the Report of the Fulton Committee on the Civil Service which concluded in 1968 that the administrative process was 'surrounded by too much secrecy' and that 'the public interest would be better served if there were a greater amount of openness'. With this in mind, the Report proposed that 'the Government should set up an enquiry to make recommendations for getting rid of unnecessary secrecy in this country. Clearly the Official Secrets Acts would need to be included in such a review' (Fulton, 1968). The matter was picked up by the Conservative Party in 1970 when in its election manifesto for that year it promised to eliminate unnecessary secrecy concerning the workings of government and to review the operation of the Official Secrets Acts.

1. The Franks Report

Despite its distinguished membership, the Franks Committee's Report was a very disappointing document, particularly in view of the absence of any theoretical analysis of the problem which it addressed. It did recognise the need for openness on the one hand (without really explaining why). But it also recognized a need for secrecy on the other, for 'Even a democratic government requires a measure of secrecy for some of its functions, as a means whereby it can better carry out its duties on behalf of the people.' The concern of Franks was to strike a proper balance between these two competing interests, which in the view of the Committee would be best achieved not by retaining or repealing section 2, but by replacing it with something more narrowly drawn which would as a result catch a much narrower range of information within the net of the criminal law, the criminal sanctions being retained 'only to protect what is of real importance'. Specifically, it was proposed that section 2 should be repealed and replaced by a new statute called the Official Information Act which would apply only to official information which:

(*a*) is classified information relating to defence or internal security, or to foreign relations, or to the currency or to the reserves, the unauthorized disclosure of which would cause *serious* injury to the interests of the nation; or

(*b*) is likely to assist criminal activities or to impede law enforcement; or

(*c*) is a Cabinet document; or

(*d*) has been entrusted to the Government by a private individual or concern.

These proposals would require the introduction of long overdue legal procedures for the proper classification of documents.

The great breakthrough of the Franks Report was the proposal that the criminal law should be withdrawn from much of the area which it occupied under section 2. One problem with the Report, however, which was to influence every subsequent proposal for reform, was that, even with reform, the criminal law would continue to cover a considerable area, while another was that the effective operation of the proposed legislation left too much input to the executive branch of government. Thus it was proposed that the question whether disclosure would cause serious injury would be left to the Minister to decide, rather than to the jury. So if a prosecution was to be brought, the Minister would issue a certificate stating that the document had been properly classified in the sense that its unauthorized disclosure would cause serious injury to the interests of the nation. Such a certificate would be conclusive evidence that the document had been classified within the meaning of the Act, that is to say that the Minister would have the power to determine what might be the central question in the case, that disclosure would cause serious injury to the national interest. Given this control over the process by the executive, it was particularly important that there should have been adequate defences available to an accused especially in cases where the Minister's stranglehold was abused. Yet a further defect of Franks was the failure to deliver an effective defence. In particular there was to be no defence that the information was already in the public domain, and no public interest defence with the provision in the old section 2 (permitting disclosure where it was the duty of the accused to disclose in the interests of the state) to go without question. Moreover, the newspapers would still be guilty of a criminal offence if they published information known to be classified. As a bench-mark for reform then, the Franks Report is not a particularly auspicious document. To say that the 1989 Official Secrets Act is more liberal is not to say a great deal.

2. The new categories of protected information

There were powerful arguments in favour of the repeal of section 2 derived from, first, the right of people to be informed by those in whom they place trust as governors, secondly the right to freedom of expression, and thirdly the fact that there were sanctions for disclosure already provided for by the law. At the very least, such arguments suggest that if section 2 was to be replaced rather than simply repealed, it should be by a very narrowly and very carefully drafted substitute. The Home Office did, indeed, suggest that the number of areas where disclosure would harm the public interest to such an extent that criminal sanctions are necessary 'is in fact small' (Home Office, 1988a: 7). But the Government has not been faithful to this concern. It has replaced the catch-all section 2 with a measure which is admittedly confined to six types of information, but which nevertheless is very widely drafted in its application to this information. So despite being aware of the need to strike a proper balance and of the dangers of legislation which is too all-embracing, it is strongly arguable that in the Official Secrets Act 1989 the Government fell far short of finding that balance in this area.

The first category of information protected by the new Act is that relating to security and intelligence. It is true that the new measure is an improvement on the Conservatives' ill-fated Official Information Bill of 1979 which proposed that the disclosure by any person of any information relating to security and intelligence would have been an offence. The new arrangements, although narrower, have nevertheless given rise to much criticism. As enacted, the 1989 Act makes it an offence for any member of the security and intelligence services to disclose any information relating to security or intelligence which he or she has acquired by virtue of his or her position as a member of these services. So it will automatically be an offence for any member (or former member) of the security services to disclose any information, whatever its nature and even though it does not cause harm. The same applies to anyone who is notified that he or she is subject to the provisions of the Act, a measure which would presumably operate to catch within the web Telecom engineers engaged in the business of wire-tapping. But that is not all. It is also an offence for a person who is or who has been a civil servant or a government contractor to make a damaging disclosure of any information relating to security or intelligence. For this purpose, a disclosure is damaging if it causes damage to the work of the security and intelligence services; or if it is information which is such that its unauthorized disclosure would be likely to cause such damage; or if it is information which falls within a class or description the unauthorized disclosure of which would be likely to cause damage to the work of the security and intelligence services. So, in this last case, disclosure may be an offence even though it too does not cause harm, and even though disclosure of the specific information in question is not likely to cause harm. Mere membership of a particular class is enough. In the White Paper, the Government explained that in order to satisfy the test of harm in some cases, evidence would have to be adduced 'which involves a disclosure which is as harmful as or more harmful than the disclosure which is the subject of the prosecution'. The class or description clause meets this concern by allowing 'the arguments before the court to be less specific'. All that need be said here is that the case would have been rather more convincing if the Government had secured the repeal of section 8 of the Official Secrets Act 1920 which allows for the hearing of official secrets cases in camera.

The second category of protection relates to the damaging disclosure by a Crown servant or government contractor of any information relating to defence. For this purpose both the terms 'damaging disclosure' and 'defence' are defined to include in the former case anything which endangers the interests of the UK abroad. In the case of the latter, the term defence is defined to mean over twenty different things from the size of the armed forces—which should surely be common knowledge—to the state of readiness of those forces. This is despite the experience of the Second World War which illustrated the danger of an absolute protection of this kind. It has been pointed out on several occasions now how important it was for government officials to leak information to Duncan Sandys and Winston Churchill in 1938 about our lack of preparedness for the Second World War. Mr Sandys was threatened with prosecution then (presumably for receiving the information), even though, in the words of Mr Edward Heath during the Commons debate on the Bill, he 'was absolutely right and was finally shown to be right'. Nevertheless, the 1989 Act does in fact retain the criminal law for cases such as this. It may also be an offence now for the *Daily Telegraph* to repeat its front page story of 20 April 1989 about a shortage of soldiers in British infantry battalions. This appeared under a headline, 'Army "frontline" battalions undermanned. Recruiting crisis causes concern over standards'. The mere possibility that this could be an offence is bizarre. It is perhaps not so strange that the Ministry of Defence should not want many of the other kinds of protected information to be disclosed such as that relating to military operations. On the other hand, the sinking of the *General Belgrano* and the Ponting affair suggest that in at least some instances it may not always be reasonable to use the criminal law to prosecute such disclosures, and that there is a need to ensure that those who fight our battles do so in a manner which does not repel those on whose behalf they purport to act.

The third category of protection relates to the damaging disclosure by a Crown servant or government contractor of any information relating to international relations or any confidential information which was obtained from another state or international organization. For this purpose a disclosure will be damaging if it endangers the interests of Britain abroad, or seriously obstructs the promotion or protection by the UK of those interests, or endangers the safety of British citizens abroad. The phrase 'the interests of the UK' is not defined but presumably the Government expects the courts to give it the same meaning as has been given to a similar phrase in sections 1 and 2 of the 1911 Act; that is to say, the interests of the UK are the interests of the UK as determined by the government of the day. So the mere disclosure of information which will seriously obstruct (in a manner unspecified) the promotion of the interests of the state as determined by the government will be an offence if it relates to international relations. This too is remarkably widely defined to mean not only information relating to relations between Britain and other states and international organizations, but also information 'relating to a state other than the United Kingdom or to an international organisation which is capable of affecting the relations of the United Kingdom with another state or with an international organisation'. So it will be an offence to disclose information about the United States if this disclosure is *capable* of affecting the relations between Britain and America if that disclosure is damaging in the sense that it seriously obstructs the promotion of the interests of the United Kingdom abroad. One effect of this generally very wide drafting is that it could be an offence to disclose information from the US to the British government that an airline hijack is suspected, or that a ship is carrying highly toxic waste if it is believed (however wrongly) that such disclosure might induce the US not to entrust Britain with confidential information in the future. Although it is an offence to disclose where the safety of the public will be endangered, public safety is not so important that disclosure will be a defence. It is true that as a result of a Lords amendment this aspect of the Act is not as far-reaching as originally drafted. Nevertheless, it still appears to place a cordon sanitaire around the Foreign Office, just as the previous section does for the Ministry of Defence, and the one before that for the security service.

The fourth and fifth categories of protection seem designed for the work of the police, the security services again, and departments in the Home Office, though it must be said immediately that the provisions seem largely if not wholly unnecessary. Thus it is an offence for a Crown servant or government contractor to disclose information which results in the commission of an offence, facilitates an escape from legal custody, or impedes the prevention or detection of offences or the arrest or prosecution of suspected offenders. The White Paper rightly pointed out that it is 'clearly sensible' to inhibit the disclosure of information of this kind. But the fact is that the disclosure of this information would in all but the most marginal cases be an offence anyway. This is particularly true given the defence under the Act that the accused did not know, and had no reasonable cause to believe that disclosure would have any of the prohibited effects. So the Act is aiming mainly at deliberate and intentional disclosure of a kind which would normally give rise to a prosecution for aiding and abetting the commission of the principal offence or for perverting the course of justice. The only possible reason for the inclusion of this provision is to give an insubstantial bill some ballast. The same criticism can be made, with only slightly less force, of the other part of section 4. This makes it an offence to disclose any information obtained by reason of the interception of any communication gathered by virtue of a warrant issued under the Interception of Communications Act 1985. It is also an offence to disclose any information obtained by reason of a warrant issued under the Security Service Act 1989. Yet by section 1 of the Official Secrets Act 1989 it is already an offence for a member of the security service to disclose any such information, and it is already an offence for any other Crown servant to disclose such information if it will cause damage to the work of the security and intelligence services.

The sixth and final category of protected information relates to information entrusted in confidence by the British government to other states or international organizations. This is in some respects a rather startling provision which seeks to prevent the publication in this country of information whose confidentiality has been blown. Specifically, section 6 applies to any information relating to security or intelligence, defence or international relations which has been communicated in confidence by or on behalf of the UK to another state or to an international organization. It is an offence to make a damaging disclosure of such information (if it is not already an offence by the preceding provisions of the Act) if the information has come into the possession of the accused by an unauthorized disclosure from the state or organization to whom the material or information has been transmitted. What this means in practice is that if a civil servant or official of a foreign state leaks information given by the British government to that state, it could be unlawful to disclose that information here. Yet the information may, for example, be reported by newspapers all over the world and as such it could be available to any British citizen who travels to any other part of the world. Yet it will be an offence for newspapers or the broadcasting authorities in this country to inform the British people of what is known to everyone else. The information in question could pose no threat to national security, but might simply be governmental position papers seeking to justify to bodies such as the ILO and the EEC why it continues to act in breach of international law. Presumably it will be for the jury to determine whether government embarrassment is sufficiently damaging to support a conviction. And it will be for the newspapers to determine whether they should take this risk. We now turn to consider some of the wider implications of the 1989 Act for the press.

3. Liability of the press

An important feature of the Official Secrets Act is that liability is not confined to the discloser, though he or she will clearly be guilty if the release of the information is contrary to his or her official duty. Not even disclosure to an MP is excused. Future Clive Pontings should beware. So far as the press is concerned, it is true that the mere receipt of information is no longer criminal. But the subsequent disclosure of information by someone to whom information has been unlawfully disclosed may be an offence with only a drafting 'cock-up' stopping liability from being as wide as the Government planned. The obvious targets here are newspaper editors who will be liable if they have reasonable cause to believe that the information is protected against disclosure. The government has explained that

what justifies making the unauthorised disclosure of certain information a criminal offence is the degree of harm to the public interest in which it is likely to result. Since the unauthorised disclosure of such information by, say, a newspaper may be as harmful as disclosure of the same information by a Crown servant, the Government believes that it would not be sufficient for the new legislation to apply only to disclosure by Crown servants. (Home Office, 1988a: 12)

On the other hand, however, the continuing place of newspapers in this net is a cause for some concern. A notable omission from the discussion in the White Paper or subsequently in the deliberations of the Government was any appreciation of the constitutional role of the press. The Franks Report was equally disappointing on this score—'A secret is a secret' and if 'the citizen knows that he is in possession of a secret but chooses nevertheless to disclose it, it is then reasonable that he should be liable to criminal penalties'. On this basis there would be no objection to the prosecution of the *Guardian* for publishing the documents leaked by Sarah Tisdall. The function of the press in Britain, it seems, is to stroke rather than censure. This failure to confront the constitutional role of the newspapers stands in sharp contrast to the position in the United States, as reflected by the Pentagon Papers case, decided in the same year that Franks was appointed.

The Pentagon Papers case[17] concerned an attempt by the US Government to restrain the *New York Times* and the *Washington Post* from publishing the contents of a classified study entitled 'History of US Decision-Making Process on Vietnam Policy'. The US Supreme Court divided 6:3 in holding that no restraining order, whether temporary or permanent, could be made, with Justice Black booming that every moment's continuance of the temporary injunction which had been granted by a lower court against the newspapers 'amounts to a flagrant, indefensible, and continuing violation of the First Amendment'. In a powerful judgment Justice Black also wrote that:

In the First Amendment the Founding Fathers gave the free press the protection it must have to fulfill its essential role in our democracy. The press was to serve the governed, not the governors. The Government's power to censor the press was abolished so that the press would remain forever free to censure the Government. The press was protected so that it could bare the secrets of government and inform the people. Only a free and unrestrained press can effectively expose deception in

---

[17] *New York Times Co.* v. *US* 403 US 713 (1971).

government. And paramount among the responsibilities of a free press is the duty to prevent any part of the government from deceiving the people and sending them off to distant lands to die of foreign fevers and foreign shot and shell. In my view, far from deserving condemnation for their courageous reporting, the New York Times, the Washington Post, and other newspapers should be commended for serving the purpose that the Founding Fathers saw so clearly. In revealing the workings of government that led to the Vietnam war, the newspapers nobly did precisely that which the Founders hoped and trusted they would do.

It may be noted in passing that these remarks contrast sharply with the remarks of Lord Ackner in the *Spycatcher* (No. 1) case. There he said, in referring to the United States, that 'There the courts, by virtue of the First Amendment, are, I understand, powerless to control the press. Fortunately the press in this country is, as yet, not above the law, although like some other powerful organisations they would like that to be so, that is until they require the law's protection.'

Support for the press in the Pentagon Papers case came not only from Justice Black, well known for his strong defence of the First Amendment. Justice Douglas conceded that the 'disclosures may have a serious impact' but concluded 'that is no basis for sanctioning a previous restraint on the press', noting that the 'dominant purpose of the First Amendment was to prohibit the widespread practice of governmental suppression of embarrassing information', and proclaiming that '[s]ecrecy in Government is fundamentally anti-democratic, perpetuating bureaucratic errors. Open debate and discussion of public issues are vital to our national health. On public questions there should be uninhibited, robust, and wide-open debate.' Justice Brennan made it clear that these values were to inform hearings not only for permanent restraining orders but for temporary ones as well. Thus, he wrote a separate opinion 'only to emphasise' the lack of propriety of even 'temporary . . . restraining orders to block the publication of material sought to be suppressed by the Government'. He continued by clearly asserting that 'The error that has pervaded these cases from the outset was the granting of any injunctive relief whatsoever, interim or otherwise.' (This contrasts again with *Spycatcher* (No. 1),[18] where, for example, Lord Donaldson

---

[18] *Attorney-General* v. *Guardian Newspapers Ltd.* [1987] 3 All ER 316.

(in the Court of Appeal) suggested that the delay imposed by a temporary restraining order was of 'no consequence', since '[Mr Wright's] disclosures relate to a period which is already long past'.) For his part, Justice White decided for the newspapers despite being unable to 'deny that [publication] will do substantial damage to public interests. Indeed, I am confident that their disclosure will have that result.' The dangers were presented by the lower court as involving 'the death of soldiers, the destruction of alliances, the greatly increased difficulty of negotiation with our enemies . . .'.

It would be expecting too much of a British government to recognize the constitutional role of the press by restricting criminal sanctions to the Crown servant or government contractor who discloses the information in the first place. But it is not too much to expect some restraint in the vigour with which the criminal law is applied to the press if only to help safeguard freedom and liberty when the professionals who purport to do so on our behalf abuse their powers in the process. In fact there is no such recognition in the 1989 Act, save only that the accused will escape conviction if he or she did not know or had no reasonable cause to believe that the information was covered by the Act. The full force of the criminal law thus applies to the press, a not insignificant problem for whom is the wide sweep and the continuing vagueness of the legislation. The Franks Committee had the advantage over the 1989 Act in that it would have applied the law to a narrower range of material, the scope of which could have been easily determined. Franks had recommended that the criminal law should operate only to protect information the disclosure of which would be seriously damaging. In practice this meant disclosure (and publication) of only two categories of classified information. Thus, the criminal law would apply to TOP SECRET (exceptionally grave damage to the nation) and SECRET (serious injury to the interests of the nation) information, but not to CONFIDENTIAL (prejudicial to the interests of the nation) or to RESTRICTED (undesirable in the interests of the nation) information. It is true that the major weakness of this system was that classification is done in the departments and that Franks also proposed that a relevant Minister could issue a certificate in legal proceedings which would be conclusive evidence that the document had been properly classified. So if the Minister certified that a document had been properly classified as SECRET, it would be (on the Franks proposal) impossible to show that disclosure would not be seriously damaging.

It may be noted, however, that Franks also recommended that regulations should be introduced to regulate the classification of documents and to review classifications. Presumably it was hoped and intended that this might help to prevent the tendency towards over-classification by Ministers which was later acknowledged by the Security Commission in 1982. It is true that a major weakness of these proposals was the heavy hand of government in classification and the lack of any independent scrutiny of the procedures. Yet even in its original form it is strongly arguable that the Franks proposal, with its ministerial certificates, was preferable to that which the Thatcher Government has finally produced. In rejecting the system of certificates, the Government feigned a commitment to liberalism; purporting to recognize the force of the argument that the proposed system placed 'too much power in the hands of Ministers', it noted that:

since the defendant would not be able to challenge the Minister's certificate, an essential element of the offence would not be considered by the courts but would be decided by the Minister alone. There would be no restraint on a Minister issuing a certificate, even if circumstances did not objectively justify it. The Minister would not be seen as disinterested and there would always be the suspicion of political bias. (Home Office, 1988a)

The reason why the Government has feigned liberalism is precisely because it has come up with something even worse.

Thus the new legislation restrains the press from publishing any information unlawfully disclosed to it if publication would be 'damaging'. In some cases—such as information unlawfully disclosed relating to telephone-tapping—the Act applies to restrain the press whether or not the publication is damaging. The overall effect is to sweep into the net of the criminal law all the categories of classified information referred to by Franks above, rather than just the first two. It could even sweep into the net information which has not been classified. It means that the Act applies to the press disclosure of any information covered by the Act (with the exception of information disclosed by retired security officers—the drafting 'cock-up' referred to above), the publication of which causes harm, however insubstantial or inconsequential. A related problem is the lack of precision as to what will constitute damage for this purpose. The protection for the press is that the Crown will have to convince a jury that damage has been caused or is likely to be caused by disclosure. But this is of little utility to a newspaper which needs to know in advance whether it is operating within the four corners of the law. The imprecision of the law and the uncertainty of how juries will respond will surely have a considerable chilling effect on freedom of expression. Although it is true that juries have refused to convict in recent Official Secrets cases, it would be a mistake to ignore the fact that instructions to the jury like the one in the Clive Ponting case will almost certainly continue to be made by a British judiciary which appears in this area at least to be more executive minded than the executive. And it would be a mistake to underestimate the impact not only of jury-vetting which operates in Official Secrets cases, but more importantly, perhaps, the attack on the jury system conducted by the Conservative Government.

4. Defences for unauthorized publication

Just as the protection of a wide category of information by criminal sanctions could be more easily justified if a demanding standard of harm or damage had been employed, so a lower standard of harm or damage could be more easily justified if the legislation was liberally sprinkled with adequate defences and safeguards. The two most commonly recognized as being necessary in this context are first (as a minimum) a defence of prior publication, and secondly a defence that publication is justifiable in the public interest. But again the Government has refused to yield. In denying a prior publication defence, the Government has repudiated a proposal to this effect which had been contained in its Official Information Bill of 1979, the reason for doing so being outlined in the White Paper (Home Office, 1989). In a passage reminiscent of the judgment of Lord Donaldson in the *Spycatcher* case, the Home Office explained that a second or subsequent disclosure may be more harmful than the original disclosure. For example, it was argued, 'a newspaper story about a certain matter may carry little weight in the absence of firm evidence of its validity. But confirmation of that story by, say, a senior official of the relevant Government Department would be very much more damaging. In such circumstances, the Government considers that the official should still be subject to criminal sanctions' (Home Office, 1988*a*: 13). The only defence, apart from the standard one based on the defendant's ignorance about the material, is that no further harm is likely to arise from a second disclosure. In the view of the Government the prior publication of the information would be relevant evidence for the courts to consider in determining whether harm was likely to result from a second disclosure, but it would by no means be conclusive.

Although there is some substance in the Government's argument on this point, the impact and effect of the absence of a defence of prior publication is in fact much greater than it appears willing to acknowledge. For it is not only a civil servant who will be liable for disclosing that which is already known: the newspapers will also be liable. Thus under section 5 of the Act, it is an offence for a person to disclose information which is protected by the Act even though the person in question is not a civil servant, and even though the person in question did not obtain his or her information from a civil servant or former civil servant. The implications of this are really quite far-reaching. As a first example, take the position of information which has been disclosed to and by a small subscription magazine circulating amongst those with an interest in the defence industry. The Government may choose not to prosecute until the same story is picked up and retold by a larger circulation weekly on the left. Take as a second example the *Spycatcher* case itself. It was by no means clear whether the *Guardian* and the *Observer* could have been prosecuted for their stories of June 1986—the stories that led to the first injunctions in the English courts for breach of confidence. Any such doubts may now be resolved. The information is protected information (relating to security and intelligence) and the fact that its source is beyond the jurisdiction of the English criminal law would not now protect the newspapers from prosecution. The fact that the information was stale and already in the public domain on account of authors such as Chapman Pincher, would merely serve to invite a jury to consider whether the publication now was damaging. And the fact that the allegations were widely known throughout the world (East and West) would be of no consequence.

As already pointed out, the Government also rejected any introduction of a public interest defence, an omission described by Mr Edward Heath as being 'integral to the bill's failure to weigh the rights of the individual against possible abuses of state powers' (Heath, 1989). Attempts to redress this balance failed at both Committee and Report stages in the Commons, and in the Lords despite support from both sides of the House. In the White Paper the Government recognized that some people who make unauthorized disclosures do so for altruistic reasons and without desire for personal gain. But it was also recognized that this is 'equally true of some people who commit other criminal offences' and that the 'general principle which the law follows is that the criminality of what people do ought not to depend on their ultimate motives—though these may be a factor to be taken into account in sentencing—but on the nature and degree of the harm which their acts may cause'. For the Government there were two 'good grounds' for not departing from this general principle in the present context. In the first place, it was argued that 'a central objective of reform is to achieve maximum clarity in the law and in its application. A general public interest defence would make it impossible to achieve such clarity.' But although this is a desirable goal, it is, as we have argued, not met by the legislation. If clarity had been the overriding consideration the Government would have retained the Franks proposals rather than gone off on a frolic of its own in a direction which is arguably less liberal, but certainly much less clear. In any event, clarity is not necessarily a virtue to be pushed at the expense of any other. If clarity in legislation is a virtue then so too is integrity in public office, and justice in the administration of the law. Many people would compromise clarity a shade in order to make room for these other virtues.

The second reason for rejecting the public interest defence is that the Government wished 'to concentrate the protection of the criminal law on information which demonstrably requires its protection in the public interest'. In the view of the Government it 'cannot be acceptable that a person can lawfully disclose information which he knows may, for example, lead to loss of life simply because he conceives that he has a general reason of a public character for doing so'. But this presumes that it is always in the public interest to protect information from disclosure regardless of the circumstances. Yet as Lord Goff of Chieveley said in the *Spycatcher* (No. 2) case, 'in a free society there is a continuing public interest that the workings of government should be open to scrutiny and criticism'. There is also a particular public interest in ensuring that those who wield executive power do not abuse that power. So much was recognized by Scott J. at first instance in *Spycatcher* (No. 2) where he said that '[t]he press has a legitimate role in disclosing scandals in government. An open democratic society requires that to be so.' In a similar vein, he was to say later in his judgment that 'the ability of the press freely to report allegations of scandal in government is one of the bulwarks of our democratic society. It could not happen in totalitarian countries. If the price that has to be paid is the exposure of the government of the day to pressure or embarrassment when mischievous and false allegations are made, then, in my opinion, that price must be paid.' In other words there may be a greater public interest than the public interest in secrecy. Indeed so much is recognized by the civil law in the action for breach of confidence: an injunction will not be granted to restrain a confidence if the public interest lies in favour of disclosure. To say the least, it seems absurd that conduct which could thus not be the subject of an injunction could nevertheless be the subject of a prosecution. Normal practice is that the standards of the criminal law (leading to a possible loss of liberty) should be more exacting than those of the civil law.

Nevertheless, the lack of a public interest defence means that the criminal law will continue to operate in this area with potentially inhibiting consequences. The following examples are an indication of how wide will be the liability of the press:

(*a*) a newspaper publishes documents showing that a Minister of the Crown has withheld information from Parliament;

(b) a newspaper publishes documents showing that a Minister of the Crown has deceived or misled Parliament;

(c) a newspaper discloses allegations published by a former security officer overseas which show members of the service to have been engaged in subversive activities.

If the source of the information is a civil servant, and if the information relates to security, intelligence, or defence (etc.) then the newspaper as well as the civil servant could be prosecuted. And, as others have pointed out, events elsewhere, such as Irangate in the United States, could not be disclosed under the 1989 Act without exposing the newspapers to the risk of prosecution. Thus, during the Second Reading in the Commons, Mr Edward Heath asked whether if the Bill was passed 'would Irangate be possible?' 'The answer', he said, 'is no. For 30 years, nothing would come out. Yet Irangate exposed the incompetence and hypocrisy of the President of the United States.'[19] The task for the Government, which was not even willing to accept a Lords amendment which would have allowed officials to reveal serious misconduct involving crime, fraud, or other gross impropriety, is to explain why it is in the public interest that the disclosure of this kind of information should be potentially a criminal offence.

5. A liberalizing measure?

It is hardly surprising then that the Official Secrets Act 1989 has been strongly condemned, though concern was as much with the manner of introducing the legislation as it was with its content. Thus, Edward Heath complained that the Government's attitude towards the drafting and passage of the legislation was 'far from satisfactory' (Heath, 1989). Debate in the Commons was restricted by guillotine, a tactic which provoked condemnation from all

[19] The parliamentary debates on the Official Secrets Act 1989 are located at 144 HC Debs. 460 (21 Dec. 1988) (2nd Reading); 145 HC Debs. 1047 (25 Jan. 1989); 146 HC Debs. 441 (2 Feb. 1989); 147 HC Debs. 69; 332; 503 (13, 15, 16 Feb. 1989) (Committee); 147 HC Debs. 1004 (Report and 3rd Reading) (22 Feb. 1989); 504 HL Debs. 1605 (9 Mar. 1989) (2nd Reading); 505 HL Debs. 906 (3 Apr. 1989) (Committee); 506 HL Debs. 698 (18 Apr. 1989) (Report); 506 HC Debs. 1065 (24 Apr. 1989) (3rd Reading); 152 HC Debs 143 (3 May 1989) (Lords amendments considered).

sides. For his part, Lord Jenkins of Hillhead complained that what was even 'more objectionable' than the guillotine was 'not so much the Government's impatience with extended debate as their unwillingness to take any notice of the arguments deployed, whether the debates be long or short'. He continued by pointing out during the Second Reading debate in the Lords that 'only a single, one-word, obscure amendment has been accepted. The others have been crushed by the unlistening, uninformed, unconcerned majority.' The fact that a few modest and largely inconsequential amendments were subsequently accepted hardly answers this charge.

But of course while the manner of introduction may be seen to betray both arrogance and a lack of commitment to the values of freedom and liberty which the Act purports to defend, the contents of the legislation also betray a lack of commitment to the ideal of liberty. Indeed it is hard to see how it can seriously or justifiably be described as a liberalizing measure at all. In the first place, it does not provide any rights to information, in sharp contrast to the position in the United States, Canada, and Australia. So although the ambit of the criminal law is in theory pulled back, the Government still controls the flow of information and has effective sanctions to prevent and restrict disclosure even where the criminal law is no longer applicable. And secondly, it may be that in practice the new Act does not in fact withdraw the boundaries of the criminal law at all; there may even be a potential extension of the criminal law. The point was made forcefully by Lord Bonham-Carter during the Second Reading in the Lords. He accepted that the new measure 'formally releases' large areas of information which had previously been within the scope of the Official Secrets Act 1911. This included leaks of information concerning education, pensions, the Budget, and water privatization. He continued:

However, it seems to me to be a largely theoretical achievement. When was the last journalist prosecuted under the Act of 1911 for leaking information of the kind that I have just mentioned? The answer is, I think, never. The earthquake that the Home Secretary spoke of, which was to shake the foundations of Whitehall, is largely a figure of speech. In practice, when the Bill becomes law, *The Times* education correspondent will not feel that a great load of anxiety has been lifted off his shoulders.

In these large areas the writ of the Act of 1911 never ran. Even in those parts covering security and defence, after Ponting a prosecution was a risky and unpredictable business. So it could be argued that this country found itself without an Official Secrets Act, and hence the necessity of the one that we have before us, which I would argue is in some respects wider in its scope and more easily enforced than the one that it succeeds.

There may thus be some substance in the claims of Lord Jenkins of Hillhead that the Home Secretary displayed 'an increasingly pathetic lack of conviction trying to proclaim that he is presenting a great liberalising measure' which owed 'too much to obsessive resentment at the outcome of the *Spycatcher* and *Ponting* cases'.

Conclusion

On a purely formal level, the *Spycatcher* saga has had a huge impact on British law and practice on national security. It has been a major factor in the introduction of the staff counsellor and in the publication of the procedures whereby security officers seek authorization to publish their memoirs—even though, by the admission of the Home Office, permission will rarely if ever be granted. More importantly, *Spycatcher* has been instrumental in producing not only the much resisted statutory recognition and regulation of the security service, but also the long overdue repeal of section 2 of the Official Secrets Act 1911. But the progress is purely formal and superficial. The introduction of this legislation has the effect in practice of extending the power of the state over the individual. The Security Service Act extends the power of the service by authorizing it to do that which was previously done unlawfully. And despite the very serious concern about its abuse of power, the service continues to operate on behalf of the executive branch without any adequate scrutiny, whether judicial or legislative. Indeed, the effect of the Official Secrets Act is further to insulate the service from any effective form of scrutiny or public accountability. In fact, the Official Secrets Act (like its sibling the Security Service Act) is notably illiberal: not only because of the scope of protection for MI5, but also because of the sheer breadth which the criminal law continues to occupy. As Lord Bonham-Carter suggested, the drafting of the Act suggests a greater rather than a reduced role for the criminal law. It will cease to apply in those areas where in practice it had no application anyway, but has been sharpened for deeper penetration in those areas where the Government feels vulnerable to attack by enemies, both real and quixotic, whether they be in the USSR, or in what was once called Fleet Street. Against this background, perhaps the most appropriate position for a Home Secretary, without the courage for real liberal reform, would be to follow the lead of Lord Jenkins of Hillhead. He too gave some thought to reforming section 2 when he was Home Secretary, but found out:

There were certain powerful departments where secrecy had become a way of life and where the Secretaries of State in charge of them, though powerful in Cabinet, did not (how shall I put it?) allow their reforming enthusiasm to lift them above their department ethos. I found the war of resistance sufficiently strong that I decided—and there may be a lesson for Mr. Hurd here—that any measure which emerged might actually make things worse and not better. In particular, I feared for the replacement of the rusty old blunderbuss of Section 2 of the 1911 Act, which, although it looked fearsome, was too cumbersome and inaccurate to be at all frequently used. I feared that its replacement by some new armoury of sharp-shooting weapons which would nonetheless splay too wide might be damaging.

Therefore, I decided to apply what I think is a good old Conservative principle, though it is one that is not much in vogue today: that if you cannot be fairly confident that you will improve matters and not make them worse, it is better to leave them as they are. I withdrew. It was not noble; but then the principles of Conservatism, at least since the great Halifax, the trimmer, rarely are noble, but they can often be sensible.

7

Legal Responses to Terrorism

AT the Lord Mayor's annual Banquet in the Guildhall in November 1988, Mrs Thatcher said the following about her Government's legislative response to terrorism:

Yes, some of those measures do restrict freedom. But those who choose to live by the bomb and the gun, and those who support them, can't in all circumstances be accorded exactly the same rights as everyone else. We do sometimes have to sacrifice a little of the freedom we cherish in order to defend ourselves from those whose aim is to destroy that freedom altogether—and that is a decision we should not be afraid to take. Because in the battle against terrorism we shall never give in. The only victory will be our victory: the victory of democracy and a free society.

To those who argued that the Government's action was undermining freedom, Mrs Thatcher had this to say:

To answer that charge, perhaps I can refer to a letter I received from the mother of a young serviceman who was murdered by the IRA. She said and I quote: 'Where is the freedom of the Press? I hear them cry. Where is my son's freedom?'[1]

It is difficult to counter the emotional power of such arguments. The Prime Minister is right to express concern about political violence in the United Kingdom. It is mainly, though not exclusively, the work of the Provisional IRA and Protestant paramilitary forces in Northern Ireland. Over 2,000 people have died since the Troubles began in 1968. In 1972, the year of 'Bloody Sunday' in Derry and 'Bloody Friday' in Belfast, 103 soldiers and 321 civilians died. After two more years of heavy

[1] *Independent*, 15 Nov. 1988.

casualties (1975 and 1976), the rate of deaths in the province has dropped to an annual average of slightly less than 100. The IRA's possession of a plentiful supply of the highly destructive plastic explosive Semtex is evidence of its continuing capacity to cause havoc. In 1987/8 alone, a relatively quiet year, compensation payments for criminal damage amounted to over £19 million. Personal injury claims also run into millions. The cost of security is quite enormous. Since Mrs Thatcher came to power, the price of policing has soared: 1987/8 expenditure by the Northern Ireland Office on law, order, protective, and miscellaneous services (LOPMS) was estimated to be about £512 million—yet this was admitted to be no more than 10.5 per cent of total government expenditure in the Province. In the same year, the cost of deploying the army in support of the police was estimated at £168 million.[2]

The Legal and Political Background

Maintaining the legal system and the debilitated economy of Northern Ireland is thus a very expensive business. But political violence has not been restricted to the Province. British soldiers have been killed in both Germany and the Netherlands. A number of barracks in the United Kingdom have been attacked. The phase of the indiscriminate murder of civilians in Britain, as epitomized by the Birmingham and Guildford pub bombs in the mid-1970s, may be over, but the IRA of the 1980s remains a lean and professional outfit willing to fight a long war and willing to exploit the political process whenever it suits them. It retains the ability to strike at 'prestige' targets at the centre of government— the outstanding example of this, of course, was the explosion in the Grand Hotel, Brighton, during the Conservative Party Conference in October 1984, which killed five people and came close to murdering nearly half the Cabinet, including the Prime Minister. The paramilitaries thus continue to pose a fundamental

[2] See a most useful survey by David McKittrick in the *Independent*, 1 Oct. 1988. The figures in this paragraph are drawn from answers to written parliamentary questions at 124 HC Debs. (WA) 77 (7 Dec. 1987); 139 HC Debs. (WA) 820–3 (4 Nov. 1988); 142 HC Debs. (WA) 431–2 (2 Dec. 1988).

question which many liberal democracies have been trying to answer for over two decades: how can a country cope with organized lawlessness pursued for ostensible political purposes?

The United Kingdom Government dabbled with some of the more militaristic answers in the late 1960s and in the first half of the 1970s. The British army first became heavily engaged in Northern Ireland in 1969. Their robust approach to security did not endear them to the Catholic communities it was their job to protect. Internment without trial was introduced on 9 August 1971. The majority of those held appear in retrospect not to have been involved with violence; the action of the security forces, therefore, seemed arbitrary and partisan and caused deep alienation throughout the Catholic community. Particularly controversial was the army's use, during long interrogation sessions with internees, of the 'five techniques' (wall-standing, hooding, continuous noise, deprivation of food, and deprivation of sleep) which led to condemnation by the European Court of Human Rights as being inhuman and degrading treatment.[3] When the leaders of the IRA were apprehended, their places outside were taken by more radical and violent fighters. Until 9 August, 30 people had died violently in Northern Ireland, but 143 were killed in the rest of 1971 alone. The initiative rebounded catastrophically by adding greatly to the IRA's popular support. The Government had no idea what to do with the 'political prisoners' it had interned and, indeed, on one memorable occasion ended up flying some of them to meet Ministers in London. Many of the fourteen million Americans who described themselves as Irish rallied to what they saw as the ancient cause of their country's freedom.

The British Government has spent years living down the political consequences of the open nature of this partially militarized response to the IRA. It may have been an honest and explicit policy—but it was also a disastrous one. The Diplock Report of late 1972 (so named after the Law Lord who was the Commission's chairman) began a slow switch of emphasis from the military to the law. Internment was to continue, but as many cases as possible were to be processed through the courts as

---

[3] *Ireland* v. *United Kingdom* (1978) 2 EHRR 25.

criminal charges; it was thought that this would make the resultant detention more acceptable. To facilitate convictions, jury trials were suspended for certain crimes judged to be 'terrorist' offences. The fear was twofold: that jurors would be intimidated and that the then predominantly Protestant juries would return perverse acquittals when faced with Loyalist paramilitary defendants. Such an extreme measure reflected continuing recognition of the unique nature of Northern Ireland's emergency and the inability of the law as it then stood to cope with it. The Province's Emergency Provisions Act in 1973, and the nationwide Prevention of Terrorism Act the following year underlined, in a similar fashion, the authorities' perception of the special threat of the IRA.

Yet, despite such explicit recognition of an abnormal situation, the policy of criminalization gathered pace when the phasing out of internment came towards the end of 1975. Special category status in prisons, available to internees and to those convicted in the Diplock courts was ended in 1976. In theory at least, members of the IRA were now to be tried and punished for offences just like ordinary criminals and according to the same rules of evidence. It was the IRA's inability to accept this that led first to their prisoners' refusal to wear prison clothes, and then, after the authorities had retaliated by denying them daily exercise and other facilities, to the 'dirty protest'. This involved the smearing of excrement on cell walls. The whole sordid business ended in compromise, but not before the death, on hunger strike, of ten republican prisoners, including Bobby Sands, who had been elected to the House of Commons during his fast. Like internment before it, the episode hugely increased support for Provisional Sinn Fein. Despite this, the idea of criminalization has, if anything, become even more firmly rooted in the mind of authority. The police have replaced the army as the primary enforcers of law throughout the Province. All counter-terrorists are said to be as subject to the same laws as those whom they try to catch—and as vulnerable to criminal proceedings if they should step outside the rules. There is, on this view, no state of emergency in Northern Ireland, just a very particular and difficult criminal situation.

Turning now to the substantive law, we shall look first at the current prevention of terrorism legislation. Then we shall examine the criminal justice system, including the 'shoot to kill' controversies of recent years. This will lead us on to a discussion of the impact on the media of the present Government's determination to deprive members of the IRA and Sinn Fein of what the Prime Minister has called the 'oxygen of publicity'. Three aspects of the law call for particular reference at this stage. First, most anti-terrorist law is of general application. Its ostensible focus, and the basis for its enactment, may be a terrorist group but its impact is felt throughout the community. It is often the case that the innocent and the uninvolved, rather than the terrorists, are the most sorely affected. Secondly, laws designed to cope with the very special problems of Northern Ireland have a habit of being extended to the rest of the United Kingdom, either immediately upon enactment or shortly thereafter. This occurs without the controversy and the debate that would ensue if the measure were entirely new. Thirdly, the lesson of the past two decades has been that temporary measures, designed to meet particular emergencies, have a tendency to become permanent and to develop a life of their own, independent of the transitory panic that gave birth to them. These various features testify to the risks inherent in too ready an acceptance of the Government's definition of necessity. They also give some indication of how general has been the erosion of our liberties under cover of this continuing fear of terrorism. The civil liberties in issue here are not those of the gunmen; they are the rights of us all.

The Prevention of Terrorism Act

The Prevention of Terrorism (Temporary Provisions) Act 1989 is the latest version of legislation that, despite its name, has been on the statute books since 1974. It emerged as a response to a campaign of violence that the IRA had sustained in Britain since early 1972. In February of that year, 7 civilians died in a bomb attack on Aldershot army barracks. In 1973, there were 86 explosions, involving 1 fatality and 380 other casualties. By the middle of November 1974, there had already been another 20 killed and over 150 injured. Then came the explosions in two public houses in Birmingham, on 21 November 1974, in which 21 died and 184 were badly hurt. This proved the last straw for a frightened government. In introducing the Prevention of Terrorism (Temporary Provisions) Bill to Parliament, the then Home Secretary, Mr Roy Jenkins, described the new powers contained within it as 'draconian'. They were 'unprecedented in peacetime' but were 'fully justified to meet the clear and present dangers'.[4] The Act was passed in forty-two hours and, with one minor exception, without amendment.

Section 12(1) declared the Act's expiry date as 28 May 1975, unless it should have been continued in force by statutory order before then. An extension of six months was duly agreed in spring 1975. Later, another extension was granted. In 1976, a new Act was passed, replicating many of the provisions of the earlier measure and adding a few more crimes. Once again temporary, the 1976 Act set out a renewal period that was one year rather than six months. Having got its legislation through Parliament, the Government then asked Lord Shackleton to review it; his terms of reference, requiring him to accept 'the continuing need for legislation against terrorism', made his ultimate conclusions less than exciting (Shackleton, 1978). As the years rolled by, the annual renewal debates became increasingly ritualistic. Another review, by a different peer (Earl Jellicoe) but with the same inhibiting terms of reference, led eventually to the Prevention of Terrorism (Temporary Provisions) Act 1984 (Jellicoe, 1983). With this measure, 'international terrorism' sneaked into the equation for the first time (and by June 1988 220 suspected 'international terrorists' had been detained). The Act required annual renewal, was regularly reviewed by a knight (Sir Cyril Philips), and given a maximum life of five years, after which, if continuance was desired, new legislation would be required. The statute not only survived but prospered so that, after yet another noble review (Colville, 1987), we now have the 1989 version, greatly expanded and no longer absolutely limited to five years, but capable, through annual renewal, to continue—temporarily of course—in happy perpetuity.

[4] 882 HC Debs. 35 (25 Nov. 1974).

IRA violence has continued throughout this period, seemingly untouched by any of Parliament's cogitations or by any legal definition of its activities. Violence was particularly serious during 1975 and 1976. In subsequent years, the organization has combined more careful targeting of victims with the occasional reminder of its capacity to terrorize, as with the Christmas bombing campaigns of 1980 and 1983. It is true that since then things have quietened down somewhat. At the end of February 1989, there had been only two incidents causing casualties (a total of one dead and nine injured) on mainland Britain since the Brighton bomb—none at all was recorded for 1985, 1986, or 1987. In the years since Mrs Thatcher took office in 1979, there has been a total of no more than seventeen incidents involving casualties in Britain which can be attributed to the IRA.[5] But it has not been obvious that these various changes in strategy and impact have been either helped or hindered by the Prevention of Terrorism Acts. The police have had many successes, attributable mainly, as a leading commentator has noted, 'to a combination of chance, incompetence on the part of the terrorists and routine police work' (Walker, 1986: 177–8). It is the ordinary criminal law that bears most of the burden, the Act being 'largely peripheral in effect' (Walker, 1986: 183). The level of violence is nothing like that which impelled Parliament to act in 1974. Despite this, the Government remains, if anything, more deeply committed than ever to its terrorist legislation. The irony is that, as political violence in Britain drops, so the 'draconian' legislation designed to counter it widens and strengthens. We have come a long way from the 'clear and present dangers' formula of more innocent times.

1. Proscription

For present purposes, the most important powers in the prevention of terrorism legislation relate to proscription, exclusion, and detention. There are three groups of crimes of relevance to the general question of proscription. First, belonging to the Irish Republican Army and the Irish National Liberation Army is an

[5] These figures are in an answer by the Home Secretary to a written parliamentary question at 148 HC Debs. (WA) 7–12 (27 Feb. 1989).

offence in Britain, punishable by up to ten years in jail. Soliciting or inviting support for the IRA or INLA is similarly dealt with. (The following groups are also banned in Northern Ireland: the Ulster Volunteer Force; the Ulster Freedom Fighters; the Red Hand Commando; Fianna na hEireann; Cumann na mBan; and Saor Eire.) Secondly, it is a crime to arrange, manage, or address any meeting of three or more persons (whether private or public) if it is known that the meeting is to support or to further the activities of the IRA or INLA or is to be addressed by someone belonging to one or other of them. The 1989 Act has added to this by introducing new laws aimed at the financing of proscribed organizations. Thirdly, any person who in a public place either (*a*) wears any item of dress or (*b*) wears, carries, or displays any article, 'in such a way or in such circumstances as to arouse reasonable apprehension that he is a member or supporter of a proscribed organisation' may incur a hefty fine or six months' imprisonment.

These laws were passed because it was felt that 'the public should no longer have to endure the affront of public demonstrations in support of' the IRA.[6] It has never been seriously claimed that they have helped to reduce terrorism; an underground IRA being harder to penetrate, it is quite possible that they have achieved exactly the reverse. It is the presentational point—the enshrinement in legislation of public aversion—that has been repeatedly emphasized. A Home Office Minister has pointed out, for example, how proscription has denied IRA supporters the opportunity 'to flaunt themselves in public'.[7] If successful, it achieves, according to Earl Jellicoe, 'the avoidance of public outrage, but also the averting of any danger of this outrage being expressed in disorder' (Jellicoe, 1983: para. 207). This is a curious, if emotionally understandable, rationale for eroding freedom of association and freedom of expression. There have, however, been no prosecutions at all in Britain for membership or organizing meetings and only a handful under the unlawful dress provision. This is hardly surprising. Routine public-order law is wide enough to cover most situations where it is likely that these powers would fall to be considered. Section 1 of the Public Order

---

[6] 882 HC Debs. 636 (28 Nov. 1974). Mr Jenkins.
[7] 38 HC Debs. 633 (7 Mar. 1983). Mr Waddington.

Act 1936, for example, prohibits the wearing of uniforms for political purposes. Under this head, the Divisional Court has upheld the conviction of republican sympathizers for marching together whilst wearing black berets and dark clothing.[8] Similarly, breach of the peace charges can often be brought and tendentious republican processions and meetings can now be restricted (or in the case of the former, banned altogether) under the Public Order Act 1986 (see Chapter 4).

It is open to question whether public disgust alone should be a basis for criminal penalties restricting political freedom. The measures under discussion do not prohibit the killings (a legislative impossibility, unfortunately), nor any overt incitements to murder (for which the criminal law has a remedy), nor any prospective breach of the peace (already covered by public order law), but rather the peaceful activities of political organisations. Unsurprisingly, this has occasionally degenerated into a more general and informal curtailment of debate about Republicanism and Irish unity. Scorer and Hewitt (1981: 18–20) note the difficulties the Troops Out Movement has had in booking halls for public meetings and in getting permission to hold rallies in Trafalgar Square. As Jellicoe has observed (1983: para. 212), it is 'asking a lot of the police to apply these provisions fully in relation to proscribed organisations themselves, while not affecting the free expression of views about Northern Ireland'. In response to this, a government circular requests of officers that they 'should take care to ensure that members of the public do not feel inhibited from the free expression of views' (Home Office, 1983: para. 8). This is a political maze that it is unfair to ask the police to enter.

2. Exclusion

The exclusion powers of the prevention of terrorism legislation are the most widely disliked, illiberal, and controversial part of the whole anti-terrorism legislation. Under section 5 of the 1989 Act, if the Secretary of State is satisfied that any person (*a*) is or has been concerned in the commission, preparation, or instigation of acts of terrorism connected with Northern Ireland; or (*b*) is

---

[8] *Whelan* v. *DPP; O'Moran* v. *DPP* [1975] QB 864.

attempting or may attempt to enter Great Britain with a view to being concerned in the commission, preparation, or instigation of such acts of terrorism, then the Secretary of State may make an exclusion order against him or her. Such an order prohibits the person from 'being in, or entering, Great Britain'. For these and the other purposes of the Act, terrorism is defined as 'the use of violence for political ends' including 'any use of violence for the purpose of putting the public or any section of the public in fear'. The order lasts for a maximum of three years, though the authorities are perfectly free to make fresh orders. A British citizen who 'is at the time ordinarily resident in Great Britain and has then been ordinarily resident in Great Britain throughout the last three years' is exempt. A mirror image provision in section 6 allows the Northern Irish Secretary to expel people to some other part of the United Kingdom. Non-British citizens may be excluded from the whole of the United Kingdom, on the same criteria as govern these earlier sections, but without regard here to the length of their period of residence in the country. In practice, this is aimed at the Irish in Britain, in respect of whom ordinary immigration law does not operate. Breaching an exclusion order, or helping to circumvent one, is an offence under section 8 which carries a maximum penalty, on indictment, of five years in jail.

The decision to exile a citizen or expel an Irish resident is the culmination of a period of bureaucratic cogitation which is as impenetrable as it is mysterious. Some light has been shed by a Home Office circular (Home Office, 1984). As we would expect, the grandly named 'intelligence sources' have pride of place. This formula embraces hearsay gossip and the revelations of paid informers. Forensic evidence and previous convictions can also play a part. The circular reveals that silence during interrogation may be used against a suspect on the ground that it indicates training in ' "anti-interrogation" techniques'. This administrative modification of the privilege against self-incrimination anticipated by some four years the formal destruction of the right to silence in Northern Ireland. It is possible that, over the years, the threat of exclusion has loosened the tongue of many recalcitrant citizens who thought that all they were doing was exercising a constitutional right. A person who objects to an exclusion order against him or her may exercise the power under the Act to write to the Home

Secretary setting out the grounds of the complaint and requesting a personal interview in order to discuss them. The Secretary of State then refers the matter 'for the advice of one or more persons nominated by' him. The Minister has an absolute discretion in choosing these people. There is no requirement that they be lawyers or that they have any familiarity with the Northern Irish situation. They could be police officers or civil servants.

What usually happens is that one of the advisers interviews the aggrieved suspect. Legal representation may be allowed but no witnesses are called. The adviser then gives the Home Office his or her view as to what should be done. When he comes to reconsider the matter, the Secretary of State will have before him this advice, together with an objective report on the interview, and the letter containing the suspect's original representations. This is the basis upon which the Home Secretary's final decision is made. It appears that nearly half the exclusion orders are now being made subject to this appeal procedure (Colville, 1987: para. 11.3). The advisers' wishes are invariably followed and, by the end of 1982, fourteen orders had been revoked after representations by forty-three people (Jellicoe, 1983: para. 169). The secrecy attaching to the initial decision, the absence of any judicial review, and the informal and restricted nature of the advisers' investigations make this a less than satisfactory procedure, especially bearing in mind the enormous consequences that internal banishment can have for some of the individuals and the families concerned. What makes it almost comically difficult to utilize the procedure is that at no stage need the authorities inform the suspect of any of the reasons why he or she is about to be exiled. Suspicions that cannot be seen are not ones that can be easily allayed. Yet, the Divisional Court has upheld this procedure, declaring that to give reasons when making exclusion orders 'would be fraught with difficulty and danger'.[9]

Between 1976 and 1 July 1987, the British police had applied for 390 exclusion orders—353 of these had been granted (Colville, 1987: para. 11.2.1). Despite the three-year time limit, as well as other factors like death and revocation, 123 orders remained in force on 6 December 1988. By 1 January 1988,

[9] *R. v. Secretary of State for the Home Department, ex parte Stitt, The Times*, 3 Feb. 1987.

seventeen people had been found guilty of breaching an order made against them and a further three had been convicted of helping an individual to evade exclusion. (The Northern Irish power has been much less used: thirty-two orders remained in place at the end of December 1988.)[10] Walker (1986: 71) has identified a tendency to use the procedure to exclude Republican activists from Britain. He points out that many of its early victims were members or officials of groups like Sinn Fein and Clann na hEireann. The most notorious example of this was in 1982, when the then Home Secretary, Mr Whitelaw, excluded Gerry Adams, Martin McGuinness, and Danny Morrison, all prominent leaders of the Belfast-based Provisional Sinn Fein, from Britain. They were to visit London at the invitation of the leader of the Greater London Council, Mr Ken Livingstone. The Prime Minister later claimed that the exclusion was based on 'intelligence about the men's involvement in terrorist activity'.[11] No other evidence was forthcoming, the ban was not challenged in court, and the order against Mr Adams was immediately lifted when he was elected to Parliament in 1983. The Government did not say that they no longer suspected Adams of any association with terrorist groups.

Despite this *cause célèbre*, most of the British orders were made in the 1970s. Recent years have seen a marked downturn in the number of applications being made (Colville, 1987: para. 11.2). Independent reviews of the legislation have welcomed this trend. Earl Jellicoe thought the power should 'be allowed to lapse as soon as it [was] no longer considered strictly necessary' (Jellicoe, 1983: para. 200). In the second of his annual reviews of the 1984 Act, Sir Cyril Philips went further by suggesting that no more internal exclusion orders should be issued (Philips, 1986: paras. 20–1). Lord Colville followed this up in 1987 with the recommendation that the power be allowed to lapse, a course that he thought was 'correct in terms of civil rights' (Colville, 1987: para. 11.6.1). A further pressure for change lies in Britain's current reluctance to ratify Protocol 4 of the European Convention on

[10] Much useful data appear in the speech made by the Home Secretary during the Commons debate on the Prevention of Terrorism Bill: 143 HC Debs. 210 (6 Dec. 1988). See also Mr Hogg's comments in Official Report, Standing Committee B, col. 115 (15 Dec. 1988).

[11] 33 HC Debs. 974 (9 Dec. 1982).

Human Rights, which declares the right to move freely and to reside where one wishes in one's own country. The existence of what a foreign diplomat on the defensive can with some justification describe as 'internal exile' must be at least occasionally embarrassing to Mrs Thatcher on her multifarious foreign travels. Despite all this, the power remains in place, its life freshly renewed in the 1989 Act. It is a continuing reminder of the difficulty of removing even the harshest and least liked of 'temporary' emergency laws.

3. Detention

Section 14 of the Prevention of Terrorism Act includes a discretion to arrest, without warrant, where a constable has reasonable grounds for suspecting an offence against any of the proscription, exclusion, or financial provisions in the legislation. Section 14 also permits arrest where the reasonable suspicion relates to 'a person who is or has been concerned in the commission, preparation or instigation of acts of terrorism'. The value of these arrest powers lies in the period of detention without charge that can follow from their exercise. The basic rule is that the suspect may be held for no more than forty-eight hours. A diluted version of the procedure under the Police and Criminal Evidence Act 1984 regulates this period of incarceration.[12] It appears in a schedule to the 1989 Act. A 'review officer', who must be someone who has 'not been directly involved in the matter', looks at the suspect's case 'as soon as practicable after the beginning of the detention', and then 'at intervals of not more than twelve hours'. Such reviews may be postponed if they are 'not practicable', if they would interrupt an interrogation to the prejudice of the investigation, or if a review officer is not 'readily available'. The job of the officer concerned is to decide whether the suspect should remain in custody. He or she is obliged to authorize continued detention if two conditions are fulfilled. First, the officer must be satisfied that it is 'necessary in order (whether by questioning him or otherwise) to obtain or to preserve evidence' relating to any of the offences covered by

[12] See ch. 2 for a discussion of the relevant provisions of the Police and Criminal Evidence Act 1984.

section 14. Secondly, the officer must also be satisfied that the investigation 'is being conducted diligently and expeditiously'. The suspect or his or her solicitor may make representations to the review officer before each decision about continuing detention is made.

This last safeguard is, however, diluted by the fact that the police can postpone communications with an outsider and access to a lawyer for the whole forty-eight-hour period. The grounds include, in addition to the regular exceptions that operate in the ordinary law, a reasonable belief that such contact 'will lead to interference with the gathering of information about the commission, preparation or instigation of acts of terrorism' or will alert people so as to make the prevention of acts of terrorism, or the apprehension of terrorists, more difficult. Recitation of these formulae, with consequent denial of access, has become a commonplace when detainees assert these rights. Where access to a lawyer is allowed, the authorities may go on to direct that the consultation be 'in the sight and hearing' of a police officer.[13] Justifying these restrictions during the passage through Parliament of the 1989 Act, the Home Office Minister, Mr Douglas Hogg, said that he had 'to state as a fact, but with great regret, that there are in Northern Ireland a number of solicitors who are unduly sympathetic to the cause of the IRA'. Seamus Mallon MP immediately asked the Minister, 'in the interests of the integrity of every solicitor operating in the North of Ireland, to provide specific support for what he has said'. Mr Hogg refused. Mr Mallon then remarked that he had 'no doubt that there are lawyers walking the streets or driving on the roads of the North of Ireland who have become targets for assassins' bullets as a result of the statement that had been made' by the Minister. Shortly afterwards, a distinguished solicitor with a record of including Republican sympathizers amongst his clients, Mr Patrick Finucane, was shot dead at his home in Belfast.[14]

[13] See the Police and Criminal Evidence Act 1984, sects. 56 and 58, both for the ordinary law on when access to a lawyer may be denied and for the special rules that govern terrorism cases. The Northern Ireland law is in the Northern Ireland (Emergency Provisions) Act 1987, sects. 14 and 15.

[14] The exchange between Mr Hogg and Mr Mallon is to be found in the Official Report of Standing Committee B on the Prevention of Terrorism Bill for 17 Jan. 1989, at cols. 508, 509, and 519.

It may be thought that this two-day detention period, with its wide arrest power, its pretence of solicitors' access, and charade of independent review, is an unhappy but necessary response to the far more dramatic erosion of our freedoms imposed on us by the political gunman. The same may also be claimed for the port and border controls set out in section 16 of the 1989 Act. These give wide powers to the authorities to stop, search, and question people travelling between Britain and Ireland. No reasonable suspicion is required as long as the travellers are not held for longer than twelve hours, though the practice is to detain people for less than one hour whenever possible. If a reasonable suspicion is formulated, the forty-eight-hour period may then come into operation. Whether these powers are acceptable may be thought to some extent to depend on the number of times they are exercised, a matter to which we shall presently turn. Before that, however, one further matter needs to be considered, since it adds enormously to the variety of options available to the authorities. The two-day detention period we have just discussed can be extended by up to five further days by simple order of the Secretary of State. The moment an application for such an extension is made, the complicated review procedure carefully set out in the Act simply ceases to exist. No British court can consider the question of the validity of this seven-day detention law and, given the subject-matter of the power involved, no judicial review of the Home Secretary's decision is likely. There are no special guarantees in the Act about the sleep, diet, or treatment of detainees, despite the greater length of time involved than is the case with the Police and Criminal Evidence Act 1984.[15]

The legislation gives no hint of the criteria that guide the Minister to his decision; in place of the conditions and magistrates and superintendents and custody officers and so on that litter the ninety-six-hour detention period in the Police and Criminal Evidence Act, we have a simple but total reliance on unnamed authorities. This is British law's black hole for civil liberties, and

[15] See Home Office, 1979: paras. 5–7, and 1984: para. 95. With regard to Northern Ireland, see Bennett, 1979, and Jellicoe, 1983: paras. 82–94. The latter details the extent to which the recommendations in Bennett have been implemented by administrative reform. See also the Police and Criminal Evidence (Northern Ireland) Order, (1989) 51 1989/1341.

it is one into which hapless suspects may be quite lawfully sucked. In *Brogan* v. *United Kingdom*,[16] the length of this detention period was considered by the European Court of Human Rights. The four applicants before the Court, all British citizens resident in Northern Ireland, were arrested under the 1984 Act equivalent of section 14. The four were held for five days and eleven hours; six days and sixteen and a half hours; four days and six hours; and four days and eleven hours. All were questioned about specific incidents, but each was released without charge. The European case revolved around Article 5(3) of the Convention, which provides that 'Everybody arrested or detained . . . shall be brought promptly before a judge or other officer authorised by law to exercise judicial power.' The Court found against the Government by 12 votes to 7. It understood the word 'promptly' as allowing only a limited degree of flexibility. Terrorism presented the authorities with special problems, and this was recognized, but the circumstances of a case could never be such as to deprive the word of any coherent meaning. To attach such importance to the special features of this case so as to justify these lengthy incarcerations would impair the very essence of the right protected by Article 5(3). Accordingly all the detention periods in the case infringed the European Convention.

The first reaction of the British Government to the ruling was one of anger and criticism. Mrs Thatcher declared in the House of Commons that 'we shall consider the judgment carefully and in doing so we shall consider the human rights of victims and potential victims of terrorism as well as the human rights of those suspected of terrorist involvement. We shall ensure that the police have the powers they need to tackle terrorism vigorously.'[17] The Court had joined the ranks of the weaklings. After a period of indecision, during which half-hearted attempts were made to interpose a judicial stage into some part of the detention period, it was announced that Britain had refused to accept the judgment and had consequently derogated from the relevant provisions of the European Convention and the International Covenant on Civil and Political Rights. There was, it seemed, a 'public emergency threatening the life of the nation', in the words of the get-out

---

[16] (1989) 11 EHRR 117.

[17] 142 HC Debs. 575 (29 Nov. 1988).

clause in the European Convention. It is curious in the light of
this emergency situation, and the crucial nature of this detention
power, to note that the authorities in Britain did not detain a
single person for over six days in the first nine months of 1988.[18]
Perhaps the threat that the section might be used has been saving
the life of the nation. The derogation, said to be temporary, was
not expressly limited by time and no promise to seek a speedy way
out of the impasse was volunteered by Ministers. It is not easy to
distinguish derogation from the decision of a particular case from
what would for ordinary litigants be described as simple
disobedience. Within a fortnight, the Home Secretary had
authorized the holding of a number of men for up to one week in
connection with a discovery of explosives in London.[19] It was as
though the judgment had never been. The rule of law applies, it
would seem, only when it is convenient.

What is the purpose of arrest and detention under the
prevention of terrorism legislation? According to a Home Office
circular the 'prime objective' is questioning so as to enable
proceedings to be instituted (Home Office, 1984: para. 92). If this
is true, then the whole business has been a dismal failure.
Between 1977 and 1989, a total of over 4,000 people were
detained in Britain under the Prevention of Terrorism Acts. The
busiest period was during the late 1970s. Numbers have dropped
somewhat since: in 1986, 202 were held; in 1987, the figure was
225. In the first three-quarters of 1988 a total of 130 were detained
in Britain. The majority of detentions occur at the ports, where if
they do not exceed twelve hours they are not entered in the
statistics; so we are on safe ground in presuming that many stops
of relatively short duration occur but go unrecorded. Very few
detainees are held longer than four days: 32 in 1986; 28 in 1987;
and 10 to 30 September 1988.[20] Northern Ireland presents a
somewhat different picture. Between 1977 and 1989, over 8,000
have been detained, of whom slightly more than half have been
held for longer that forty-eight hours. The use of this legislation

[18] See the figures given by the Home Secretary in his written parliamentary
answer at 145 HC Debs. (WA) 141–2 (17 Jan. 1989).

[19] *The Times*, 1 Jan. 1989.

[20] See the figures given by the Home Secretary in his written parliamentary
answer at 145 HC Debs. (WA) 141–2 (17 Jan. 1989).

in the Province has shown no signs of decline; on the contrary the highest figures of all have been in 1986 and 1987—this has certainly something to do with the decline in the availability of other arrest powers in the Province during this period (Hogan and Walker, 1989: 54–8). Yet, despite these huge numbers, between 1977 and 1984, only 186 charges under the legislation were brought in Britain—this represents slightly more than 4 per cent of the total detained during this period. A further 228 were charged with other offences. The Northern Ireland Office produces a global figure of 110 charges under the Act since 1974, and 2,750 further charges relating to other crimes since that date: neither figure is very impressive when one bears in mind the greater use to which the Act has been put in the Province.

The pursuit of a prosecution is not, however, the whole story. As Walker says (1986: 137), the 'rate of charging betokens a dominant police interest in gathering background information through questioning a detainee about his political views, friends and colleagues'. As Lord Shackleton (1978: para. 135) admitted, the Act 'is not simply a question of arresting people who can promptly be charged with offences'. Such surveillance may make perfect sense to army and police strategists, but inherent in its arbitrariness is the risk that large sections of the Irish community will be politically estranged. Despite Home Office advice to the contrary, the police have occasionally allowed the impression to develop that those arrested have been chosen more for the radical nature of their politics than for their connections with political violence (Scorer and Hewitt, 1981: 39–45). Walker (1986: 138) reports on police sweeps, whereby 'everyone connected with a person against whom there is firm evidence may be arrested'. He refers to two large operations in the mid-1970s, in which 122 people were detained, but only 4 were convicted of any offence. Similar exercises also occurred before Christmas in 1979, 1981, and 1983. The problems are especially acute in Northern Ireland. Nowhere is the absurdity of separating security from politics more evident than in the self-defeating results of a large-scale practice of detention for interrogation. The more that people are dragged in for questioning, the greater will be the number of those who feel alienated and oppressed by British law. And the greater this number is, the more there is to survey and the more questions there are to be answered. So the pressure builds up for even more wholesale use of arrest, detention, and interrogation—and so on, *ad infinitum*. It is the spiral of repression beloved by terror strategists, and rightly so, because, in such a chaos of increasing alienation, constitutional nationalism is likely to disappear and militant republicanism emerge as the only winner.

The Criminal Justice System

Detention for interrogation is not at such a level in either Britain or in Northern Ireland that one could say that the IRA are guaranteed the estrangement from the authorities of the local nationalist communities which it is their ambition to achieve. They have seized on other opportunities to exploit disgruntlement and to increase political alienation. For in the campaign against the IRA sweeping measures other than the Prevention of Terrorism Acts have been employed. One is the use of emergency powers legislation and a second is the introduction of major changes to criminal procedure. A third significantly alienating factor are the allegations—whether or not well founded—that the security forces are operating a 'shoot to kill' policy which the public authorities seem unable or unwilling to control.

1. Aspects of emergency powers

The most recent version of the emergency powers legislation was passed in 1987, and deals with such questions as bail, the transfer of cases to non-jury courts, the closure of roads, the search of homes for weapons, and the arrest and detention of persons suspected of offences. These powers may be essential in any battle against terrorism but their exercise has given rise to repeated complaints. In 1988, for example, a total of 4,136 premises were searched by the police under one provision alone (section 15 of the Emergency Provisions Act 1978)—no warrants were required for any of these intrusions.[21] Often, it is the army that does the actual work and some of their house searches in West Belfast have

---

[21] 149 HC Debs. (WA) 297 (16 Mar. 1989) (Mr Ian Stewart).

caused particular controversy. One search attracted a great deal of media attention: it lasted thirty-one hours, involved teams of soldiers working in relays, and included the digging of a 5-foot hole in the kitchen and the removal of all household furniture. Nothing untoward was found and the family concerned were compensated for the damage done—a new floor, new kitchen units, new foundations, and new insulation were required.[22] The use of plastic bullets has always caused rancour. Their inefficient deployment caused fifteen deaths between 1972 and 1988. In 1987, 2,575 rounds were fired, a figure already exceeded by 500 in the first ten months of 1988. In 1986, £245,250 was paid out as compensation in respect of rubber and plastic bullet injuries.[23] The security services say that these weapons are essential, and this point of view appears to be supported by the European Commission of Human Rights.[24] These statistics ensure, however, that they remain a continuing source of aggravation to the communities affected by them.

2. Changes in criminal procedure

So far as the criminal justice system is concerned, many important rules have been changed over the years in ways which have eroded the traditional rights of the defendant, and undermined claims that the rule of law is being impartially applied. To the forefront of this debate are the Diplock courts. The abolition of juries for a wide range of crimes may have been justified in the early 1970s, but, over time, the single-judge courts that replaced them have carved their own niche in Northern Irish law, with the result that they are now viewed more as an integral part of the legal system than as a temporary emergency exception to it. A large number of the cases before these courts involve offences clearly unrelated to terrorism and the Government has displayed a marked reluctance to utilize an available statutory procedure to expand the number of situations in which the Attorney-General may certify an individual case as suitable for jury trial. There has

[22] *Independent*, 6 Feb. 1989.
[23] For these figures, see the written parliamentary answers by Mr Ian Stewart at 138 HC Debs. (WA) 571–4 (28 July 1988); 142 HC Debs. (WA) 431 (2 Dec. 1988); 143 HC Debs. (WA) 195. (7 Dec. 1988).
[24] *Stewart* v. *United Kingdom*, Application no. 10044/82.

been a similar lack of enthusiasm for various proposals, like having a court with three judges or with two or three assessors of fact, which would have the effect of diluting the power that the system presently reposes in the single presiding judge. Meanwhile, in the years from 1980 to 1986, an average of 630 defendants per year were proceeded against on serious charges without a jury. It is noteworthy how quickly even this dramatic break with our ancient traditions has been assimilated.

The same successful process of integration may well be underway in relation to the right to silence, relied upon for generations by suspects in the police station and by defendants in court, but eroded to the point of oblivion by sudden government action towards the end of 1988. The background and rationale of the right have been explained in our chapter on police powers. In Northern Ireland, the judge (or jury, if there is one) may now draw inferences from a suspect's silence under interrogation, and may use that silence as corroboration of other evidence for the purpose of obtaining convictions, in the following three specific situations:

(*a*) The suspect fails to mention a fact when he or she is being questioned about or charged with an offence later, at his or her trial, he or she seeks to rely on this fact in his or her defence, and the court decides that it is one which in the circumstances existing at the time the accused could 'reasonably have been expected' to mention.

(*b*) The suspect fails or refuses to explain 'any object, substance or mark' on his or her person, clothing or in his or her possession which the police inform him or her they reasonably believe 'may be attributable' to a crime he or she has committed.

(*c*) The suspect fails or refuses to explain why he or she was found in a particular place or why he or she was there at a particular time, after the police have informed him or her that they reasonably believe that his or her presence may have been attributable to a crime he or she has committed.

The court may also now draw adverse inferences from an accused's failure to give evidence in court on his or her own behalf. The law requires that a silent accused be publicly called to give evidence, notwithstanding his or her declared intention not to do so. It is hard to see what the purpose behind this piece of contrived theatricality could be; its effect is to prejudice further the standing of the defendant in the eyes of the court. These changes to the rules leave very little of the right to silence intact. They apply to all prosecutions in Northern Ireland, and may be the model for the expected British legislation. Terrorism may be the justification for such alterations in the law—but it in no way restricts the breadth of the law that it is said to necessitate.

3. Deaths caused by the security forces

The most serious alienation of recent years has been caused by none of these measures. Between 1969 and 1 March 1984, 233 people were killed by the security forces in Northern Ireland.[25] An Amnesty International Report published in 1988 (Amnesty International 1988) drew attention to the fact that, between November 1982 and April 1988 alone, 49 people had been killed by the RUC and the army. In 19 of the 32 incidents identified, the victims had been unarmed. The vast majority of those killed were Catholic. Since 1969, over 20 members of the security forces have been tried for killings caused by the use of firearms while on duty, but only one conviction has been obtained. This was in the case of Private Thain, who was found guilty of murder and was given the mandatory sentence of life imprisonment by the trial judge. He was subsequently released on licence after being in prison for three and a half years (this includes his time spent in custody before trial). He is still a member of the armed forces, though he is not expected to serve in Northern Ireland. The circumstances behind some of these figures and controversies have given rise to a widespread belief in nationalist communities that an unofficial policy of 'shoot to kill' has been operated by elements within the security forces, particularly during the early 1980s.

Whatever the truth behind such a claim, and it is strenuously denied by the Government, the number of unarmed people killed by the RUC and the army, and the lack of convictions in court despite the suspicious context of many of these fatalities, has been one of the running sores in community relations and in Anglo-

[25] 56 HC Debs. (WA) 493–4 (21 Mar. 1984).

Irish diplomacy during the last ten years. It offers the clearest evidence, to those who want to believe it, that, within the ostensibly common umbrella of the rule of law, the police and the army are playing by different rules. Part of the problem lies in the law, as it has been interpreted by the judges. A police officer or a member of the army who shoots a person usually desires to kill or to cause grievous bodily harm; their expertise and training make it unlikely that the gun has been accidentally discharged or that the injury caused was unforeseen by the user of the gun. That being the case, a murder charge can hardly be avoided if a prosecution is to be launched. The reason for the curious disparity between deaths and convictions lies in the nature of the various defences available to accused persons in these situations. The most important of these are the use of reasonable force in self-defence and section 3(1) of the Criminal Law Act (Northern Ireland) 1967, which states that a 'person may use such force as is reasonable in the circumstances in the prevention of crime or in effecting or assisting in the lawful arrest of offenders or suspected offenders or of persons unlawfully at large'.

There are three important judicial glosses to these defences. 'Reasonable' is a vague word at the best of times, and the courts have been content to define it pragmatically, on a case by case basis. They have, however, stipulated that the relevant circumstances are those in which the accused finds himself or herself at the moment of shooting; they do not include any period of operational planning or tactical surveillance.[26] This is irrelevant as far as the ordinary civilian is concerned—the situation is normally thrust upon him or her; he or she does not usually contrive to have to shoot to survive or to prevent some crime. It is, however, relevant to the RUC, who may have forgone earlier opportunities for a peaceful arrest. Deliberately being put into the position where killing is 'reasonable force' under section 3(1) could, therefore, result in an acquittal. Secondly, there is the question whether killing is a proportionate response to the harm that has been done or the crime that is about to be committed. Killing someone solely to prevent the offence of failing to stop for questions is wrong; just as is such action where the only crime at

---

[26] *Farrell* v. *Secretary of State for Defence* [1980] 1 All ER 166.

issue is a minor assault.[27] In *Attorney-General for Northern Ireland's Reference (No. 1 of 1975)*,[28] a soldier shot and killed an unarmed man who had run away when challenged. The refusal to answer the soldier's challenge was a minor offence under Northern Ireland's terrorism laws. It was clear that the man had had no weapons at the time and the court accepted that he was an 'entirely innocent person who was in no way involved in terrorist activity'.

In considering the soldier's acquittal for murder in the Northern Irish courts, the House of Lords did not focus on the crime committed by the victim in turning away from his questioner. This would have led to further tricky questions about whether such a misdemeanour warranted death. Their Lordships looked instead at the larger issue of the victim's perceived potential for future wrongdoing. As Lord Diplock put it, the soldier could reasonably have apprehended an 'imminent danger to himself and other members of the patrol if the deceased were allowed to get away and join armed fellow-members of the Provisional IRA who might be lurking in the neighbourhood'. It was not unreasonable to assume that the harm to be averted by preventing the victim's escape was even graver than the harm caused by shooting him—i.e. 'the killing or wounding of members of the patrol by terrorists in ambush, and the effect of this success by members of the Provisional IRA in encouraging the continuance of the armed insurrection and all the misery and destruction of life and property that terrorist activity in Northern Ireland has entailed'. This dilution of the notion of imminent danger has the effect of exculpating those defendants whose killings are committed in anticipation of some unspecified violence at some unspecified time in the future. There is a very thin line between this and an open season on all those who fail to stop.

Thirdly, the tendency in the law on self-defence as it has been developed in both Britain and Northern Ireland has been to judge reasonableness on the basis of the facts as the accused knew or honestly believed them to be. Unlike section 3, the defendant does not have to convince the judge that the mistake that was

[27] *R. v. Thain* [1985] 11 NILR 31.
[28] [1977] AC 105.

made was a reasonable one. The subjective rule is fair as far as the ordinary accused goes. People should not be imprisoned for mistakes, even for foolish ones. Juries can be relied upon to separate the bogus from the genuine: the surrounding circumstances will usually give a strong indication of what the accused really believed or knew. A police officer in the dock relies on this rule to argue that he or she believed that either the officer or a colleague was about to be attacked. He or she does not have to have been right; nor does the mistake, if it was one, have to have been reasonable. It is enough that the officer erred. It is a question not of law, but of credibility. A police officer is more likely to be believed than the usual sort of citizen who ends up in the dock on charges like this, particularly in Northern Ireland, where there will often be no jury. Right across the law, judges have shown themselves understandably reluctant to question the judgment of police officers on matters of fact. There will usually be few objective circumstances and many conflicting versions of events. There is an understandable deference to the 'constable on the spot', and a great reluctance to prefer a story that would put such an officer behind bars for life.

These three aspects of the criminal law have meant that, in a succession of controversial cases, it has looked as though the law has unduly favoured the police or the army. In *R.* v. *Bohan and Temperley*,[29] a soldier shot dead a boy who was at an arms cache and whom they believed had been aiming a rifle at them. In fact, the rifle was unloaded and the boy had previously reported the arms cache to the police. The soldiers were acquitted. In *R.* v. *Robinson*,[30] the police shot dead two unarmed men in a car who were, according to the police, about to fire at them. The marksman was acquitted. In another case,[31] three more unarmed men were shot dead by the RUC. The police said that the men had driven through a checkpoint and that the officers involved had feared an immediate attack. Gibson LJ ruled that the defendants had no case to answer and acquitted them of the charge, declaring that the police should be commended for their 'courage and determination in bringing the three deceased men to justice; in this case to the final court of justice'. (Three years after

[29] [1979] 5 NILR.   [30] [1984] 4 NILR.
[31] *Guardian*, 5 June 1984.

the case, Gibson LJ and his wife were murdered by the IRA when the car in which they were travelling was blown up). In yet another case, a young man was shot dead by the RUC when he entered a hay-shed which was under police surveillance after firearms had been discovered in it.[32] The police, who claimed that the victim had pointed a gun at them, were not charged with any offence. In early 1988 an unarmed Catholic, Aidan McAnespie, was shot dead at a border checkpoint in County Tyrone. A charge of manslaughter was brought against the soldier who had allegedly fired the shot, but it was dropped after the DPP decided that there was not enough evidence to warrant a prosecution.

These various structural weaknesses in the law, together with the controversial executive decisions that complement them, are carrying members of the security forces, notionally the same as the rest of us, beyond the reaches of the law. Disquiet over these and other incidents, and in particular suspicions that a covert assassination, or 'shoot to kill', policy was being or had been followed by elements within the security forces, led to a complaint being made under the European Convention on Human Rights, but this was thwarted when the complaint was settled by the Government.[33] Continued disquiet led to the setting-up of an internal police inquiry, under the Deputy Chief Constable of Greater Manchester, John Stalker. Close to the completion of his investigations, disciplinary allegations emerged against Mr Stalker himself. He was suspended from duty pending the outcome of inquiries into his activities and his personal life. He was also removed from the inquiry, his place being taken by Colin Sampson, the Chief Constable of West Yorkshire, whose report found no evidence of murderous activity by officers in the Province. Stalker himself wrote later that the evidence 'pointed to a police inclination, if not a policy, to shoot suspects dead without warning' (Stalker, 1988: 253). Both Stalker and Sampson did conclude, however, that there was evidence that certain police officers had conspired to pervert the course of justice and had obstructed police investigations. In January 1988, the Attorney-General, Sir Patrick Mayhew, announced in the Commons that, despite this evidence, the DPP for Northern Ireland, in consultation

---

[32] *R.* v. *McAuley* [1985] 2 NILR 48.
[33] *Farrell* v. *United Kingdom* (1983) 5 EHRR 466.

with him, had decided not to bring charges against any of the RUC officers implicated by the Report.[34] This was stated to be for reasons of 'national security', though what these were was not further explained by Sir Patrick. There was uproar in the Republic of Ireland and allegations there that the spirit of the Anglo-Irish Agreement was being disregarded.

Perhaps with a view to meeting some of these Irish criticisms, a further investigation into the appropriateness of initiating disciplinary proceedings against certain officers was announced. The Northern Ireland Police Authority decided in June 1988 not to take any action against the Chief Constable and two other senior policemen in the Province. On 4 July 1988 it was revealed that, after an inquiry by Charles Kelly, the Chief Constable of Staffordshire, twenty lower-ranking RUC officers were to be disciplined for their role in the Stalker affair. After another long delay, these hearings eventually got under way in March 1989. Reprimands were delivered to eighteen of the officers; one was cautioned and the charges against the last officer were dismissed. The hearings against all the officers took less than two days and were held in secret. Meanwhile, no disciplinary charges against Mr Stalker were ever forthcoming. Within a short period, however, he left the service altogether. At the time of writing, the affair rumbles on, with litigation still current on the proper scope of the much delayed coroners' inquests at which some of the shootings are to be re-examined. (Special rules apply to inquests in Northern Ireland and these restrict the role of the jury to ascertaining who the deceased was and 'how, when, and where' he or she came by his or her death. Unlike Britain, there is no power to return a verdict of unlawful death.)

Terrorism and the Media

1. 'Death on the Rock'

The most dramatic and controversial 'shoot to kill' occurred not in Northern Ireland but in Gibraltar. The facts need to be recounted in some detail. On Sunday, 6 March 1988, three

---

[34] 126 HC Debs. 21 (25 Jan. 1988).

persons entered the colony from Spain. One, Sean Savage, arrived in a white Renault car sometime between 12.30 and 1 p.m. He parked in Ince's Yard, a place where soldiers of the Royal Anglian Regiment were known to assemble before and after the changing of their guard, a ceremony which was a regular occurrence on Tuesday mornings. The other two, Daniel McCann and Mairead Farrell, entered the territory on foot early in the afternoon. All three met up near where the white Renault was parked and began to walk together towards the Spanish border. Before they had reached the frontier, Savage parted from the other two and headed back towards the town centre. At about 3.40 p.m., a stationary police car near the three of them sounded its siren. At almost exactly the same time, McCann and Farrell were shot dead. Savage was followed and was shot several times. He died instantly. By 3.45 p.m., all three were dead. The men who did the shooting were SAS soldiers in plain clothes. Their victims were later admitted to be members of an active service unit of the IRA.

In the House of Commons on the Monday after the incident, the Foreign Secretary, Sir Geoffrey Howe, gave the official version of what had happened. In fact, there had been no bomb in the car or anywhere else on Gibraltar; a vehicle in Spain which had been hired by the victims had indeed been found—it contained 'three false passports and items of equipment including insulating tape, electrical screwdrivers, a number of pairs of gloves, wire and an alarm clock'. (Later in the week, a bomb was found 40 miles away on the Costa del Sol.) Nor were any of the three IRA members armed when they were shot. Sir Geoffrey explained the killings in the following way:

On their way towards the border, [the three of them] were challenged by the security forces. When challenged, they made movements which led the military personnel operating in support of the Gibraltar police to conclude that their own lives and the lives of others were under threat. In the light of this response, they were shot. Those killed were subsequently found not to have been carrying arms.

The Foreign Secretary ended with a tribute to the Spanish police for having helped to prevent 'a dreadful terrorist act':

I am equally confident that the House will wish me to extend our gratitude to the Spanish authorities, without whose invaluable assistance the outcome might have been very different. This co-operation underlines once again the importance of international collaboration in the fight against terrorism.[35]

Apart from an inquest to be held in Gibraltar, there was, according to the Foreign Secretary, to be no further investigation into the events of the preceding day. In particular, there was to be no criminal inquiry into the circumstances of the killings. When Amnesty International announced their own investigation at the end of the month, the Prime Minister joined an angry Tory back-bencher in castigating it as a 'stunt without status'.[36] The inquest was the place where all was to be examined.

Shortly after the Foreign Secretary's statement to the House of Commons, a team from Thames TV's current affairs programme, *This Week*, began to research a possible television programme on the killings. The programme's editor, Roger Bolton, and the company's Director of News and Current Affairs, Barrie Sales, considered that the 'basic unresolved question at the heart of Sir Geoffrey Howe's statement' was 'why three unarmed terrorists, when challenged by armed security personnel, should make suspicious movements, which gave the impression they were a threat? . . . It did not make sense; there was no logic to it' (Windlesham and Rampton, 1989: 18). In the event, the Thames team uncovered a range of interesting material. New witnesses, previously uncontacted by the local police, came forward to suggest that the three had been shot without warning and without making the threatening movements emphasized in the ministerial statement. The Spanish police co-operated with Thames in order to demonstrate how acute their surveillance had been and how 'a constant flow of information about the terrorists' movements [had been] radioed directly to British officials in Gibraltar' (Windlesham and Rampton, 1989: 46). If true, this would have implied either that the police had knowingly allowed a car that they thought was full of explosives to drive into and around the island, or that they were aware throughout the operation that the car was not dangerous. Finally, a former commander of bomb disposal in

[35] 129 HC Debs. 21 (7 Mar. 1988).
[36] 130 HC Debs. 1274 (30 Mar. 1988). The back-bencher was Mr Ian Gow.

Northern Ireland suggested that the appearance of the Renault driven by Savage would have indicated to the army that it did not contain a significant amount of explosives.

The programme, entitled 'Death on the Rock', was aired on ITV on Thursday, 28 April, between 9 p.m. and 9.45 p.m. At this time, the date for the inquest had still not been fixed and it was not known if the SAS would attend. The following week, a similar programme on BBC Northern Ireland, *Spotlight*, tended to support the Thames version of events. Both transmissions provoked immediate controversy. The Foreign Secretary wrote to the Chairman of the IBA expressing his 'deep regret and serious disquiet' that the inquest would be prejudiced and that the evidence of witnesses would be contaminated by their being forced to take public positions in advance of their testimony. The Prime Minister spoke of her preference for believing that she could 'rely on the television authorities properly to uphold the rule of law'. Meanwhile, one of her senior advisers was reported as declaring that 'the standards of the media [had] declined to the point of institutionalised hysteria'.[37] Others were similarly unrestrained. Their new focus was 'Death on the Rock'. Tory backbenchers spoke of 'a stab in the back for the nation' and the need 'to prevent the media from providing gratuitous support for acts of terrorism'.[38] Many newspapers rallied to the Government's side. The *Sunday Times* covered the story in a way that caused internal dissent amongst journalists. Forthright as ever, at least one tabloid newspaper engaged in a personal attack on a key witness which led to the initiation of libel actions.[39]

Notwithstanding its obvious importance as the only forum in which the killings would be examined, the inquest took an immensely long time to organize. Unlike in Northern Ireland, the scope of an inquest in Gibraltar remains the same as in Britain. For much of the summer, it seemed as though the SAS men would not be in attendance. The Government's request that they be screened from the court was turned down by Gibraltar's coroner, Mr Felix Pizzarello, who insisted that the jury and

[37] *Observer*, 8 May 1988.
[38] See in particular 133 HC Debs. 1083–92 (19 May 1988). The comments quoted in the text came from Mr Stokes and Mr Marlow respectively.
[39] See the *Independent*, 17 Dec. 1988.

counsel for the dead should be able to see them. This was the arrangement that pertained when the inquest finally started on 6 September. The proceedings took a total of nineteen days, and the various allegations about what precisely happened were exhaustively analysed. The soldiers continued to assert that they had killed to protect themselves and also the lives of others, who would have died had their victims pressed the bomb detonators that the soldiers said they believed they possessed. The inquest received written evidence from a Spanish police officer that the IRA unit had been lost by the undercover team following it during the crucial period immediately prior to the entry of the victims into Gibraltar. The officer did not appear in person and was therefore not cross-examined on this statement. It has been consistently contradicted by elements within the Spanish police, and in March 1989 the Spanish authorities honoured twenty-two of their police officers for the role they had played in the surveillance operation. This action seems more in line with Sir Geoffrey Howe's original praise for the 'invaluable assistance' of the Spanish than the subsequent claim of local neglect in losing the IRA trio at Malaga airport.

The inquest heard the stories of those who had appeared earlier on television. One of these witnesses retracted the information he had given to the *This Week* team. The coroner gave his summing-up on 30 September.[40] He told the jury of eleven men that there were three verdicts available to them: 'unlawful killing', 'lawful killing', and an 'open' verdict. 'Unlawful killing' would be appropriate if the jury found that the soldiers had used force when it was not necessary; or more force than was reasonably necessary; or if the soldiers had been 'unwitting tools of a plot to dispose of the three suspects'. If they were not satisfied beyond reasonable doubt about one of these, they should, he said, return a verdict of lawful killing. Mr Pizzarello urged that an open verdict be avoided if at all possible. The eleven men retired at 11.30 a.m. to consider their verdict. They returned at 5.20 p.m. to say that they were unable to agree. The coroner said they were 'reaching the edge' of a reasonable time to produce a decision. They retired once more. At 7.15 p.m. the jury re-emerged and

[40] The full summing-up to the jury by Mr Pizzarello was published in the *Irish Times*, 1 Oct. 1988.

delivered a verdict of lawful killing, by a majority of 9 to 2. This was regarded by the Government as a vindication of the SAS action and as confirmation that neither a real trial—in a proper court of law—nor a formal tribunal of inquiry had ever been necessary. Neither Amnesty International nor the NCCL were so sanguine, with both publishing critical accounts of the procedure at the hearing.

The inquest also refocused attention on the 'Death on the Rock' and *Spotlight* programmes. Thames TV in particular feared a resuscitation of the earlier attacks on them. Partly to circumvent this, and also because they were concerned at the gaps that now seemed to have appeared in 'Death on the Rock', they asked Lord Windlesham, a former Tory Home Office and Northern Ireland Office Minister and one-time Leader of the House of Lords, to conduct an inquiry into the whole affair. Assisted by Richard Rampton QC, Lord Windlesham spent four months receiving and assessing submissions from all the relevant interested parties, including the Foreign Office and the Ministry of Defence, and writing up his conclusions. His report exonerated Thames from violating the due impartiality requirements of the IBA contained in the Broadcasting Act 1981. The programme was 'trenchant and avoided triviality'. Its makers did 'not bribe, bully, or misrepresent those who took part'. They acted 'in good faith and without ulterior motives'. The vast majority of allegations against the programme were dismissed. This view of the film's quality was supported by the BAFTA and Broadcasting Press Guild awards for best single documentary which 'Death on the Rock' later won. Lord Windlesham's reward for such independence was to be subject to a campaign of personal and political attack. The Prime Minister simply dismissed the report *in toto* and repeated her view that there had been 'many serious and damaging inaccuracies' and a conscious failure 'to pursue the truth'.[41] In the Lords, the Minister of State for Defence, Lord Trefgarne, thought Lord Windlesham had 'singularly failed' to draw the 'proper conclusions'—his report was a 'sad commentary on the standards now expected of the media'. His Tory colleague, Lord Beloff, wondered 'what business is it of a young television

[41] *Independent*, 27 Jan. 1989.

producer to decide that he has the right to cast doubt on what is going on, because it does not seem to his tender conscience that justice has been done or the law has been fully observed?'[42]

2. The media ban

There can be little doubt that the events of the first half of 1988 crystallized the Government's mistrust of the way in which television approached the reporting of political violence. In a succession of different situations, the medium had shown itself to be in the hands of those who, if not on the other side in Mrs Thatcher's straightforward moral lexicon, were at any rate shuffling half-heartedly in the middle—and this was almost as bad. After the Omagh bomb in which eight British soldiers were killed, the Prime Minister appears to have decided to launch a new offensive against the IRA, and Provisional Sinn Fein in particular. One of the inevitable targets, innocent but accessible, were the media. Existing law was vague on the question of the degree of contact journalists could have with proscribed organizations. Section 11 (now section 18) of the Prevention of Terrorism Act criminalized the failure, without reasonable excuse, to contact the authorities where a person had information which he or she knew or believed might be of material assistance in preventing acts of terrorism or in apprehending terrorists.

This measure had been used in the past to intimidate journalists who had got too close to the IRA in their pursuit of a story. After an incident in 1979, during which an IRA road-block in Carrickmore was filmed (but not broadcast) by a *Panorama* crew, the Attorney-General wrote to the Chairman of the BBC, drawing attention to section 11. It was by threatening prosecutions under this provision that the RUC obtained the pictures of the West Belfast funeral at which two army corporals were brutally killed in 1988. The reluctance of ITN and the BBC to hand the material over voluntarily caused the Prime Minister to remark that either 'one [was] on the side of justice in these matters or one [was] on the side of terrorism'.[43] The film of Michael Stone's

[42] See the debate in the House of Lords on 1 Mar. 1989. These comments are recorded at 504 HL Debs. 1103 and 1130.
[43] 130 HC Debs. 194 (22 Mar. 1988).

attack on the burial ceremony at Milltown cemetery in March 1988 was also obtained by invocation of section 11.[44] Walker (1986: 110–11) recounts one story about an American crew from ABC News which was arrested in 1979 after interviewing members of Provisional Sinn Fein. Film was confiscated but no charges were brought. This was hardly surprising. It would not have been particularly astute diplomacy to jail an American broadcaster (in this case, the renowned Pierre Salinger, formerly President Kennedy's press spokesman) for talking to a legal political party in Northern Ireland. Similar considerations may have been behind the decision not to bring charges against another American journalist, Donna Foote, for interviewing an IRA man for the weekly magazine, *Newsweek*, in September 1988. A further factor behind the lack of actual use of the section lies in the difficulties of proof; its construction shows clearly that it was never Parliament's intention to target the provision against journalists, and, indeed, the most recent review of the Act had suggested its repeal (Colville, 1987: para. 15.1.3).

Most serious of all in Mrs Thatcher's eyes, however, was the fact that the provision could do little to prevent members of Provisional Sinn Fein appearing on British television screens, thereby enjoying the media publicity which was, in her view, their life-blood. There was little evidence, however, that the organization had been particularly successful in this regard over the years. Quite apart from the law, Northern Ireland has always been an extremely sensitive topic for the broadcasting authorities. Complicated referral systems have operated for years so as to ensure that controversy does not get out of hand. There have been many examples since the early 1970s of programmes being withdrawn because of anxiety about their presentation of the conflict in Northern Ireland. The most famous of these was *Real Lives* in 1985, which was first delayed and then altered by the BBC, after pressure from the Home Office. The film involved a portrait of one of Sinn Fein's leaders, Martin McGuinness. In

[44] *Guardian*, 23 Feb. 1989. The RUC would now presumably rely on sect. 17 of the 1989 Act. The police in England and Wales have a similar power under the Police and Criminal Evidence Act 1984 to order journalists to give up evidence relevant to the police investigation. See *R.* v. *Bristol Crown Court, ex parte Bristol Press and Picture Agency Ltd.* (1987) 85 Cr. App. R. 190.

September 1988, Channel 4 dropped a programme in the *After Dark* series when it became apparent that Gerry Adams was to be one of its guests. In early October the same year, a *Panorama* documentary on the SAS was transmitted in an edited form after the BBC, having received the advice of the D-notice Committee, had refused to show the original programme.[45]

Despite these demonstrations of good faith and responsibility, as the authorities would describe it, the Government acted to reinforce the law. On 19 October 1988, the Home Secretary, Mr Hurd, issued a notice to both the BBC and the IBA, under the Licence and Agreement section and section 29(3) of the Broadcasting Act 1981 respectively, requiring both organizations to:

refrain from broadcasting any matter which consists of or includes—any words spoken, whether in the course of an interview or discussion or otherwise, by a person who appears or is heard on the programme in which the matter is broadcast where—

    (*a*) the person speaking the words represents or purports to represent an organisation specified in paragraph 2 below, or

    (*b*) the words support or solicit or invite support for such an organisation, other than any matter specified in paragraph 3 below.

Paragraph 2 makes clear that all the proscribed organizations under either the Prevention of Terrorism or Emergency Provisions Acts are caught by the ban; this covers the IRA, the INLA, the UVF, the Ulster Freedom Fighters, the Red Hand Commando, Fianna na hEireann, Cumann na mBan, and Saor Eire. Three legal organizations are also included: Sinn Fein, Republican Sinn Fein, and the Ulster Defence Association. The matter specified in paragraph 3 as being exempt from the ban is:

any words spoken—(*a*) in the course of proceedings in Parliament, or (*b*) by or in support of a candidate at a parliamentary, European Parliamentary or local election pending that election.

Mr Hurd presented the ban to Parliament as a *fait accompli*. There was no consultation with any interested party before it was issued and no requirement that either House should approve it. The measure is not temporary, nor in any way linked to the level of violence in Northern Ireland; even if the IRA were disbanded

---

[45] *Guardian*, 13 Oct. 1988.

tomorrow, there is no obvious mechanism to force the Government to review it; the hope is that the Government would then deign to lift it. From its birth through to its demise (if there is one), this act of censorship exists entirely as a creature of executive discretion. It applies throughout the kingdom and is specifically designed to include lawful political parties. At the outset, the Government explained the ban by pointing to 'the occasional appearance of representatives of paramilitary organisations and their political wings' on television and radio, justifying their criminal activities.[46] This had 'caused widespread offence to viewers and listeners throughout the United Kingdom, particularly just after a terrorist outrage'. The 'offence' caused by such appearances, after the Enniskillen bomb for example, generally leads to a massive drop in Provisional Sinn Fein support: there are few more powerful images than that of a supposedly respectable 'politician' refusing to discuss the murder of innocent civilians by men or women whom he or she explicitly supports. It is curious that the Government should take these drastic steps specifically in order to save such terrorist frontmen from their own embarrassment.

It may be because of such arguments that the Government saw fit to develop two further justifications for the ban. The first, which only emerged during a Commons debate three weeks after the banning Order was introduced, highlighted the 'use of the media to deliver indirect threats'. The Home Secretary gave no examples of such exploitation; what he discussed was 'the ripple of fear' caused by the appearance of supporters of violence 'on the screen and thus in the homes of their victims'. This generalized anxiety is not, of course, the same as individual threats, the issuance of which is already covered by the criminal law. It is vague and nebulous, and something to which the people mainly threatened have sadly become accustomed. Even if true, it would only apply in Northern Ireland, not throughout Britain. Such wide-ranging warnings as the Home Secretary seems to have had in mind verge on a type of hoodlum propaganda, have been occurring on and off for twenty years, are rarely if ever voiced

---

[46] The Home Secretary's original statement about the ban is at 138 HC Debs. 885–95 (19 Oct. 1988). The debate on the banning Order is at 139 HC Debs. 1075–157 (2 Nov. 1988).

directly by spokesmen for the IRA or Sinn Fein, and may, in any event, still be effectively communicated through the newspapers. It is hard to see why, at this point in time rather than any other, they should have provoked the Government into acting in such a dramatic fashion.

The same is true of the third reason for the ban offered by the Home Secretary, namely that the 'terrorists themselves draw support and sustenance from access to radio and television'. The number of appearances of 'terrorists' (i.e. those who commit or are involved in violent crimes for political purposes) is minute and each will generally involve the journalist concerned in potential liability under section 11 (now Section 18). Equally, members of the IRA or other proscribed organizations have rarely if ever appeared on British television in the 1980s. The Home Secretary must have been referring to members of the legal organization, Provisional Sinn Fein. As a result we must now add to our lexicon this new, ill-defined, and open-ended category of 'government designated' terrorists, against whom no charges are brought, but various draconian administrative actions may be directed. All three reasons, both individually and collectively, reflect a breath-taking insensitivity, almost an ignorance, of the countervailing value of freedom of expression, and a remarkable lack of confidence in the intelligence of the public and its ability to detect terrorist propaganda when it sees or hears it.

Gagging Sinn Fein in this fashion has serious consequences for any society whose politics are structured around fair elections and the free exchange of ideas. It is a truism that television and radio are immensely powerful media, and that access to them is crucial to any group that wants to communicate a political message. Denial of such a platform is a clear act of political censorship (unless the Government thinks that neither medium matters much politically, in which case it should stop selling its own case so extravagantly on both, and withdraw the ban, justified as it is by references to the power of television). Embarrassing though it might be for the Government and for constitutional parties throughout Ireland, Sinn Fein is an established political organiza-tion, with around 11 per cent of the votes cast at the 1989 local elections (despite the ban), one elected MP, and dozens of local councillors. The majority of the Province's twenty-six councils have or have had some Sinn Fein representation, and the Party has supplied the chairmen of local councils from time to time. Its members may support the objectives of the IRA, but they represent much more than this in the politics of Northern Ireland. Issues like housing, social welfare, employment, and so on preoccupy the public life of a Sinn Fein councillor far more than the 'armed struggle'. Their local constituency clinics are visited not by gunmen calling for closer links with Libya, but voters demanding better services from their council. We may deplore that Provisional Sinn Fein functions at all or that it does so in a reasonably popular way. We may also be indignant at the cynical manipulation of the electorate represented by their chilling tactic of using both the 'armalite and the ballot box'. But the one thing we cannot afford to do is to pretend that they do not exist.

This is precisely the fantasy encouraged by the ban. As with proscription in the 1970s, we are being invited to join an unreal world of suburban bliss, in which the villains have been legislated into non-existence and the closest thing there is to a real 'bad egg' is Seamus Mallon MP. Rather than face up to the horrendous alienation implied by such strong electoral support for Sinn Fein, the Government has closed its eyes and now compels the population to do the same. Such blindness distorts truth; such political irresponsibility stores up trouble for the future. And, quite apart from this, the ban of course goes far beyond Sinn Fein, and reaches (as censorship invariably does) into the inner recesses of absurdity. Archive footage of the former Irish Taoiseach and President, Mr de Valera, during his days as a fighter for Irish freedom, may not be shown. Nor may any documentary be broadcast in full if it contains reminiscences by ancient statesmen of their contribution to Irish politics during that period. A large part of the life of the late Sean McBride is now completely taboo; he was IRA Chief of Staff in the 1930s; his Nobel and Lenin peace prizes are unlikely to save him from a media extinction to match his corporeal demise. Robert Key's series on Ireland and the ITV programmes on the Troubles may not now appear in their complete form. Henceforth, the British are to see and hear only sanitized versions of Irish history. Drama and other works of fiction are probably not caught, since the 'words spoken' are not those of the actor, but rather those of the writer. The speaker therefore, being little more than a thoughtless voice for another's ideas, can be as subversive as his or her writer wants. (There is as yet no requirement that he or she act badly when presenting the 'wrong' point of view.)

It is clear that an individual does not need to be a member of any group to get caught by the ban; it is enough that his or her words 'support or solicit or invite support' for any of the affected organizations. This includes the obvious chants at a Glasgow Celtic game, or a political rally in Hyde Park. No speech by a foreign leader giving support to Sinn Fein may appear on British television. The ban also catches campaigners like Pat Arrowsmith and Ken Livingstone, if their backing for the Troops Out Movement should drift too close to support for the banned political parties who follow this line. (It is still fine, of course, to talk with or about Abu Nidhal, ETA, Hizbollah, and all the other countless groups across the world with murderous records that match the grisly statistics of the IRA.) As drafted, the Order also dispenses with any news reporting of Sinn Fein (or IRA) statements about their intentions and desires, since these will invariably be 'words spoken . . . by a person . . . which support or solicit or invite support' for the organization. The matters excluded from the ban merely draw attention to its breadth. Were Mr Adams to take his seat in Westminster, his words could be broadcast. During election time, whether it be European, parliamentary, or local, the media are free to interview and report, as long as what is broadcast is 'by or in support of a candidate', rather than the party he or she represents. No election night speech by a Sinn Fein candidate may appear or be heard, however, even if he or she has just won the election. The proceedings of the European Parliament or of any court in the world may not be broadcast if the subject-matter infringes the ban. Cable and satellite television are nowhere covered in the banning Order. Gerry Adams may speak to us about Sinn Fein from outer space—but not from West Belfast.

When Mr Hurd introduced the ban, he declared that it placed broadcasters in the same position as the written press in relation to its reporting on Ireland. The controversy which this provoked forced some modifications in the weeks that followed. No amendment to the Order occurred and on one occasion a Minister casually wondered why confused journalists should not simply ring up the Home Office for clarification of any difficulties that they might encounter! Eventually, however, the Government accepted that mere indirect reporting of words spoken by someone else was not the same as the person himself or herself being broadcast actually speaking them, and was therefore not impermissible. Thus, news reports on the IRA and Sinn Fein and so on were still possible. Furthermore, it became apparent that the authorities did not mind such reporting of words appearing on television accompanied by a picture of the person who uttered them. Then it emerged that it was also possible to synchronize the words spoken by an actor or reporter, with the lip movements of the person in front of the camera as he or she actually said them; the crucial thing was not to hear the actual speaker. A *Panorama* programme in early 1989 was one of the first to play this naughty game. The Government also announced that Sinn Fein councillors could appear on radio and television as long as they were speaking in a personal capacity or purely in a capacity as members of a local council. It was in his role as a constituency MP welcoming investment in his area that a BBC Northern Ireland's *Spotlight* programme in February 1989 risked a few seconds of Mr Gerry Adams. Such suspensions of the full force of the Order by executive discretion are very welcome but the operation of these liberal concessions will require a pedantic accuracy of the sort that has given moral theology a bad name. How far can you go? is now asked in an editing room rather than a confessional.

In practice, the main impact of the ban has been as a stimulus to the self-censorship which we have already described. Both the IBA and the BBC have promulgated rules with a view to ensuring its efficient operation. Interviews with relatives campaigning for the release of the four Irish people convicted of the Guildford and Woolwich bombings have been cancelled,[47] and a pop song by the Pogues, declaring the four prisoners' innocence, has been refused airtime.[48] An independent television company has denied access to a labour councillor who is also a member of the Troops Out Movement.[49] Such instances of censorship in the first months of the ban bode ill for the future. Nor did the BBC or the IBA see fit

[47] *Independent*, 11 Nov. 1988. [48] *Observer*, 20 Nov. 1988.
[49] *Independent*, 13 Feb. 1989.

to challenge the ban in court. This task was left to Sinn Fein, the National Union of Journalists, and a few individuals working within the media. The application for judicial review which was launched before the English Divisional Court was unsuccessful— a somewhat surprising outcome, in view of the uncertainty of the Order, the failure to consult in advance of its issuance, its apparent conflict with the broadcasters' duty of impartiality, and its erosion of the presumption in favour of free expression which the textbooks say operates as a guide to interpreting secondary legislation.

In a judgment delivered on 26 May 1989, the Divisional Court (Watkins LJ, Roch, Judge JJ.) considered that the Home Secretary's decision 'was not perverse or absurd or a decision which no reasonable minister properly directing himself in law could reach'.[50] The Court also volunteered its view that the ban complied with Article 10 of the European Convention—it was a restriction 'necessary in a democratic society in the interests of national security, territorial integrity or public safety'. If it survives appeal, it is to be hoped that the European Court will take a more robust view of its own law that did the Divisional Court. If these absurdly wide and poorly drafted restrictions are 'necessary in a democratic society', it is hard to imagine anything that could not be brought within this umbrella. If the ban does finally succumb to the critical gaze of the judiciary, it will be no thanks to a media establishment more concerned with its own future than with the freedom of expression which it exists to exercise and promote.

The Government may argue that Sinn Fein has been in-convenienced by the ban, that they have lost some media attention that would otherwise have been theirs during 1989, the twentieth anniversary year of the Troubles. This may be true, but the cost has been severe. The principle of freedom of expression has been carelessly jettisoned. As Dworkin noted in his article in *Index on Censorship* (Dworkin, 1988), it is in Britain a dispensable commodity, occasionally useful, but never likely to survive where its consequences are remotely unpleasant for Government. Apart from principle, there is precedent. Other groups may follow Sinn

[50] R. v. *Secretary of State for the Home Department, ex parte Brind* (1989) 139 NLJ 1229.

Fein into media invisibility. Some foreign governments relish the opportunity to push for a curtailment of the activities of the BBC's World Service and it may well be that the media ban will reinforce their misapprehension that the Corporation is under government control. The prevention of terrorism legislation shows how powers special to Northern Irish terrorism can quickly be broadened to cover the whole globe. Finally there are the political consequences. The whole edifice of the 'rule of law' is severely dented. Those who support the Sinn Fein analysis of British oppression have further confirmation of their enemies' characteristic contortion of the law to suit their needs. The 'politicos' within the IRA and Sinn Fein are reminded of how weak they are when they try to draw away from violence and into mainstream politics—it can hardly have helped their credibility underground. To many Northern Irish nationalists, the ban is further justification of their political estrangement. And all for what? So that the BBC has to use an actor to pretend to be Gerry Adam's voice when he speaks about Sinn Fein on television. It is a curious victory.

Conclusion

The Government's policy of criminalization has the useful political consequence that the IRA can be presented at home and (more importantly) abroad as a criminal problem devoid of political ramifications being coped with by the ordinary processes of the law. This has never had a ring of complete truth to it. Residues from the days of militarization, like the emergency provisions law, remain in place. The Diplock courts are a continuing reminder of the abnormal nature of criminal justice in the Province. Allegations about the ill-treatment of suspects, which reached a peak in the late 1970s, continue to surface occasionally. In February 1989, for example, a report submitted to the UN Commission on Human Rights by one of its rapporteurs expressed concern 'over the level of complaints of assault and other improper practice during police interrogation of suspected terrorists'.[51]

[51] *Independent*, 15 Feb. 1989. The Government responded by saying that all complaints were investigated and prosecutions were ordered where appropriate.

The huge 'supergrass' trials of the early 1980s, in which the conviction of dozens of men was being sought on the basis of the uncorroborated evidence of RUC informers, were anything but commonplace criminal cases. Provisional Sinn Fein has occupied an anomalous situation since the withdrawal of its banning Order in 1974—neither illegal nor (in the eyes of the Government, if not of many of the electorate) part of the political mainstream. All this may be capable of being explained away as essential modifications, necessitated by violence, to a basic approach that remains rooted in law and justice. With the sequence of events catalogued in this chapter, however, this proposition has become even harder to maintain. Gibraltar, Stalker, the early release of the soldier convicted of murder, the *Brogan* case, the erosion of the right to silence, the new terrorism legislation, the narrow scope of coroners' inquests, and the media ban are all clear evidence of an abnormal rule of law. There have been other developments on top of these. The law on searches has been widened and tougher remission rules have been introduced, but for 'terrorist criminals' only (i.e. those convicted of 'scheduled offences' in the Diplock courts and sentenced to five years or more). If the IRA are no more than a bunch of criminals, then it is hard to see why such draconian and highly selective action is warranted.

The international difficulties that can arise out of fighting what amounts to a covert war under cover of the rule of law are well illustrated by the Ryan affair. Fr. Ryan was apprehended in Belgium and held as a suspected quartermaster for the IRA. The British requested his return to face charges which included the curious offence of 'conspiring with persons unknown to murder persons unknown'. The Belgians thought the allegations unspecific and sent Ryan to Ireland, where there was a delay of some days while the British authorities filed valid warrants and the Irish Attorney-General examined the case. Events were not moving fast enough for the Prime Minister; she declared that 'we are utterly dismayed' at the Belgian action. As for the Irish, their tardiness was inexcusable. It was 'no use governments adopting great declarations and commitments about fighting terrorism if they then lack the resolve to put them into practice . . . although the Government of the Republic of Ireland make fine-sounding speeches and statements, they do not always seem to be backed by appropriate deeds.'[52] Mrs Thatcher used an EEC summit in Rhodes later in the same week to bring home to both countries the extent of her anger. All this was of no avail, however; in fact, in many ways it was counter-productive.

The Irish Attorney-General, Mr Murray, refused to return Ryan for trial in England, referring in his statement to attacks in the British media on the suspect's 'general character, often expressed in intemperate language and frequently in the form of extravagantly worded headlines'. Mr Murray also mentioned certain statements in Parliament which he thought carried 'an assumption or inference of guilt'.[53] Behind his decision lies a concern shared by many in Ireland that it is difficult for an Irish person facing terrorist charges to secure a fair trial in Britain. There is great concern that those convicted of the Birmingham and Guildford pub bombings in the 1970s were not in fact responsible for these attacks, a concern fully vindicated by the release of the Guildford Four. There is a similar doubt over the Maguire family's conviction for explosives offences in the same period. More recently, the severity of the sentences meted out to three persons convicted of conspiracy to murder after they were apprehended in the vicinity of the home of the Secretary of State for Northern Ireland surprised many lawyers. At the core of the problem are Irish misgivings that the Anglo-Irish Agreement's recognition of the connection between security policy and politics has been quietly jettisoned. These have not been allayed by the Prime Minister's colourful insinuations of moral turpitude.

The state's response to the violence that emanates from Northern Ireland is based upon a fundamental contradiction. On the one hand, it gives itself broad and wide-ranging powers on the basis of needing to deal with a type of violence—'terrorism'—that is explicitly defined by reference to political motivation. On the other hand, the moment it gets these powers, it forsakes the political dimension and goes on to operate them as though all that had to be dealt with was a criminal problem. The IRA are terrorist (i.e. political) when it comes to arguing for new laws;

[52] 142 HC Debs. 574–5 (29 Nov. 1988).

[53] The full text of the Attorney-General's statement is published in *The Times*, 14 Dec. 1988. Prosecution in Ireland under the Criminal Law (Jurisdiction) Act 1976 is now being considered.

criminal when it comes to applying them. Yet to deny the political context of IRA violence is to close our eyes to the depths of antagonism and hostility that are exhibited towards the British state in certain parts of Northern Ireland. The killing does not come from nowhere; nor is it sustained in a vacuum of criminal isolation. The IRA receives at least the passive support of a proportion of members of those communities which have, through generations of discrimination, unemployment, and neglect, found few others to stand up for them. The electoral support for Provisional Sinn Fein speaks for itself. The failure to accommodate this political dimension has desensitized the army and the police to the alienation caused by the exercise of many of their powers. The systematic search of houses over a wide area, detention for interrogation, exclusion, the use of plastic bullets, the abolition of the right to silence, and so on make perfect security sense; but the extent to which they are adding to political estrangement will not be noticed by the officer who thinks himself to be doing no more than pursuing some dangerous criminals. By defining politics out of the equation at this stage, the authorities are merely adding to the breeding-ground of alienation from which the next crop of violent subversives will be drawn.

Rather than pretend that such a situation does not exist, the task for Government is to wean these inactive supporters away from the gunman, so as to reduce by a process of political reconciliation the core of his support. This does not mean dealing with the IRA. But it does involve looking at the problem in the round, as one involving political and economic solutions as well as military ones. The goal should be to isolate the politically violent, by showing that there is an alternative to their sad and destructive message. The Anglo-Irish Agreement and recent legislation on fair employment show that the Government is occasionally aware of the need for this broader thrust to its policy. The rule of law should also have a role in helping to create this culture of reconciliation, by being demonstrably fair, even-handed, and responsive to the community in which it is applied. Instead, however, we have this blinkered policy of criminalization which largely denies these broader strands and which sunders 'law and order' and security issues from politics. Such narrowness may purchase peace of mind and a sense of moral superiority over the estranged communities of Northern Ireland. The price paid for this deceit is the continuation of islands of alienation within the state and the maintenance of a cycle of violence emanating from them which the security forces can contain, but which they will never end, because it is their supposed solutions, together with decades of deprivation, that perpetuate it.

8

Conclusion

IT should now be clear that civil liberties in Britain are in a state of crisis. We have charted the unprecedented extension of police powers; a far-reaching statute for the interception of communications by the state; wide-ranging restrictions on the freedom of assembly and public protest; the growth of a national security consciousness used to justify major limitations on press freedom in particular; the extension of the powers of the security service and the lack of any effective accountability for the way these powers are exercised and, finally, the assumption of quite extraordinary powers to deal with the troubles in the north of Ireland, admittedly an issue of immense complexity. And these are only some of the setbacks of the last ten years. We have said nothing of the notorious 'clause 28' which reduces the right to freedom of expression of gay men and women by providing that local authorities shall not promote the teaching in any maintained school of the acceptability of homosexuality as a pretended family relationship.[1] We have said nothing of the use of customs legislation to stop the import of classics of gay literature even though some of the material is published and legally sold here. And we have said nothing of the discriminatory legislation (and the discriminatory application of such legislation) dealing with questions of nationality, immigration, and citizenship. But it all adds up, providing further evidence of a widespread spirit of intolerance.

The major source of the problem in our view is a political system which has allowed the concentration of power in the hands of the executive (and the Prime Minister in particular) and the absence of any effective checks and balances. The position is perhaps all the more remarkable for the fact that power has concentrated in the hands of an executive branch which by all

[1] Local Government Act 1988, sect. 28.

accounts enjoys the support of less than half the voting public, and certainly much less than half the total adult population. Although the Conservatives won the General Election in 1979 they did so by polling only 43·9 per cent of the vote. And they won again in 1983 and 1987 by polling only 42·4 per cent and 43·3 per cent of the vote. Traditionally the problem for civil liberties has been to protect the minority from the oppression of the majority. In Britain, paradoxically, the problem is increasingly one in which there is a need to protect the majority from the behaviour of an increasingly small minority. Yet, notwithstanding the questionable legitimacy of the electoral system, the leader of a majority party in an election has, on becoming prime minister, quite enormous power.

By control over appointment to and dismissal from the Cabinet the prime minister is subject to little restraint from his or her immediate colleagues. Party discipline gives almost complete control over the House of Commons which has become simply the medium through which the prime minister governs rather than a forum for holding government to account. Paradoxically again it is the unelected House of Lords which has been the major institutional bulwark to executive power, though, as we noted in Chapter 1, even this can be outmanœuvred by the strategic use of backwoodsmen when the need arises. The concentration of power has been helped enormously by a passive press, a most disappointing institution which has surrendered any claim that it might have had as a public watch-dog to become the lap-dog of the administration. There are of course a few notable exceptions to this, and a few notable incidents which suggest that the embers have not been completely extinguished. But for the most part our press is greedy and titillating, concerned to defend the attack on our liberties rather than to expose them.

The BBC, on the other hand, has been intimidated and harassed, with dependence on government goodwill for funding inhibiting its presence as a virile political force. The difficulties are illustrated by a number of events over the last ten years, including the *Real Lives* broadcast in 1985; the Zircon affair in 1987; the injunction restraining the radio broadcasting of *My Country Right or Wrong*; and finally the broadcasting ban on Sinn Fein. Although the IBA has not been attacked as aggressively as the BBC, it has not escaped the attention of the Government, with the Foreign Office expressing concern about the showing of 'Death on the Rock'. Also controversial has been the appointment of Lord Rees-Mogg to chair the non-statutory Broadcasting Standards Council, formed to draw up a code on the portrayal of sex and violence and to monitor and report on these and other questions. This development was said by Mr Roy Hattersley to 'cause great disquiet among those who believe in the freedom of broadcasting and broadcasters', and was condemned as being 'the thin end of a highly authoritarian wedge'.[2]

Parliamentary Scrutiny

One potential response to the present crisis is to improve the techniques for parliamentary scrutiny in areas of civil liberties and human rights. A major initiative, if albeit a belated response to the growing power of the executive at the expense of the Commons, was the introduction of a new Select Committee system in 1979. The Committees are appointed each session to investigate the 'expenditure, administration and policy' of the major departments of state. The Committees investigate a wide range of topics, and the Home Affairs Committee in particular has dealt with issues which have a bearing on civil liberties, such as the 'Sus' laws, immigration rules, and deaths in police custody. But the Committees do not generally examine legislative proposals in the manner of Congressional Committees. Nevertheless, in order to enhance parliamentary scrutiny of civil liberties issues an initiative introduced in Australia may repay careful study.

The Australian Senate Standing Committee for the Scrutiny of Bills was first established by resolution of the Senate on 19 November 1981. It has since been re-established by resolution at the commencement of subsequent Parliaments. The Committee consists of six Senators, three government and three non-government, the chair being taken by one of the government members. The Committee, which operates on a non-partisan basis, is appointed to scrutinize bills for five different purposes.

[2] For details of the Broadcasting Standards Council, see 133 HC Debs. 689 (16 May 1988).

The first three of these are whether a bill will trespass unduly on personal rights and privileges; make rights, liberties, and/or obligations unduly dependent upon insufficiently defined administrative powers; or make rights, liberties, and/or obligations unduly dependent upon non-reviewable administrative decisions. According to one Senator who has taken an active interest in the work of the Committee, its task is purely 'a watching brief', 'to alert the Senate to the possibility of infringements of rights and liberties', expressing no concluded view on whether the clauses on which it comments do in fact constitute such infringements (Tate, 1985: 2). The experiment has, apparently, been successful. Thus it has been claimed that:

On average [the Committee] has drawn attention to a clause or clauses in just over one third of the Bills introduced into the Parliament. It has received some response to roughly three-quarters of its comments and over a tenth of the clauses it has commented upon have been amended to answer its concern in the course of the passage of the Bills in question through the Parliament. (Tate, 1985)

At an early stage of its life, the Committee developed a set of guidelines to give some indication to those responsible for drafting legislation of the matters which it might consider to trespass on rights and liberties. Thus, in a report of 1982, the Committee indicated that in considering bills it would have regard to matters such as whether the legislation:

(a) placed the onus of proof on a defendant in a criminal prosecution;
(b) conferred a power of entry onto land or premises other than by warrant according to law;
(c) conferred a power of search of the subject, land or premises other than by warrant issued according to law;
(d) conferred a power to seize goods other than by warrant issued according to law;
(e) purported to legislate retrospectively;
(f) affected the liberty of the subject by controls upon freedom of movement, freedom of association, freedom of expression, freedom of religion, or freedom of peaceful assembly.

The Committee has since determined that it is not possible to categorize all the problems and that 'the possible set of provisions which may trespass unduly on personal rights and liberties is as extensive as those rights and liberties themselves' (Tate, 1985: 13).

The same author continued by asserting that 'In many instances debate, particularly at the Committee stages, has been enhanced . . . [and] the existence of the Committee and its performance of a monitoring function in respect of all Bills have immeasurably improved the execution by the Parliament of its legislative functions' (Tate 1985: 2–3). So far as results are concerned success must be determined by the impact which the Committee has on legislation. It seems that the Committee does at least force the department to have a second look at a clause. In most cases the department in question will respond to the Committee, usually to justify the clause commented upon. In many cases the Committee has not accepted the justification advanced by the Minister and has continued to draw attention to the clause at issue. In other cases (albeit a small number) the Minister will give an undertaking that the proposed legislation will be reviewed, while in still other cases the Minister may promise amendments to the clauses to which the Committee has drawn attention. In fact some 10 per cent of clauses commented on have led to government amendment, though it is not clear if the Committee's comments were a factor and if so the only factor in the Government's decision. Nevertheless, it has been claimed that 'the executive gives close attention to the comments made by the Committee' (Tate, 1985: 63) and that 'it is only through the existence of a specialist Committee performing the scrutiny function that this re-examination of legislation will take place and that such improvements in legislation will be made' (Tate, 1985: 64).

A Human Rights Commission?

A second possible response to the crisis is the introduction of some external administrative scrutiny of human rights questions. The idea is not a new one, having been proposed by Sam Silkin as long ago as 1971 and revived by him in a public lecture in Belfast in 1977. There he proposed the incorporation of the European Convention into British law and the creation of a Commission of Rights to 'investigate, report and recommend to Parliament, in the same way as does the [Ombudsman], but like him it would have no power to enforce'. This, he thought, would be 'a substantial step forward', even if he also thought that something more had become necessary (Silkin, 1977). The Ombudsman to whom Silkin referred is an office created in 1967 on the model of earlier Scandinavian initiatives. His function essentially is to investigate complaints of maladministration and report on these complaints to Parliament. Although he may make recommendations he is ultimately unable to enforce them and must rely on Parliament to do so. The office is not one particularly concerned with civil liberties and indeed many civil liberties issues are expressly excluded from his jurisdiction. But presumably what Silkin had in mind here is that his Commission would investigate complaints alleging a breach of the European Convention on Human Rights and refer these to Parliament with recommendations for action. The weakness of course arises where the alleged breach is clearly authorized by legislation only recently passed or universally approved on the government benches. Whereas complaints of maladministration can be resolved without amending legislation, this will rarely be true of European Convention violations.

Nevertheless, a device not unlike that proposed so long ago by Silkin now operates in Australia where the Human Rights Commission Act 1981 provides for the creation of a Human Rights Commission to promote and protect human rights. In fact the Commission, which is appointed by a government Minister, has a wide range of duties. First, it is to examine statutes (and when requested by the Minister proposed enactments) to establish whether they are (or would be) inconsistent with human rights. Secondly, it is to enquire into any government conduct which may be inconsistent with or contrary to human rights and to report on any such inquiry to the Minister. These inquiries may arise as a result of complaints referred to it by an aggrieved citizen. Thirdly, on its own initiative, or when requested by the Minister, it may issue reports as to legislation which is necessary on matters relating to human rights. Fourthly, on request from the Minister it may report on what measures are necessary in order to comply with various international human rights documents. And on top of all of this, the Commission has responsibility for the administration of the Racial Discrimination Act 1975 and the Sex Discrimination Act 1984, mirroring functions in this respect which are performed in Britain by the Commission for Racial Equality and the Equal Opportunities Commission respectively. But on the human rights questions the Commission thus has a mixture of functions: it scrutinizes; it takes complaints and conducts inquiries into these complaints; and it proposes law reform initiatives. There is nothing on such a scale in Britain.

The standard of human rights to which the Commission must aspire are to be found in a number of international instruments annexed to the Act. These are the International Covenant on Civil and Political Rights, the Declaration of the Rights of the Child, the Declaration on the Rights of Mentally Retarded Persons, and the Declaration on the Rights of Disabled Persons. (If a similar arrangement operated in Britain it would be possible to add the European Convention on Human Rights to the list or indeed to make it the only item on the list. And in view of our currently dismal record at the ILO, it would be appropriate to do the same with selected ILO Conventions, particularly No. 87 which figures so prominently in the GCHQ case.) Since 1981 the Commission has in fact examined a number of statutes and reported on their consistency with international obligations. The statutes or proposed statutes included the Australian Citizenship Act 1948; proposals to amend the Racial Discrimination Act to render incitement to racial hatred unlawful; and the Queensland Electricity (Continuation of Supply) Act 1985 restricting freedom of association during a bitter strike in the Queensland electricity industry. More recently the Commission examined the Broadcasting and Television Act 1942 and concluded that freedom of expression was violated by a provision which gave broadcasting time during an election only to political parties which at the time were represented in Parliament. The Commission has also dealt with a large number of individual complaints from citizens about the conduct of public bodies alleged to violate the international instruments. In 1985 these complaints related to matters as varied as the deportation of Australian-born children; the rights of the disabled; freedom of association; and privacy concerning application forms.

It may well be that this is a model which could be built upon in Britain, though it is far from ideal. One problem is that the members of the Australian Commission are appointed by the Government, in this case the Attorney-General, without any indication as to who should be appointed. Such a power in the UK would defeat the very purpose of independent scrutiny and review. The power of appointment can be used very effectively to neuter any potentially effective administrative agency. Apart from the composition of the Commission, there is the question of what is to be done with its work. So far as the Australian body is concerned any reports to the Minister must be laid before Parliament. A similar arrangement in Britain would not guarantee that the report would be widely noticed, not to mention debated on the floor of the House, far less acted upon by the Minister. If any such Commission was working diligently and efficiently, there would be several reports each year. But they would simply compete for time with the reports of other bodies reporting to Parliament. And even if controversial reports were debated, party discipline is such that the more critical the report, the more likely it is that the Government would be supported in the House by its own back-benchers. And quite apart from difficulties of this kind, it remains true that the experience of commissions in the field of civil liberties has not been a uniformly happy one in Britain. The Equal Opportunities Commission in particular has taken a fair amount of criticism about its reluctance to use the powers given to it by the Sex Discrimination Act 1975. Although some commentators have risen to the defence of the Commission, not all of the critics have been convinced.

A Bill of Rights?

Perhaps the reform which has been most frequently proposed in recent years in response to the growing threat to political freedom is the introduction of a bill of rights. Such a document would list the political freedoms which are cherished in many liberal democracies. These would include freedom of association and peaceful assembly, freedom of expression (including freedom of the press), and freedom of conscience and religion. Parliament would not be permitted to pass laws which violated the terms of the bill of rights, while existing legislation would be capable of challenge if it contravened the guaranteed freedoms. It is unlikely, perhaps, that the wide terms of the old Official Secrets Act 1911, section 2, would have survived such scrutiny. In fact all powers of government would be subject to the bill of rights, the terms of which would be a form of higher law applied by the courts to whom citizens could go if they had a grievance. A number of countries already have such provisions in their constitutions, including the United States and Canada, which recently introduced a Charter of Rights in 1982 at the time the Canadian Constitution was repatriated. A number of countries, on the other hand, have recently rejected serious proposals to follow the Canadian example, though the Australians only did so at the eleventh hour. In October 1983 the Federal Parliament approved a proposed Australian Bill of Rights which passed all stages in the House of Representatives only to be withdrawn after it had gone to Committee in the Senate.

For us, however, there exists a tailor-made document in the form of the European Convention on Human Rights, which we referred to in Chapter 1. This international treaty is not yet part of our domestic law, though if it were it would serve the same function as, say, the Canadian Charter, with which it shares many common features. Several attempts have in fact been made to introduce the European Convention into British law. A Bill introduced into Parliament with this end in view has been passed by the House of Lords, and a recent attempt to secure Commons approval for such a measure only narrowly failed. There is indeed much to be said for such an initiative. Apart from the fact that it could impose a major limitation on the arbitrary power of government, it would at the same time permit individuals to take steps to protect their political freedoms without having to take the long and tortuous road to Strasburg. By signing the European Convention in Rome in 1950 we as a nation accepted the principle that there should be some limits on the power of big government to frustrate civil liberty. That being so, we should facilitate the effective safeguarding of these liberties rather than build obstacles in the paths of those who are aggrieved. Although the European Convention is unusual in permitting citizens to have direct access to its enforcement machinery, the road is time-consuming and expensive for those who have a right to expect a speedy settlement of what may be an issue of major importance.

The movement in favour of formally incorporating the European Convention (or an equivalent document) into domestic law has been growing rapidly since the early 1970s. There is now support from a number of quite different sources, including a large number of academic lawyers. The old SDP–Liberal Alliance formally adopted the proposal and used it as a prominent campaigning theme during the 1987 General Election. Perhaps more significantly the cause has attracted the attention of several judges, though as Lord McCluskey demonstrated in his Reith Lectures, not all judges desire this sort of sovereign power, or believe it justifiable in principle that such power should reside with them. But still there are those who think otherwise. Lord Scarman has long been an advocate of a bill of rights, and the campaign enjoys support at the other end of the judicial political spectrum. And as we saw in Chapter 5, Lord Bridge of Harwich expressed concern during the *Spycatcher* affair in the ability of the common law to protect liberty and indicated that he too may now be persuaded by the case for incorporation of the European Convention, having been against it in the past. But as might be expected those who presently wield near-absolute political power, particularly the Prime Minister, have voted against the introduction of any such intiative. It is perhaps tempting to believe that the proposal must therefore be an admirable one. There are, however, major difficulties associated with such an initiative, though we suspect that our concerns are not those of the Prime Minister or her Government.

1. Problems of entrenchment

The first problem is a technical problem of constitutional law which perhaps ought not to be exaggerated. But equally it cannot be ignored or dismissed. In Chapter 1 and again in our discussion of the security service in Chapter 6 we encountered one of the fundamental principles of the British Constitution—the rule of law. The other is the doctrine of parliamentary sovereignty or supremacy, a legal principle which bears no relationship to political practice. It means that one Act of Parliament cannot bind Parliament in the future if the subsequent Parliament should wish to change the law. It also goes further than this. If an Act of Parliament is impliedly inconsistent with an earlier one, the courts have a duty to uphold and give effect to the one most recently passed. If this doctrine were applied to an incorporated European Convention or a bill of rights, it would mean that earlier legislation inconsistent with the Convention would be repealed (expressly or impliedly) to the extent of the inconsistency. But it would also mean that the Convention or the bill of rights could not govern future legislation and that the Government would be free through its control of Parliament to secure the passage of legislation which contravened the terms of the bill of rights. The duty of the courts would be to uphold the legislation despite the fact that it contravened the incorporated European Convention. Indeed they would be required to do so even if the later measure was only implicitly inconsistent with the bill of rights, without there being an expressed intention to deviate from its terms.[3]

This is a problem which has been faced by several Commonwealth countries. In Canada a federal Bill of Rights was introduced in 1960, some twenty-two years before the Charter. In order to be effective, it provided that the Bill of Rights would apply to render ineffective any law passed before or after the commencement date unless the law should state expressly that it was to apply despite the terms of the Bill. In 1970 the Supreme Court of Canada accepted that legislation passed after the introduction of the Bill of Rights would be ignored to the extent of any inconsistency, thereby departing from the rule of parliamentary sovereignty that one Parliament cannot bind its successors.[4] The reality is, however, that until the introduction of the Charter, which traversed much of the same ground as the Bill of Rights, this power was never in fact used and indeed the 1960 document had

[3] *Ellen Street Estates Ltd.* v. *Minister of Health* [1934] 1 KB 590.
[4] *R.* v. *Drybones* [1970] SCR 282.

become a rather sterile measure in the hands of the Canadian judges. Although the Charter itself has been enthusiastically embraced by the courts, it should not be taken as an example of what would happen in Britain. The political circumstances surrounding the introduction of the Charter profoundly changed the legal basis of Canadian government. The incorporation of the European Convention in Britain would not take place in such a political context with the result that it is the judicial response to the Bill of Rights and not the Charter which may be a more appropriate yardstick for likely behaviour in Britain. It must also be said that although the Charter has helped to breathe life into the Bill of Rights (both operate simultaneously), so that it has now been used to render ineffective post-1960 legislation,[5] the difficult questions of principle relating to the binding of successor Parliaments have been avoided but will ultimately have to be confronted.

The problem is also one which confronted New Zealand when it was considering the introduction of a bill of rights. A White Paper suggested that steps would have to be taken to make it difficult for the judges to avoid giving effect to an attempt at entrenchment. Such steps would include a referendum demonstrating widespread political consensus behind such an initiative. In Australia the then Chief Justice warned that the problem could not be taken lightly. In a public lecture in 1982 he said that effective entrenchment is 'difficult to reconcile with formal legal theory' and that it 'remains a matter of conjecture' whether the Australian judges would be prepared to mould the theory to accommodate new arrangements of the kind under discussion. And in Britain too we have already had a taste of the problem through our inability to come to terms with the attempt to entrench EEC law as part of domestic law. When we joined the EEC in 1973, legislation was on the books providing that in the event of conflict between domestic law and EEC law, the latter should prevail and it should do so even over legislation passed by Parliament after the European Communities Act. So far some courts have said that they would ignore EEC law in favour of domestic law in the event of conflict.[6] Others have said that they

---

[5] *Singh* v. *Minister of Employment and Immigration* [1985] 1 SCR 177.

[6] *Felixstowe Dock and Railway Co.* v. *British Transport Docks Board* [1976] 2 CMLR 655.

would give effect to EEC law unless Parliament should say expressly that the legislation is to apply over any inconsistency.[7] And others have taken a middle ground saying that the legislation will apply over inconsistent EEC law if Parliament indicates an intention, expressly or impliedly, that its will is to prevail over any inconsistent EEC law.[8] This view—of a senior member of the House of Lords—seems simply to be another way of restating the traditional rule.[9] Such is the nature of the problem.

2. Questions of principle

Even if the knotty legal problems can be unravelled, there is a further difficulty with entrenchment. This is whether such an initiative can be justified as a matter of political principle and democratic theory. Three problems arise here. The first is that it would involve conferring the ultimate sovereign power upon a group of people who are appointed and not elected. The final political decision on major questions would be made by people who have no mandate to make such decisions. This in itself would be a cause for great concern. Any such concerns, however, pale in light of the fact that appointment to these key positions is by the Prime Minister. Senior judges in Britain (including all the members of the House of Lords) are appointed without any parliamentary scrutiny or approval. If Robert Bork had been proposed for high judicial office in the UK there is nothing like a Senate Committee to expose weaknesses and block his elevation to the bench. Appointment by the executive when so much would be at stake might well be seen to be unacceptable. But any notion that the appointment process could be changed to eliminate the possible abuse of patronage, is fanciful. For the fact is too that these appointed judges will continue to be recruited mainly from the practising Bar. And given the social and economic decay of Britain, and with it the lack of equal opportunity for all of its children, the Bar is likely to become more rather than less élitist and unrepresentative.

[7] *MacCarthys Ltd.* v. *Smith* [1981] QB 180.
[8] *Garland* v. *British Rail Engineering Ltd.* [1983] 2 AC 751.
[9] See now *Factortame Ltd.* v. *Secretary of State for Transport* [1989] 2 All ER 692.

So one question of principle is whether it is legitimate or justifiable to have the final political decision, on say a woman's right to abortion, to be determined by a group of men appointed by the Prime Minister from a small and unrepresentative pool. Related to this is a second problem that these appointed people who make the major political decisions are not accountable in any way for what they do with this quite enormous power. Once appointed, judges have security of tenure until death or retirement, and although there are procedures for the removal of senior judges, these have never been used in modern times. Judges are thus given the power to disrupt decisions and adjustments made by the process of persuasion, compromise, and agreement in the political arena. Difficult ethical, social, and political questions would be subject to judicial preference rather than the shared or compromised community morality. While politicians must account for these decisions, the judges would exercise this power without any such constraint. Personal policy preferences can thus be imposed on a nation in the manner of a feudal king. The problem can become particularly acute when the power of executive appointment is heavily politicized as it has been during the Reagan era in the United States. There (subject to Senate confirmation which despite the Bork affair has been usually granted), it is open to the President to fill spaces on the court as they fall vacant with people who share his particular political vision. These people will remain on the court long after the President has gone from office and perhaps long after the political values of the nation have changed. Still they will be there to stamp an increasingly unrepresentative and largely unwanted ideology on contemporary political life.

The third and perhaps the most bizarre problem of principle is that not only would we be giving the final say on the big political questions to people who are appointed rather than elected, and to people who are not accountable for their decisions, but we would do so without any clear idea of what we expect of them. We would be giving to these people the freedom to determine the limits and scope of their own power. It is the judges, and not we the people, who would determine whether they would be activists or conservatives in their interpretation of the Constitution. For the judges are not only the guardians of the Constitution: they are also its masters. Bear in mind the point made in Chapter 1 that bills of rights are very loosely drafted so that it is possible in almost any case to decide for or against the party bringing the action. Recent cases in Canada, for example, have asked whether the constitutional protection of freedom of association extends to protect the right to strike;[10] whether the protection of freedom of religion extends to invalidate the Sunday trading laws;[11] and whether the protection of life, liberty, and security of the person guarantee a woman's right to have an abortion.[12] The answer to these questions will depend to a large extent on the agenda which the judges set for themselves. More remarkable, perhaps, is that the judges may choose to be activist in some areas but to show restraint in others. Thus, the Canadian Supreme Court has become as frisky as a spring lamb with its new Charter. Significantly, however, the area of visible restraint so far has been where trade unions have sought to defend themselves through the Charter from governmental attack. In these areas, say the judges, the matter must be left to the legislature. The judges are thus free not only to determine how actively they will intervene, they are free to determine which constitutional freedoms they are willing to read broadly, and they are also free to determine which groups and interests they are willing to defend. It is open to question whether the ultimate political power should depend in this way on the whims, prejudices, and vision of a handful of citizens.

3. No difference in practice

But still it is argued that despite any such problems of principle, the practical results in securing the protection of liberty are such that any theoretical objections can easily be waived. Look for example at the famous US Supreme Court case, *Brown* v. *Board of Education of Topeka*[13] in 1954 which by constitutional interpretation signalled the end of apartheid laws in America. Another way of looking at the *Brown* case, however, is much less flattering of the judiciary. Despite the existence of the Bill of Rights apartheid

[10] *Re Public Service Employee Relations Act* [1987] 1 SCR 313.
[11] *R. v. Big M Drug Mart Ltd.* [1985] 1 SCR 295.
[12] *R. v. Morgentaler* [1988] 1 SCR 30.
[13] 347 US 483 (1954).

laws flourished until only very recently. For hundreds of years the Bill of Rights did nothing but condone the practice. Indeed it was only 100 years before *Brown* that the Supreme Court had held that the rights and privileges in the Constitution did not apply to blacks![14] This is not to deny that in some countries, the courts have, on some issues, played a helpful role in the development of social progress and in the safeguarding of civil liberties. Some of the decisions of the (exceptional) Warren Court in the United States in the 1960s were clearly of great importance. And it would be churlish to ignore the great strides made by the Canadian Supreme Court in elevating—with a little prompting from the legislature—the human rights statutes (which guarantee protection from discrimination on grounds of race and sex) into a form of quasi-constitutional status.[15] But what happens in other countries is not guaranteed to happen here. Our third concern is that in the hands of the English judges a bill of rights would make very little difference to the condition of political freedom in this country.

Look at the facts. First, many of the legislative developments of the Thatcher years were anticipated by judicial developments. One example of this is the police power to regulate public assemblies in the Public Order Act 1986, section 14, a power recognized by the courts in a line of cases starting as long ago as 1936.[16] Indeed, in some respects the legislation paradoxically modifies some of the worst excesses of common-law rules, one example of this being section 78 of the Police and Criminal Evidence Act which seems to be a response to a decision of the House of Lords which on one view would appear to have allowed the police to admit non-confession evidence in criminal prosecutions, regardless of the means by which the evidence was obtained.[17] Secondly, many of the restrictions on political freedom which have taken place in the 1980s have not been as a result of legislation but have been judge-made initiatives authorizing the extension of executive power. Some of the most significant restrictions on the freedom of assembly, freedom of movement, and the freedom of the press were imposed by the courts, not by Parliament. The harsh reality is that we need to be protected by

[14] *Dred Scott* v. *Sandford* 60 US (19 How.) 393 (1857).
[15] *Ontario Human Rights Commission* v. *Simpsons-Sears Ltd.* [1985] 2 SCR 536.
[16] *Duncan* v. *Jones* [1936] KB 218.   [17] *R.* v. *Sang* [1980] AC 402.

Parliament from the courts, as much as we need to be protected from the abuse of executive power. Indeed, as the *Sunday Times* case[18] vividly illustrated, we also need to be protected by the European Convention from decisions of the English courts, as much as we need to be protected from the abuse of executive power. And thirdly, while even the conservative members of the Supreme Court of Canada proclaimed human rights legislation to be of 'a special nature',[19] the English courts and the Court of Appeal in particular have construed the already narrow Race Relations Act 1976 in very restrictive terms. The Chief Justice of Canada has asserted that the courts 'should not search for ways and means to minimise those rights and to enfeeble their proper impact'.[20] There has been no such recognition by English judges who, unlike their Canadian counterparts, have made few attempts to use the law in a creative way to help eradicate the cancer of systemic discrimination.

It is sometimes argued that the judges would be more creative with a bill of rights and the conferring on them of such a power would make a big difference as to how they responded. But again, look at the facts. The House of Lords (called for this purpose the Privy Council) has for a long time been the final court of appeal for an admittedly dwindling number of Commonwealth countries. Many of these countries have a bill of rights, and many appeals on these bills of rights come to London for final adjudication. So the constitutional rights of the people of Antigua, Jamaica, Singapore, and Trinidad and Tobago have depended in recent years to some extent on the decisions of the Privy Council. This experience has led some commentators to reinforce their case for a bill of rights on the ground that the senior English judges are well experienced in constitutional adjudication of the kind which a bill of rights would require. It must be pointed out, however, that the most notable feature of these cases is the narrow reading down of the constitutions which leads in turn to many appeals being dismissed. In one case the Privy Council held that the right to freedom of association did not guarantee the right to collective bargaining

---

[18] (1974) AC 273; (1980) 2 EHRR 245.
[19] *Winnipeg School Division No. 1* v. *Craton* [1985] 2 SCR 150.
[20] *Action Travail des Femmes* v. *Canadian National Railway* [1987] 1 SCR 1114.

and the right to strike,[21] despite the surely correct assertion by counsel that without such protection the constitutional guarantee would be empty of worthwhile content. In another case it was held that constitutional protection for freedom of expression did not invalidate laws banning the use of loudspeakers at public meetings without police permission.[22] In 1948 the US Supreme Court had said that a more effective previous restraint is hard to imagine, with loudspeakers being today 'indispensable instruments of effective public speech'.[23]

More recently still, in 1975, the Privy Council was confronted by a statute on an appeal from Antigua which made it unlawful to publish a newspaper without a licence from the Cabinet and without depositing $10,000 with a public official as a surety against libel.[24] In a remarkable decision their Lordships unanimously reversed the trial judge and the Court of Appeal in upholding this legislation against a constitutional protection for freedom of expression. Yet a more blatant restraint on press freedom is hard to imagine. In the view of the Privy Council, however, the surety could be justified as being necessary for the protection of the reputations and rights of others (see the comparable provision in Article 10(2) of the European Convention on Human Rights). But as if to demonstrate that this was no mere aberration, or to remind us that judicial attitudes do not change significantly with the passage of time, in 1986 we encounter an even more remarkable decision.[25] Frank Robinson was convicted of murder by a court in Kingston, Jamaica, on 2 April 1981. He was then sentenced to death, the death penalty having already been upheld by the Privy Council against a constitutional challenge from Singapore.[26] For various reasons, Robinson had been tried, convicted, and sentenced without legal representation, despite a constitutional guarantee that every person who is charged with a criminal offence 'shall be permitted to defend himself in person or by a legal representative of his own choice'. Yet the Privy Council

---

[21] *Collymore* v. *Attorney-General* [1970] AC 538.
[22] *Francis* v. *Chief of Police* [1973] AC 761.
[23] *Saia* v. *New York* 334 US 558 (1948).
[24] *Attorney-General* v. *Antigua Times Ltd.* [1976] AC 16.
[25] *Robinson* v. *The Queen* [1985] AC 956.
[26] *Ong Ah Chuan* v. *Public Prosecutor* [1981] AC 648.

upheld the conviction taking the view that the constitutional guarantee was not an absolute right and that it was not necessary always to grant an adjournment to ensure that the defendant (on trial for his life) was properly represented. Other factors, such as the present and future availability of witnesses, also had to be considered. Perhaps all that can be said about this case, which rightly led to international condemnation, is that it is so shocking that it would have been best left unreported.

But while advocates of a bill of rights or incorporation of the European Convention might acknowledge these decisions of the Privy Council, they might still cry foul in the sense that the evidence is unfair and therefore inconclusive. The Privy Council is acting as a final court of appeal from territories thousands of miles away with which its members have no local connection, knowledge, or understanding. It is thus appropriate that their Lordships adopt a restrictive and non-interventionist policy, with the result that the position taken in the interpretation of Commonwealth constitutions offers no guidance as to how their Lordships (and their younger brethren in the lower courts) would construe a British bill of rights or an incorporated European Convention. Well, supposing that there is substance in this argument (which of course hardly explains the *Antigua Times* case,[27] in which the Privy Council overturned both the local courts below) it is increasingly the case that the English courts are providing a valuable insight into how they would respond if the Convention did form part of English law. For the fact is that the courts are increasingly anticipating the Convention, in some cases deciding disputes as if the Convention was already part of English law, though always in such a way as to justify restrictive and illiberal decisions. So quite apart from the evidence provided by the Privy Council decisions, we also have direct evidence of British judicial responses to the Convention itself. And it has to be said that the record here is as equally disappointing as the record of the Privy Council. For evidence it is necessary to look only at the *Spycatcher* case, though ample corroboration is provided, if any is needed, by

[27] *Attorney-General* v. *Antigua Times*.

the Jeremy Warner press disclosure case,[28] and by the judicial response to the media ban on Sinn Fein.[29]

The *Spycatcher* case is discussed fully in Chapter 5. Of particular interest for present purposes is the speech of Lord Templeman in the first House of Lords decision, in which the interlocutory injunctions were maintained and made more restrictive.[30] According to Lord Templeman, the case involved a direct 'consideration of the European Convention on Human Rights'. But any optimism that this would consequently liberate the press from the injunctions was shattered when his Lordship proceeded to use the Convention to justify the continued restrictions. According to his Lordship, the question for the House was whether the interference with freedom of expression constituted by the continuation of the injunctions on the press was necessary in a democratic society in the interests of national security, for protecting the reputations or rights of others, for preventing the disclosure of information received in confidence, or for maintaining the authority and impartiality of the judiciary. In a notable response, Lord Templeman answered simply and without explanation that the continuance of the injunctions 'appears to be necessary for all these purposes'. This is despite jurisprudence of the European Court (including the *Sunday Times* case) which has stressed that the word 'necessary' in this context is not to be confused with the words 'desirable' or 'useful'; despite the fact that the British market had become saturated with copies of the book; and despite the fact that according to Lord Bridge of Harwich in the *Spycatcher* case, 'the intelligence and security services of any country in the world can buy the book *Spycatcher* and read what is in it'. If the Convention can be used in this way to justify a restriction on press freedom in circumstances where the Government seemed determined to look foolish, how can it possibly be seriously suggested that incorporation of the Convention would make a significant contribution to political freedom in this country?

[28] *Re an Inquiry under the Company Securities (Insider Dealing) Act 1985* [1988] 1 All ER 203.

[29] *R. v. Secretary of State for the Home Department, ex parte Brind* (1989) 139 NLJ 1229.

[30] *Attorney-General v. Guardian Newspapers Ltd.* [1987] 3 All ER 316.

Conclusion

In our view the crisis facing civil liberties in Britain is much too serious to be met by glib proposals for the introduction of a bill of rights as a panacea of all our problems. In many ways it is understandable that lawyers should be in the vanguard of the proposals for such a reform. There are undoubtedly those who are guided by the most honourable of motives. But it is also the case that a bill of rights would be big business financially which at the same time would move the legal profession even closer to the centre of political power. Yet neither lawyers nor judges have any special skills which equip them to make the great political decisions which a bill of rights requires. As we hope we have shown in the last few pages, to address the present problems of civil liberties with a bill of rights (or indeed with any of the other devices discussed in this chapter) would be like treating a heart attack with a used Band-aid. The condition is much too serious and the prognosis much too grim. The need is for major surgery to the body politic to reduce the load on an overworked House of Commons and to introduce some real and effective political constraints on the power of the Prime Minister. The enormous range of prescribed options currently available merely reflects the scale of the underlying problem. We have seen demands for electoral reform; devolution; an elected second chamber; reform of the judiciary; and freedom of information. It is, however, in such proposals to redress the balance of political power, rather than in such cosmetic changes as a bill of rights, that the protection of civil liberties in this country ultimately depends. But the task will be hopeless unless a serious commitment is made to the constitution, and given the inexorable drift to the centre, the commitment will have to be as great as that which brought down the Stuart despots in the seventeenth century. Some have spoken and written of the need to establish a culture of liberty in this country. But liberty flows only from democracy, and despite the rhetoric of liberalism, there never has been a democratic culture in England. Should it ever emerge, we will then have cause to be optimistic about the future of political freedom in Britain generally. We look forward to writing a much different book but fear that we will never have the opportunity to do so.

Table of Cases

Bibliography

ABRAHAM, H. J. 1988. *Freedom and the Court. Civil Rights and Liberties in the United States.* 5th edn. Oxford: Oxford University Press.

ABRAMS, F., KIRBY, Mr Justice M., and SCARMAN, Lord. 1985. *The Right to Know.* The Granada–Guildhall lectures 1984. London: Granada.

ADENEY, M., and LLOYD, J. 1986. *The Miners' Strike 1984–5. Loss Without Limit.* London: Routledge & Kegan Paul.

AITKEN, J. 1971. *Officially Secret.* London: Weidenfeld and Nicolson.

AMNESTY INTERNATIONAL. 1988. Northern Ireland: Killings by the Security Forces and 'Supergrass' Trials. London.

ANDREW, C. 1986. *Secret Service. The Making of the British Intelligence Community.* London: Sceptre.

APPLEBEY, G., and ELLIS, E. 1984. 'Formal Investigations: The Commission for Racial Equality and the Equal Opportunities Commission as Law Enforcement Agencies.' *Public Law* 236.

ASMAL, K. 1985. Shoot to Kill? Report of an International Lawyers' Inquiry into Lethal Use of Firearms by the Security Forces in Northern Ireland. Cork: Mercier.

ATLAS, J. 1989. 'Thatcher Puts a Lid On: Censorship in Britain.' *The New York Times Magazine*, 5 March.

AUBREY, C. 1981. *Who's Watching You?* Harmondsworth: Penguin.

BAILEY, S. 1987. 'Wilfully Obstructing the Freedom to Protest.' *Public Law* 495.

BAILEY, S. D. (ed.). 1988. *Human Rights and Responsibilities in Britain and Ireland: A Christian Perspective.* London: Macmillan.

BAILEY, S. H., HARRIS, D. J., and JONES, B. L. 1985. *Civil Liberties: Cases and Materials.* 2nd edn. London: Butterworths.

BAKER, Sir George. 1984. Review of the Operation of the Northern Ireland (Emergency Provisions) Act 1978 (Cmnd. 9222).

BARENDT, E. 1985. *Freedom of Speech.* Oxford: Oxford University Press.

—— 1987. 'Free Speech in the Universities.' *Public Law* 344.

BAYEFSKY, A. F. 1987. 'The Judicial Function Under the Canadian Charter of Rights and Freedoms.' (32) *McGill Law Journal* 791.

BELL, J. B. 1978. *A Time of Terror: How Democratic Societies Respond to Revolutionary Violence.* New York: Basic Books.

BELL, J. B. 1979. *The Secret Army: The IRA 1916–1979*. Dublin: Academy Press.

BENNETT, H. G. 1979. Report of the Committee of Inquiry into Police Interrogation Procedures in Northern Ireland (Cmnd. 7497).

BENYON, J. (ed.). 1984. *Scarman and After. Essays reflecting on Lord Scarman's Report, the Riots and their Aftermath*. Oxford: Pergamon Press.

BERLIN, M. L., and PENTNEY, W. F. 1987. *Human Rights and Freedoms in Canada: Cases, Notes and Materials*. Toronto: Butterworths.

BEVAN, V. 1980. 'Is Anybody There?' *Public Law* 431.

BINDMAN, G. 1989. 'Spycatcher: Judging the Judges.' *New Law Journal*, 20 January.

BIRKETT, Sir NORMAN. 1957. Report of the Committee of Privy Councillors Appointed to Inquire into the Interception of Communications (Cmd. 283).

BIRKINSHAW, P. 1988. *Freedom of Information: The Law, the Practice and the Ideal*. London: Weidenfeld and Nicolson.

BIRTLES, W. 1973. 'Big Brother Knows Best: The Franks Report on Section 2 of the Official Secrets Act.' *Public Law* 100.

BISHOP, P., and MAILLIE, E. 1987. *The Provisional IRA*. London: Heinemann.

BLACK, R. 1987. 'JPs, Sheriffs and Official Secrets.' (32) *Journal of the Law Society of Scotland* 138.

BLACKSTONE, W. 1830. *Commentaries on the Laws of England in Four Books. The First Book*. (1st pub. in 1765.) 17th edn. with notes and additions by E. Christian. London: Thomas Tegg.

BOLLINGER, L. C. 1986. *The Tolerant Society. Freedom of Speech and Extremist Speech in America*. Oxford: Oxford University Press.

BOYLE, K., and HADDEN, T. 1985. *Ireland. A Positive Proposal*. Harmondsworth: Penguin.

—— —— and HILLYARD, P. 1975. *Law and State. The Case of Northern Ireland*. London: Martin Robertson.

—— —— and —— 1980. *Ten Years on in Northern Ireland: The Legal Control of Political Violence*. London: Cobden Trust.

—— and HANNUM, H. 1972. 'Ireland in Strasburg.' (7) *Irish Jurist* 329.

—— and —— 1976. 'Ireland in Strasburg: Final Decisions in the Northern Irish Proceedings before the European Commission of Human Rights.' (11) *Irish Jurist* 243.

BRADLEY, A. W. 1987a. 'Parliamentary Privilege and the Zircon Affair.' *Public Law* 1.

—— 1987b. 'Parliamentary Privilege, Zircon and National Security.' *Public Law* 488.

—— 1989. 'Judicial Enforcement of *Ultra Vires* Byelaws.' *Public Law* 1.

BRENNAN, W. 1989. 'The Right Weapon against an Elective Dictatorship in Britain.' *Independent*, 26 May.

BRODER, D. S. 1989. 'Queen Maggie I. Is Thatcher destroying British Democracy?' *Washington Post*, 23 July.

BROOKS, R., and HARRIS, R. 1988. 'Television on Trial.' *Observer*, 1 May.

BROWN, D. 1989. Detention at the Police Station under the Police and Criminal Evidence Act 1984 (Home Office Research Study no. 104).

BROWNE-WILKINSON, N. 1989. 'The UK's Alice-in-Wonderland Position on Human Rights.' *Independent*, 27 April.

BUCHAN, N., and SUMNER, T. (eds.). 1988. *Glasnost in Britain: Against Censorship and in Defence of the Word*. London: Macmillan.

BUNYAN, T. 1977. *The History and Practice of the Political Police in Britain*. London: Quartet.

BURNS, P. 1976. 'The Law and Privacy: The Canadian Experience.' (54) *Canadian Bar Review* 1.

CAMERON, I. 1986. 'Telephone Tapping and the Interception of Communications Act 1985.' (37) *Northern Ireland Legal Quarterly* 126.

CAMERON, Lord. 1969. Disturbances in Northern Ireland. Report of the Commission appointed by the Governor of Northern Ireland (Cmd. 532). Belfast.

CAMPBELL, C. M. (ed.). 1980. *Do We Need a Bill of Rights?* London: Temple Smith.

CAMPBELL, D. 1980. 'Big Buzby is Watching You.' *New Statesman*, 1 February.

—— 1981. 'British Teletap Inc.' *New Statesman*, 3 April.

CHARTER 88. 1988. *New Statesman and Society*, 2 December.

CHRISTIAN, L. 1983. *Policing By Coercion*. London: GLC Police Committee Support Unit.

—— 1985. 'Restriction Without Conviction: The Role of the Courts in Legitimising Police Control in Nottinghamshire.' In B. Fine and R. Millar (eds.), *Policing the Miners' Strike*. London: Lawrence and Wishart.

CHRISTIAN, T. J., and EWING, K. D. 1988. 'Labouring Under the Canadian Constitution.' (17) *Industrial Law Journal* 73.

Civil Service Department. 1979. Open Government (Cmnd. 7520).

COLVILLE, Lord. 1987. Review of the Operation of the Prevention of Terrorism (Temporary Provisions) Act 1984 (Cm. 264).

COMFORT, N. 1988. 'Is the State becoming too Powerful?' *Daily Telegraph*, 27 October.

Commission for Racial Equality. 1985. Review of the Race Relations Act 1976: Proposals for Change. London.

COMPTON, Sir EDWARD. 1971. Report of the Enquiry into Allegations against the Security Forces of Physical Brutality in Northern Ireland arising out of Events on 9 August 1971 (Cmnd. 4823).

COOGAN, T. P. 1987. *The I.R.A.* 3rd edn. London: Fontana.

CORBY, S. 1986. 'Limitations on Freedom of Association in the Civil Service and the ILO's Response.' (15) *Industrial Law Journal* 161.

COULTER, J., MILLER, S., and WALKER, M. 1984. *State of Siege. Miners' Strike 1984. Politics and Policing in the Coalfields.* London: Canary Press.

COX, A. 1987. *The Court and the Constitution.* Boston: Houghton Mifflin.

CRANE, P. 1982. *Gays and the Law.* London: Pluto Press.

Criminal Law Revision Committee. 1972. Eleventh Report, Evidence (General) (Cmnd. 4991).

CRIPPS, Y. 1984. 'Judicial Proceedings and Refusal to Disclose the Identity of Sources of Information.' *Cambridge Law Journal* 266.

CURRAN, J., and SEATON, J. 1988. *Power without Responsibility. The Press and Broadcasting in Britain.* 3rd edn. London: Routledge.

DASH, S. 1972. Justice Denied. A Challenge to Lord Widgery's Report on 'Bloody Sunday'. The Defence and Education Fund of the International League for the Rights of Man in association with the NCCL. London.

DEACON, R. 1980. *A History of British Secret Service.* London: Panther Books.

DENNING, Lord. 1963. Lord Denning's Report (Cmnd. 2152).

DICEY, A. V. 1959. *An Introduction to the Study of the Law of the Constitution.* (1st pub. in 1885.) With an Introduction by E. C. S. Wade. London: Macmillan.

DIPLOCK, Lord. 1972. Report of the Commission to Consider Legal Procedures to Deal with Terrorist Activities in Northern Ireland (Cmnd. 5185).

—— 1981. The Interception of Communications in Great Britain (Cmnd. 8191).

DREWRY, G. 1985. 'The Ponting Case—Leaking in the Public Interest.' *Public Law* 203.

DUFFY, P. J. 1980. 'English Law and the European Convention on Human Rights.' (29) *International and Comparative Law Quarterly* 584.

DWORKIN, R. 1988. 'Devaluing Liberty.' (17) *Index on Censorship* 7.

ELIAS, P. 1981. *The British Constitution: Time for Reform?* The Cambridge–Tilburg Law Lectures. Deventer: Kluwer.

EWING, K.D., and FINNIE, W. 1988. *Civil Liberties in Scotland: Cases and Materials.* 2nd edn. Edinburgh: W. Green & Son.

FINDLAY, M., and DUFF, P. 1988. *The Jury under Attack.* London: Butterworths.

FISHER, Sir HENRY. 1977. Report of an Inquiry into the Circumstances leading to the Trial of Three Persons arising from the Death of Maxwell Confait and the Fire at 27 Doggett Road, London SE6 (HC 90).

FLICK, G. A. 1981. *Civil Liberties in Australia.* Sydney: The Law Book Company.

FORDE, M. 1983. 'The European Convention on Human Rights and Labor Law.' (31) *American Journal of Comparative Law* 301.

FORGAN, L. 1988. 'A Gag that Hurts Us All.' *The Times*, 5 November.

FRANKS, Lord. 1972. Departmental Committee on Section 2 of the Official Secrets Act 1911. Volume 1. Report of the Committee (Cmnd. 5104).

FULTON, Lord. 1968. The Civil Service. Report of the Committee (Cmnd. 3638).

GALLIGAN, D. J. 1988. 'The Right to Silence Reconsidered.' (41) *Current Legal Problems* 69.

GARDINER, Lord. 1975. Report of a Committee to Consider, in the Context of Civil Liberties and Human Rights, Measures to deal with Terrorism in Northern Ireland (Cmnd. 5847).

GARTON ASH, T. 1988. 'Real War, Phoney Reflection.' *Independent*, 25 November.

Gay London Policing Group. 1988. Gay Men and Bindovers. London.

GEARTY, C. 1987. 'The Courts and Recent Exercises of the Prerogative.' *Cambridge Law Journal* 372.

GIBBS, Sir HARRY. 1982. 'Constitutional Protection of Human Rights.' (9) *Monash University Law Review* 1.

GOLD, M. 1987. 'The Rhetoric of Rights: The Supreme Court and the Charter.' (25) *Osgoode Hall Law Journal* 375.

GOODRICH, P. 1981. 'Freedom of the Phone.' (3) *Liverpool Law Review* 91.

GORDON, P. 1983. *White Law. Racism in the Police, Courts and Prisons.* London: Pluto Press.

GOSTIN, L. (ed.). 1988. *Civil Liberties in Conflict.* London: Routledge.

GREER, S. C., and WHITE, A. 1986. *Abolishing the Diplock Courts: The Case for Restoring Jury Trial to Scheduled Offences in Northern Ireland.* London: Cobden Trust.

GRIFFITH, J. A. G. 1985a. *The Politics of the Judiciary.* 3rd edn. London: Fontana.

—— 1985b. 'Judicial Decision-Making in Public Law.' *Public Law* 564.

—— 1987. Review. (50) *Modern Law Review* 982.

HAILSHAM, Lord. 1978. *The Dilemma of Democracy: Diagnosis and Prescription.* London: Collins.

HAIN, P. (ed.). 1979. *Policing the Police. Volume 1.* London: J. Calder.

—— (ed.). 1980. *Policing the Police. Volume 2.* London: J. Calder.

HALL, R. V. 1987. *A Spy's Revenge*. Harmondsworth: Penguin.

HARDEN, I., and LEWIS, N. 1986. *The Noble Lie. The British Constitution and the Rule of Law*. London: Hutchinson.

HASSON, R. A. 1988. 'The Charter and Social Legislation'. Unpublished paper delivered at the University of Edinburgh, 21 May.

HATTERSLEY, R. 1989. 'A Fatally Flawed Approach to Protecting Fundamental Liberties.' *Independent*, 4 May.

HAZELL, R. 1989. 'Freedom of Information in Australia, Canada and New Zealand.' (67) *Public Administration* 189.

HEATH, E. 1989. 'A State of Secrecy.' *New Statesman & Society*, 10 March.

HEWITT, P. 1982. *The Abuse of Power. Civil Liberties in the United Kingdom*. London: Martin Robertson.

HILLYARD, P., and PERCY-SMITH, J. 1988. *The Coercive State*. London: Fontana-Collins.

HILTON, I. 1989. 'Where is the Remedy for those Caught in the Web of MI5?' *Independent*, 23 March.

HINTON, J. 1989. *Protest and Visions. Peace Politics in 20th Century Britain*. London: Hutchinson Radius.

HOGAN, G. 1987. 'Free Speech, Privacy and the Press in Ireland.' *Public Law* 509.

—— and WALKER, C. 1989. *Political Violence and the Law in Ireland*. Manchester: Manchester University Press.

HOGG, P. W. 1984. 'Canada's New Charter of Rights.' (32) *American Journal of Comparative Law* 283.

—— 1985. *Constitutional Law of Canada*. 2nd edn. Toronto: Carswell.

—— 1987. 'The Charter of Rights and American Theories of Interpretation.' (25) *Osgoode Hall Law Journal* 87.

HOLME, R., and ELLIOTT, M. (eds.). 1988. *1688–1988: Time for a New Constitution*. London: Macmillan.

Home Affairs Committee. 1980. The Law Relating to Public Order (HC 756).

—— 1989. Report on Higher Police Training and the Police Staff College (HC 110).

Home Office. 1976. Legislation on Human Rights. With Particular Reference to the European Convention. A Discussion Document.

—— 1978. Reform of Section 2 of the Official Secrets Act 1911 (Cmnd. 7285).

—— 1979. Circular dealing with Aspects of the Prevention of Terrorism Legislation (no. 114).

—— 1980*a*. The Interception of Communications in Great Britain (Cmnd. 7873).

—— 1980*b*. Review of the Public Order Act 1936 and Related Legislation (Cmnd. 7891).

—— 1983. Circular dealing with Aspects of the Prevention of Terrorism Legislation (no. 90).

—— 1984. Circular dealing with Aspects of the Prevention of Terrorism Legislation (no. 26).

—— 1985*a*. The Interception of Communications in the United Kingdom (Cmnd. 9438).

—— 1985*b*. Review of Public Order Law (Cmnd. 9510).

—— 1985*c*. Code of Practice for the Detention, Treatment and Questioning of Persons by Police Officers.

—— 1985*d*. Code of Practice for the Identification of Persons by Police Officers.

—— 1985*e*. Code of Practice for the Searching of Premises by Police Officers and the Seizure of Property found by Police Officers on Persons or Premises.

—— 1988*a*. Reform of Section 2 of the Official Secrets Act 1911 (Cm. 408).

—— 1988*b*. Code of Practice on Tape Recording.

HOOPER, D. 1987. *Official Secrets: The Use and Abuse of the Act.* London: Secker and Warburg.

HUME, D. 1906. *Political Discourses.* (1st publ. in 1752.) New York: Walter Scott Publishing Co.

HUTCHINSON, A., and PETTER, A. 1988. 'Private Rights/Public Wrongs: The Liberal Lie of the Charter.' (38) *University of Toronto Law Journal* 278.

Index on Censorship. 1988. 'Britain.' (17) *Index on Censorship* 1.

ISON, T. G. 1985. 'The Sovereignty of the Judiciary.' (10) *Adelaide Law Review* 3.

IVAMY, E. R. H. 1949. 'The 'Right of Public Meeting.' (2) *Current Legal Problems* 183.

JACK, I. 1988. 'Gibraltar.' (25) *Granta* 13.

JACONELLI, J. 1976. 'The European Convention on Human Rights—The Text of a British Bill of Rights?' *Public Law* 226.

—— 1980. *Enacting a Bill of Rights: The Legal Problems.* Oxford: Oxford University Press.

JANSEN, S. C. 1988. *Censorship. The Knot that Binds Power and Knowledge.* Oxford: Oxford University Press.

JELLICOE, Earl. 1983. Review of the Operation of the Prevention of Terrorism (Temporary Provisions) Act 1976 (Cmnd. 8803).

JENKINS, S. 1988. 'The Oversight and the Limits on Intelligence Work in a Democracy.' Ditchley Conference Report No. D 88/11.

JENNINGS, A. (ed.). 1988. *Justice Under Fire. The Abuse of Civil Liberties in Northern Ireland*. London: Pluto Press.

JOHNSON, F., and VERITY, C. 1989. 'Liberty and the Pursuit of Thatcher.' *Sunday Telegraph*, 12 March.

JOWELL, J., and OLIVER, D. 1985. *The Changing Constitution*. Oxford: Oxford University Press.

KAIRYS, D. (ed.). 1982. *The Politics of Law. A Progressive Critique*. New York: Pantheon Books.

KAVANAGH, D. 1987. *Thatcherism and British Politics. The End of Consensus?* Oxford: Oxford University Press.

KEITH, K. J. 1985. 'A Bill of Rights for New Zealand? Judicial Review versus Democracy.' (11) *New Zealand University Law Review* 307.

KETTLE, M. 1985. 'The National Reporting Centre and the 1984 Miners' Strike.' In B. Fine and R. Millar (eds.), *Policing the Miners' Strike*. London: Lawrence and Wishart.

—— and HODGES, L. 1982. *Uprising!: The Police, the People and the Riots in Britain's Cities*. London: Pan.

KITCHIN, H. 1989. Gibraltar Report: An Independent Observer's Report of the Inquest into the Deaths of Mairead Farrell, Daniel McCann and Sean Savage, Gibraltar, September 1988. London: NCCL.

Labour Party. 1989. Democracy, the Individual and the Community. London

Labour Research. 1984. 'Phone Tapping.' April.

LAMBERT, J. 1980. 'Executive Authority to Tap Telephones.' (43) *Modern Law Review* 59.

LAQUEUR, W. 1987. *The Age of Terrorism*. London: Weidenfeld and Nicolson.

Law Commission. 1982. Offences against Public Order (Working Paper no. 82).

—— 1983. Criminal Law. Offences relating to Public Order (Report no. 123) (HC 85).

LEE, S. 1988. 'Bicentennial Bork, Tercentennial Spycatcher: Do the British need a Bill of Rights?' (49) *University of Pittsburgh Law Review* 777.

—— 1989. 'The Court of Reagan's Revenge.' *Independent*, 7 July.

LEIGH, I. 1986. 'A Tappers' Charter?' *Public Law* 8.

LESTER, A. 1984. 'Fundamental Rights: The United Kingdom Isolated?' *Public Law* 46.

LEVIN, B. 1985. 'Who will Defend Us against the Bullies in Blue?' *The Times*, 17 December.

LLOYD, C. 1985. 'A National Riot Police: Britain's "Third Force"?' In B. Fine and R. Millar (eds.), *Policing the Miners' Strike*. London: Lawrence and Wishart.

LLOYD, I. J. 1986. 'The Interception of Communications Act 1985.' (49) *Modern Law Review* 86.

LLOYD, Lord Justice. 1987. Interception of Communications Act 1985, chapter 56. Report of the Commissioner for 1986 (Cm. 108).

—— 1988. Interception of Communications Act 1985, chapter 56. Report of the Commissioner for 1987 (Cm. 351).

—— 1989. Interception of Communications Act 1985, chapter 56. Report of the Commissioner for 1988 (Cm. 652).

LUSTGARTEN, L. 1986. *The Governance of Police*. London: Sweet and Maxwell.

MACAULAY, T. B. 1861. *The History of England from the Accession of James the Second*. 5 vols. London: Longman, Green, Longman and Roberts.

McCABE, S., and WALLINGTON, P. 1988. *The Police, Public Order, and Civil Liberties. Legacies of the Miners' Strike*. London: Routledge.

McCLUSKEY, Lord. 1987. *Law, Justice and Democracy*. London: Sweet and Maxwell: BBC Books.

MacCORMACK, N. 1977. 'Civil Liberties and the Law.' A public lecture delivered at Heriot-Watt University. Edinburgh: Heriot-Watt University.

MacDONALD, Mr Justice D. C. 1981. Freedom and Security under the Law. Commission of Inquiry Concerning Certain Activities of the Royal Canadian Mounted Police. Report. Ottawa: Ministry of Supply and Services.

MACKINTOSH, J. P. 1982. *The Government and Politics of Britain*. 5th edn. by P. Richards. London: Hutchinson.

Magill Magazine. 1988. 'The Birmingham Six—the Complete Judgement.' (11) *Magill*, February.

Manchester City Council. 1985. Leon Brittan's Visit to Manchester University Students' Union. 1 March 1985. Report of the Independent Inquiry Panel.

MANDEL, M. 1989. *The Charter of Rights and the Legalization of Politics in Canada*. Toronto: Wall and Thompson.

MEIKELJOHN, A. 1960. *Political Freedom*. New York: Harper.

Metropolitan Police Commissioner. 1987. Annual Report 1986 (Cm. 158).

—— 1988. Annual Report 1987 (Cm. 389).

—— 1989. Annual Report 1988 (Cm. 670).

MICHAEL, J. 1982. *The Politics of Secrecy*. Harmondsworth: Penguin.

Ministry of Justice (NZ). 1985. A Bill of Rights for New Zealand. A White Paper. Wellington: Government Printer.

MORRIS, G. 1985. 'The Ban on Trade Unions at Government Communications Headquarters.' *Public Law* 177.

MULLIN, C. 1986. *Error of Judgement. The Birmingham Bombings.* London: Chatto & Windus.

National Council for Civil Liberties (NCCL). 1980. Southall. 23 April 1979. The Report of the Unofficial Committee of Enquiry. London.

—— 1984. Civil Liberties and the Miners' Dispute. 1st Report of the Independent Inquiry. London.

—— 1986. Stonehenge. A Report into the Civil Liberties Implications of the Events relating to the Convoys of Summer 1985 and 1986. London.

NICOL, A. 1979. 'Official Secrets and Jury Vetting.' *Criminal Law Review* 284.

NORTHAM, G. 1985. 'A Fair Degree of Force?' *Listener*, 31 October.

—— 1988. *Shooting in the Dark. Riot Police in Britain.* London: Faber and Faber.

NORTON, P. 1982. *The Constitution in Flux.* Oxford: Basil Blackwell.

O'HIGGINS, P. 1972. *Censorship in Britain.* London: Thomas Nelson & Sons.

—— 1980. *Cases and Materials on Civil Liberties.* London: Sweet and Maxwell.

PANNICK, D. 1982. *Judicial Review of the Death Penalty.* London: Duckworth.

—— 1985. *Sex Discrimination Law.* Oxford: Oxford University Press.

PARKER, Lord. 1972. Report of the Committee of Privy Counsellors Appointed to Consider Authorised Procedures for the Interrogation of Persons Suspected of Terrorism (Cmnd. 4901).

PECK, S. R. 1987. 'An Analytical Framework for the Application of the Canadian Charter of Rights and Freedoms.' (25) *Osgoode Hall Law Journal* 1.

PETTER, A. 1986. 'The Politics of the Charter.' (8) *Supreme Court Law Review* 473.

PHILIPS, Sir CYRIL. 1981. Royal Commission on Criminal Procedure (Chairman: Sir Cyril Philips). 2 vols Volume I: Report (Cmnd. 8092).

—— 1986. Report on a Review of the Prevention of Terrorism (Temporary Provisions) Act 1984. London: Home Office.

Police Complaints Authority. 1987. Annual Report 1986 (HC 295).

—— 1988. Annual Report 1987 (HC 465).

—— 1989. Annual Report 1988 (HC 307).

PONTING, C. 1985. *The Right to Know: The Inside Story of the Belgrano Affair.* London: Sphere.

—— 1987. 'R. v. Ponting.' (14) *Journal of Law and Society* 366.

Post Office Engineering Union. 1980. 'Tapping the Telephone' (mimeo).

POWELL, E. 1989. 'The Rights Trampled under Panicky Feet.' *Guardian*, 23 February.

Prime Minister's Office. 1982. Statement on the Recommendations of the Security Commission (Cmnd. 8540).
—— 1983. Report of the Security Commission, May 1983 (Cmnd. 8876).
—— 1985. Report of the Security Commission, May 1985 (Cmnd. 9514).
RANKIN, M. 1986. 'National Security: Information, Accountability and the Canadian Security Intelligence Service.' (36) *University of Toronto Law Journal* 249.
REINER, R. 1985. *The Politics of the Police.* Brighton: Wheatsheaf.
ROBERTSON, G. 1989. *Freedom, the Individual and the Law.* 6th edn. (earlier edns. by H. Street). Harmondsworth: Penguin.
ROBERTSON, J. C. 1989. *The Hidden Cinema. British Film Censorship in Action, 1913–1972.* London: Routledge.
ROBILLIARD, St. J. A., and McEWAN, J. 1986. *Police Powers and the Individual.* Oxford: Basil Blackwell.
Royal Commission on the Police. 1962. Final Report (Chairman: Sir Henry Willink QC) (Cmnd. 1728).
SAID, E. 1988. 'Identity, Negation and Violence.' (171) *New Left Review* 46.
SCARMAN, Mr Justice. 1972. Government of Northern Ireland. Report of a Tribunal of Inquiry into Violence and Civil Disturbances in Northern Ireland in 1969 (Cmd. 566). Belfast.
SCARMAN, L. 1974. *English Law—The New Dimension.* London: Stevens.
SCARMAN, Lord. 1975. The Red Lion Square Disorders of 15 June 1974 (Cmnd. 5919).
—— 1981. The Brixton Disorders, 10–12 April 1981: Report of an Inquiry by the Rt. Hon. Lord Scarman (Cmnd. 8427).
—— 1987. 'Human Rights in an Unwritten Constitution.' *Denning Law Journal* 129.
—— 1988. 'Flaws in the Field of Human Rights.' *Guardian,* 27 June.
SCORER, C., and HEWITT, P. 1981. *The Prevention of Terrorism Act: The Case for Repeal.* London: NCCL.
SCRATON, P. 1985. *The State of the Police.* London: Pluto Press.
Senate Standing Committee on Constitutional and Legal Affairs (Australia). 1985. A Bill of Rights For Australia? An Exposure Report for the Consideration of Senators. Canberra: Australian Government Publishing Service.
SHACKLETON, Lord. 1978. Review of the Operation of the Prevention of Terrorism (Temporary Provisions) Acts 1974 and 1976 (Cmnd. 7324).
SHARPE, R. J. 1987. 'The Charter of Rights and Freedoms and the Supreme Court of Canada: The First Four Years.' *Public Law* 48.
SHAW, T. 1988. 'Justice: Cracks in the Image.' *Daily Telegraph,* 7 December.

SHEPHERD, R. 1989. 'The Court of Queen Margaret.' *Guardian*, 29 July.

SHERR, A. 1989. *Freedom of Protest, Public Order and the Law*. Oxford: Basil Blackwell.

SIBRAA, K. W. 1987. 'National Security—Parliamentary Scrutiny of Security and Intelligence Services in Australia.' (68) *The Parliamentarian* 120.

SIEGHART, P. (ed.). 1988. *Human Rights in the United Kingdom*. London: Pinter Publishers.

SILKIN, S. 1977. 'The Rights of Man and the Rule of Law.' (28) *Northern Ireland Legal Quarterly* 3.

SMITH, A. T. H. 1987. *The Offences Against Public Order including the Public Order Act 1986*. London: Sweet and Maxwell.

SMITH, J. C., and HOGAN, B. 1988. *Criminal Law*. 6th edn. London: Butterworths.

STALKER, J. 1988. *Stalker*. London: Harrap.

STONE, R. 1989. *Entry, Search and Seizure*. 2nd edn. London: Sweet and Maxwell.

STREET, H. 1982. *Freedom, the Individual and the Law*. 5th edn. Harmondsworth: Penguin.

SUPPERSTONE, M. 1981. *Brownlie's Law of Public Order and National Security*. 2nd edn. London: Butterworths.

TARNOPOLSKY, W. S. 1978. *The Canadian Bill of Rights*. 2nd edn. Toronto: Macmillan.

TATE, Senator M. 1985. The Operation of the Australian Standing Committee for the Scrutiny of Bills 1981–1985 (Parliamentary Papers No. 317/1985). Canberra: The Government Printer.

TAYLOR, P. 1980. *Beating the Terrorists? Interrogation at Omagh, Gough and Castlereagh*. Harmondsworth: Penguin.

—— 1987. *Stalker: The Search for the Truth*. London: Faber and Faber.

THOMAS, R. 1982. 'The Secrecy and Freedom of Information Debate In Britain.' (17) *Government and Opposition* 293.

THORNTON, P. 1985. *We Protest. The Public Order Debate*. London: NCCL.

—— 1989. *Decade of Decline. Civil Liberties in the Thatcher Years*. London: NCCL.

TOWNSHEND, C. 1983. *Political Violence in Ireland: Government and Resistance since 1848*. Oxford: Oxford University Press.

TRIBE, L. H. 1985. *God Save This Honorable Court: How the Choice of Supreme Court Justices Shapes our History*. New York: Random House.

TURNBULL, M. 1988. *The Spycatcher Trial*. London: Heinemann.

WACKS, R. 1980. *The Protection of Privacy*. London: Sweet and Maxwell.

—— (ed.). 1988. *Civil Liberties in Hong Kong*. New York: Oxford University Press.

WADE, E. C. S., and BRADLEY, A. W. 1985. *Constitutional and Administrative Law.* 10th edn. by A. W. Bradley with T. St. J. N. Bates and C. M. G. Himsworth. London: Longman.

WADE, H. W. R. 1980. *Constitutional Fundamentals.* London: Stevens for the Hamlyn Trust.

—— 1988. *Administrative Law.* 6th edn. Oxford: Oxford University Press.

WALKER, C. 1980. 'Shooting to Kill—Some of the Issues in *Farrell* v. *Secretary of State for Defence.*' (43) *Modern Law Review* 591.

—— 1984. 'Irish Republican Prisoners—Political Detainees, Prisoners of War or Common Criminals?' (19) *Irish Jurist* 189.

—— 1986. *The Prevention of Terrorism in British Law.* Manchester: Manchester University Press.

WALLINGTON, P. 1976. 'Injunctions and the Right to Demonstrate.' (35) *Cambridge Law Journal* 82.

—— (ed.). 1984. *Civil Liberties 1984.* Oxford: Martin Robertson.

—— 1985. 'Policing the Miners' Strike.' (14) *Industrial Law Journal* 145.

—— and MCBRIDE, J. 1976. *Civil Liberties and a Bill of Rights.* London: Cobden Trust.

WALSH, D. 1983. *The Use and Abuse of Emergency Legislation in Northern Ireland.* London: Cobden Trust.

WEST, N. 1981. *MI5. British Security Service Operations 1909–1945.* London: Bodley Head.

WIDGERY, Lord. 1972. Report of the Tribunal Appointed to Inquire into the Events on Sunday 30 January 1972 which led to Loss of Life in Connection with the Procession in Londonderry on that day (HL 101, HC 220).

WILLIAMS, D. G. T. 1965. *Not in the Public Interest. The Problem of Security in Democracy.* London: Hutchinson.

—— 1967. *Keeping the Peace. The Police and Public Order.* London: Hutchinson.

—— 1970. 'Protest and Public Order.' *Cambridge Law Journal* 96.

—— 1978a. *The Law and Public Protest.* The Cambridge–Tilburg Law Lectures. Deventer: Kluwer.

—— 1978b. 'Official Secrecy and the Courts.' In P. Glazebrook (ed.), *Reshaping the Criminal Law. Essays in honour of Glanville Williams.* London: Stevens.

—— 1979. 'Telephone Tapping.' *Cambridge Law Journal* 225.

—— 1981. 'Civil Liberties and the Protection of Statute.' (34) *Current Legal Problems* 25.

WILSON, H. 1977. *The Governance of Britain.* London: Sphere.

WINDLESHAM, Lord, and RAMPTON, R. 1989. *The Windlesham/Rampton Report on Death on the Rock.* London: Faber and Faber.

WORSTHORNE, P. 1988. 'Can They Forgive Her?' *Sunday Telegraph,* 27 November.

WRIGHT, J. S. 1981. 'The Bill of Rights in Britain and America: A Not Quite Full Circle.' (55) *Tulane Law Review* 291.

WRIGHT, P. 1987. *Spycatcher: The Candid Autobiography of a Senior Intelligence Officer.* New York: Viking.

ZANDER, M. 1985. *A Bill of Rights?* 3rd edn. London: Sweet and Maxwell.

—— 1985. *The Police and Criminal Evidence Act 1984.* London: Sweet and Maxwell.

Index

OXFORD

MORE OXFORD PAPERBACKS

Details of a selection of other Oxford Paperbacks follow. A complete list of Oxford Paperbacks, including The World's Classics, Twentieth-Century Classics, OPUS, Past Masters, Oxford Authors, Oxford Shakespeare, and Oxford Paperback Reference, is available in the UK from the General Publicity Department, Oxford University Press (RS), Walton Street, Oxford, OX2 6DP.

In the USA, complete lists are available from the Paperbacks Marketing Manager, Oxford University Press, 200 Madison Avenue, New York, NY 10016.

Oxford Paperbacks are available from all good bookshops. In case of difficulty, customers in the UK can order direct from Oxford University Press Bookshop, 116 High Street, Oxford, Freepost, OX1 4BR, enclosing full payment. Please add 10 per cent of the published price for postage and packing.

LAW AND MODERN SOCIETY

P. S. Atiyah

'The Oxford University Press has done well to publish this brief, lucid and stimulating appraisal by P. S. Atiyah of English law as it operates in our society today. And it is refreshing to find that Professor Atiyah describes the law in action before he asks his questions. His study is critical, but not damning. Though Atiyah is careful not to state his own position and sensibly emphasizes that without judges educated by training and experience to handle and develop constitutional safeguards a Bill of Rights is unlikely to achieve its purpose, I find the conclusion to be drawn from his reasoning inescapable. It points to the need for constitutional reform. Atiyah leaves it to his readers to decide what they want. It is good, therefore, that the book is designed to be read by all who are interested; that it is written in a style which all can appreciate; that it is brief; and that it is modestly priced.' Leslie Scarman in the *Times Literary Supplement*

'The author surveys the legal system rather than substantive law and has views on judges, the legal profession generally, the way lawyers themselves regard law, law and the state and "Bad law". Throughout the text he tries to be fair where there are two political viewpoints . . . the book is a stimulating introduction to the legal system for the intelligent layman.' *Solicitors Journal*

An OPUS book

REBIRTH OF A NATION
Wales 1880–1980

Kenneth O. Morgan

This comprehensive survey of Wales during the past century was described by the *Times Literary Supplement* as 'a crowning achievement', while the *Guardian* said that it would 'serve as a fulcrum of historical debate for a generation'.

THATCHERISM AND BRITISH POLITICS

The End of Consensus?

Dennis Kavanagh

Second Edition

Mrs Thatcher has cited the breaking of the post-war political consensus, established with the support of dominant groups in the Conservative and Labour parties, as one of her objectives. In this penetrating study of her style and performance, she emerges both as the midwife of the collapse of consensus and also as its product.

This new edition has been fully revised and updated to include an analysis of development since the Conservative Party's third election victory in 1987.

THE THATCHER EFFECT

Edited by Dennis Kavanagh and Anthony Seldon

For over a decade Margaret Thatcher has been the dominant force in British politics, and the changes brought about by her successive governments have provoked widespread and heated discussion.

This superb collection of analytical essays by distinguished academics and journalists examines the effects of Thatcherism on British society, covering such areas as the arts, the media, the Civil Service, trade unions, local government, the churches, education, and the law. Each essay looks at the principal changes that have occurred since 1979, and the role of the Thatcher government in promoting these changes.

These timely and original essays will stimulate thinking and provide a comprehensive picture of Thatcher's Britain as it moves into the 1990s.

LAW, LIBERTY, AND MORALITY

H. L. A. Hart

Professor Hart deals in this book with the use of the criminal law to enforce morality, in particular sexual morality. He first considers John Stuart Mill's famous declaration: 'The only purpose for which power can be rightfully exercised over any member of a civilized community is to prevent harm to others.'

The author then examines the arguments of Sir James Fitzjames Stephen, the great Victorian judge, and Lord Devlin, that the use of the criminal law to enforce morality is justified. He sets out to demonstrate that these challenges fail to recognize distinctions of vital importance for legal and political theory.

'All who lay claim to an educated conscience should make themselves familiar with the issues presented in these incisively argued lectures.' *Twentieth Century*

THE LAWFUL RIGHTS OF MANKIND

An Introduction to the International Legal Code of Human Rights

Paul Sieghart

In the course of a veritable legal revolution since 1945, a detailed code of human rights has been installed in international law. If one wants to know what *legal* human rights there are, how far they extend, and whether any particular nation adequately protects them, this code now provides a single and universally agreed standard.

This book explains for the general reader what lies behind the code, how it was made, how it works, and what it says. In addition, the governing texts of the code are set out in an appendix.

An OPUS book

POLICING LIBERAL SOCIETY

Steve Uglow

In recent years we have seen the British police involved in pitched battles with miners, youths, even hippies. All this is a long way from the comforting image of George Dixon and of the 'friend in blue' of the 1960s.

Steve Uglow argues that our expectations of our police are no longer realistic: they are presented as crime fighters when their ability to affect crime rates is only marginal. Although the police portray themselves as acting within, and accountable to the 'the rule of law', their relationship with the State is complex and ill-defined. Under the guise of the 'public interest', the police can—and do—involve themselves in all areas of life. What then is the proper province of the police within a liberal society? Are they crime-fighters, social workers, maintainers of public order, or even definers of the 'moral' or 'normal'?

The author suggests that the police have become vulnerable to the authoritarianism of governments. What is needed is a proper constitutional status for the force, protecting its independence, giving substance to its neutrality, and extending its accountability.

An OPUS book

THE REAL WORLD OF DEMOCRACY

C. B. Macpherson

In the Massey Lectures, delivered over the Canadian Broadcasting Corporation in 1965, Professor Macpherson examines what he considers to be three legitimate forms of democracy: the liberal democracy of the West, the kind of democracy practised in the Soviet block countries, and the mass democracy of the newly independent states of Africa and Asia. The work is attractively written and the argument is provocative: it should stimulate discussion on an important subject. At another level it seeks to question the validity of all the acquisitive and competitive motives that have characterized human survival and progress in the past.

THINKING ABOUT PEACE AND WAR

Martin Ceadel

In the nuclear age the ethics of war, and the policies of pacifism, have become matters of increasingly urgent concern. Martin Ceadel analyses the various arguments and describes, rather than prescribes, the standpoints of the twentieth century's most crucial debate.

The author is Tutor in Politics and a Fellow of New College, Oxford.

'a masterly analysis' *Reconciliation Quarterly*

'The book sets out to remedy what the author rightly describes as "an astonishing deficiency in popular or international-relations theory". It does this in a lively and perceptive manner ... an admirable book.' Adam Roberts, *New Society*

An OPUS book

THREE ESSAYS

John Stuart Mill

On Liberty
Representative Government
The Subjection of Women

Introduced by Richard Wollheim

The three major essays collected in this volume, written in the latter half of the life of John Stuart Mill (1806–73), were quickly accepted into the canon of European political and social thought. Nothing that has occurred in the intervening years has seriously affected their standing as classics on the subject. Today, although many of Mill's measures have been adopted, the essays are still relevant—still liberty and representative government are in collision with other principles, and women still have to gain unprejudiced general acceptance of their equality.

In this introduction Richard Wollheim describes the essays as 'the distillation of the thinking of one highly intelligent, highly sensitive man, who spent the greater part of his life occupied with the theory and practice of society'.